LEGAL PROTECTION
THE SINKING ISLANDS REFUGEES

LEGAL PROTECTION OF
THE SINKING ISLANDS REFUGEES

COSMIN CORENDEA

LEGAL PROTECTION OF THE SINKING ISLANDS REFUGEES

Cosmin Corendea

Published by:

Vandeplas Publishing, LLC – July 2016

801 International Parkway, 5th Floor
Lake Mary, FL. 32746
USA

www.vandeplaspublishing.com

ISBN 978-1-60042-280-5

TABLE OF CONTENTS

I feel very pleased to contribute the foreword to an important book on an important subject whose research and writing I have had the opportunity of following closely with keen interest and strong expectation for its final publication. In recent years, climate change has become an increasingly urgent universal concern. Probably the most significant environmental challenge in the history of the modern world is now widely recognized to be a result of increases in carbon dioxide and other greenhouse gas emissions, generally produced by human activity.

It is now obvious and well accepted that climate change will have serious environmental, economic and geopolitical consequences. The scientific projections of increased global temperatures presented the prospect of rising sea levels and associated risks for coastal areas, increased risks of floods and droughts, new and exacerbated public health issues and threats to biodiversity, and the viability of numerous ecosystems around the world. Economically, the impact of climate change could be dramatic, considering that 50 to 250 million people who could be displaced in the next 50 years. Nevertheless, the impact of climate change also involves the geopolitical sphere, several states being directly threatened by increased pollution activities of other countries and facing imminent disappearance.

In this context, the complex problem of the Sinking Islands represents a relatively controversial and new aspect of climate change. The crisis faced by multiple island nations, owing to rising sea levels that are in turn a result of climate change in principal, is also exacerbated by a general passivity of the international community regarding the lives of the Pacific Islanders, with severe overall costs, as ecological disasters and civilizations collapse.

This book analyzes the case of Sinking Islands as a scientifically demonstrated fact from the environmental point of view, mainly focusing on climate change as the primary cause. With quality and a good progressive abstract interpretation of law, the book also attempts to legally expose the refugee/migration process, as a subsidiary effect. The legal analysis will be naturally corroborated with international human rights law and the related supporting documents, offering legal solutions under the umbrella of international law to this cutting-edge global problem.

It is obligatory that these branches of international law, from which perspectives the problems are analyzed (environmental, refugee and human rights), are interpreted as interdependent and interconnected fields. They together constitute the legal core of the problem. Furthermore, only intrinsically connected and not viewed in isolation from each other, the three main "perspectives" could provide a better legal identification, collating and enforcement of the international obligations to protect the Pacific Islanders, along with more sustainable and equitable policy responses to this global predicament.

In addition, one of the purposes of this book is to support the previous works in the "Climate Refugee" field, in regard to a broad recognition and acceptance of the term in international (refugee) law and to explore the potential application of the "Economic Refugee" idiom, *sui generis* and its inevitability of use in the Pacific Islanders' context.

The present work strives to extract its innovative component from the research and analysis of the problem itself, supported by developed action-oriented case studies on different Pacific Islands, bringing *inter alia* an academic insight from the field of international law.

The salient objective of the book is to evaluate the challenge of the Sinking Pacific Islands, supported by research and policy analysis of the legal or legislative developments at international and national level for countries within the region (e.g., new domestic legislation, constitutional amendments, significant case law), finally aiming at the global aspect of the issue, its worldwide concern and the eventual international comprehensive plans of action, proposed in the conclusions and recommendations of the book.

Dr. Cosmin Corendea has done an excellent job of committing his well-researched work on a very critical and important subject matter, based on his convictions and in a manner that all its readers can benefit from. It is strongly hoped that the author will continue to research and publish in this field in which he is eminently well qualified.

Christian Nwachukwu Okeke, Ph.D.
Professor of International & Comparative Law

Director, LL.M & S.J.D. International Legal Studies & Director, Sompong
Sucharitkul Center for Advanced International Legal Studies, Golden Gate
University School of Law,
San Francisco California,
Pro-Chancellor and Chairman of the Governing Council
Godfrey Okoye University, Ugwuomu, Nike, Nigeria

In recent years, climate change has become an increasingly urgent universal concern.

Probably the most important environmental challenge in the history of the modern world is now widely recognized to be a result of increases in carbon dioxide and other greenhouse gas (GHG) emissions, generally produced by human activity.

It is widely accepted that climate change will have serious environmental, economic and geopolitical consequences. The scientific projections of increased global temperatures presented the prospect of rising sea levels and associated risks for coastal areas, increased risks of floods and droughts, new and exacerbated public health issues and threats to biodiversity, and the viability of numerous ecosystems around the world. Economically, the impact of climate change could be dramatic, considering only the prospective 50 to 250 million displaced people in the next 50 years. Nevertheless, the impact of climate change also involves the geopolitical arena, with several states being directly threatened by increased pollution activities of other countries and facing imminent disappearance.

In this context, the complex problem of the Sinking Islands represents a relatively controversial and new aspect of global warming. The crisis faced by multiple island nations, due to rising sea levels that are in turn a result of climate change in principal, is also supported by a general passivity of the international community regarding the lives of the Pacific Islanders, with severe overall costs, as ecological disasters and civilizations collapse.

This book aims to analyze the case of Sinking Islands as a scientifically demonstrated fact from the environmental point of view, mainly focusing on climate change as the primary cause. With quality and academic progressive interpretation of law, the book will also legally thrash out the refugee aspect of the problem and the forced migration process, as a subsidiary effect. The legal analysis will be naturally corroborated with international human rights law and the related supporting documents, conclusively offering legal solutions under the umbrella of international law to this cutting-edge global problem.

It is obligatory that these branches of international law, from which perspectives the problem will be analyzed (environmental, refugee, and human rights), are to be regarded and interpreted as interdependent and interconnected fields, as they together constitute the legal core of the problem. Furthermore, only if intrinsically connected and not viewed in isolation from each other could the three main "perspectives" provide a better legal identification, collating and enforcement of the international obligations to protect the Pacific Islanders, along with more sustainable and equitable policy responses to this global predicament.

In addition, one of the purposes of this book is to extend the previous work in the "Climate Refugee" field regarding a broad recognition and acceptance of the term in international (refugee) law as well as to explore the potential application of the "Economic Refugee" idiom, *sui generis* and its inevitability of use in the Pacific islanders' context.

The present work shall also extract its innovative component from the research and analyze the problem itself, supported by developed action-oriented case studies on specific Pacific Islands, contributing *inter alia* with an academic insight in the field of international law.

Hereby, the salient objective of the book is to evaluate the challenge of the Sinking Pacific Islands, supported by research and policy analysis of the legal or legislative developments at international and national level for countries within the region (e.g., new domestic legislation, constitutional amendments, significant case law), finally aiming at the global aspect of the issue, its worldwide concern and the eventual international comprehensive plans of action, proposed in the conclusions and recommendations of this book.

SINKING ISLANDS OR RISING SEAS?

The book proposes two relatively controversial concepts: the increasing numbers of officially unaccepted type of refugees, e.g., the ones affected by climate change, and the notion of "Sinking Islands," a very disputed view regarding the islands whose lands have already started to become covered by water, in particular in the Pacific Ocean and the Indian Ocean. The theory of "Climate Refugees" will be discussed more intensively in the refugee part of the book together with the definition of "Economic Refugees," which is also unaccepted by international institutions.

The "Sinking Islands" concept first appeared in relation to the rising of sea levels, with most scholars being preoccupied to acknowledge the first "victims" of climate change, which are the low-lying lands around the world, in particular, the Pacific Islands. The controversy around this definition arose when skeptical scientists initially believed that the climate change phenomenon is not a consequence of human activities, but represents the "normal" evolution of the climate during millions of years of evolution. Their strongest argument at that time was the non-existence of any historical data, which may prove that these types of warming processes did not occur before the first meteorological measurements that started at the end of the nineteenth century. In the last years, the scientists' positions became weaker due to the overwhelming scientific evidence discovered and demonstrated by the Intergovernmental Panel on Climate Change (IPCC). However, their position maintains the same direction when the discussion moves to the Sinking Islands. This happens mainly due to the theory that supports the tectonic shifts or land subsidence as representing the key factor in the Pacific Islands sinking process. *Stricto sensu*, the Pacific tectonic plate, one of the most active seismological plates of our planet, is the primary line of reasoning behind the submerging phenomenon. That is why the tectonic shifting corroborated with the land composition (as a result of the structural crust these islands are created from dead coral reefs) does stand for the main contra-argumentation of the Sinking Islands theory.

Nonetheless, since 2011, Geoscience Australia, the National Agency for Geosciences Research and Geospatial Information, has been conducting the South Pacific Sea Level Climate Monitoring Program (SPSLCMP). For this program, Continuous Global Positioning Systems (CGPS) were installed across the Pacific Islands. This network of gauges allows the scientists to accurately measure the vertical and horizontal movement of the land. The data collected also permits the scientists to determine the absolute sea level variation. The program will take at least a decade before a final report is produced. However, one of the last periodical reports of the agency, the 2013 IPCC report, describes the continuous monitoring as being very accurate[1]. The report also shows that the sea levels have drastically increased, by more than one or two millimeters than initially predicted. Without any doubt, the sea level rising is due to climate change in principal, as the tectonic shifts did not significantly change since the Great Sumatra-Andaman Earthquake, in December 2004.[2] Furthermore, the report also acknowledges the effect of the rising sea level. Therefore, there is no doubt that the Pacific Islands are directly affected by rising sea levels due to climate change.

As mentioned before, this book does not intend to debate the accuracy of the sea level change, and does not intend to become strictly environmental science-oriented, but a legal analysis of the Sinking Islands problem, using the tools of international environmental law, corroborated with the refugee and human rights law. It is a state-centered *de jure* and human-oriented *de facto* document.

Hence, the reasoning behind the use of the term "Sinking Islands" is the human aspect of the problem, in particular referring to the inhabitants of the respective islands. The justification is quite simple: if a Pacific Islander, who faces the danger of his or her own land being submerged, is asked what is his/her opinion about the rising sea level process he or she will firstly answer that the land is sinking. Additionally, a Pacific Islander will say that his or her home is in danger, and together with the land itself, the culture, history, and the Pacific

---

1   Church J.A, Clark, P.U., Cazenave, A., and Gregory, J.M., ed. *Climate Change 2013: Sea Level Change. The contribution of Working Group I to the Fifth Assessment Report of the Intergovernmental Panel on Climate Change.* Cambridge, 2013. PDF report. http://www.ipcc.ch/pdf/assessment-report/ar5/wg1/WG1AR5_Chapter13_FINAL.pdf

2   Thorne Lay et al., "The Great Sumatra-Andaman Earthquake of 26 December 2004," *Science* 308, no. 5725 (2005): 1127.

civilization are sinking too. From the Pacific Islander's perspective, it is not the ocean that is rising, but his or her home that is sinking. The inhabitants of those islands are not afraid of the ocean mainly due to their previous experience with ocean-related meteorological events such as cyclones, tsunamis, etc. They are afraid, however, of losing their homes, which are sinking.

Naturally, this subjective engagement does not necessarily imply a legal argument and perhaps only a political debate, which does not represent the purpose of the present book. Yet, the human factor of the Sinking Islands still stands as the reasoning *inter alia* behind the general principles of international law.

Consequently, without any arguments against the sea-level rise notion, the book will continue to use this term, as a well-accepted perception. However, due to the human factor of the problem argued above, the book will also continue to use the "Sinking Islands" concept, a legally unique application from this perspective.

Finally, this book will advocate for the general admittance of this view, as a part of the embraced progressive interpretation of international law theory and as a part of the development of the modern notion of complementary protection.

HISTORICAL AND LEGAL BACKGROUND

The research starts with a historical retrospective, emphasizing the role of the Polynesian, Melanesian and Micronesian cultures in the past, their role in the history of human evolution, and their significance within the international cultural heritage. A retrospective of the consequences of "civilized nations" in the historical context will be conducted through the example of Rapa Nui (Easter Island or Isla de Pascua), as a Polynesian settlement of cultural values. The actual development of Rapa Nui will represent an example of human activities' impact on the environment and Polynesian civilization.

Later, the study will focus on the three proposed case studies of Tuvalu, Republic of Marshall Islands (RMI) and Maldives, the last one being an example from outside the Pacific, but extremely similar in nature to the case of the Pacific Islands. For the purpose of the introduction, the following brief analysis is conducted using the generalities of the clustered islands; however the study will reveal an individual and separate examination of each island.

The research will articulate the present political situation of fragile states (Tuvalu and RMI) as well as failing states (Maldives) that have experienced human rights violations and lack self-governance. Within an unstable political setting, the environmental aspects will be revealed, demonstrating a vulnerable and weak ecosystem. This situation contributes to severe social and economic impacts: the shores are eroding, coral reefs are becoming bleached,[3] Water supplies are contaminated, and due to the environmental degradation of the ocean surrounding the islands, the surge system has been more or less nonexistent for the past 25 years. Consequently, important immediate economic sources, such as fishing, are compromised. With their homes vulnerable and few natural resources, the Pacific Islanders rely on foreign financial aid from Japan and the United Kingdom. In addition they often seek temporary solutions to meet their needs (e.g., Tuvalu sold the ".tv" internet domain and the "900" phone numbers for over $20 million[4]). With a population of just over 400,000 people, the respective islands are struggling regionally to find solutions in respect to climate displacement. The discussion will also focus on the activity of the Secretariat of Pacific Environmental Program (SREP) and all other important actions taken by these islands (e.g., the Male Declaration on the Human Dimension of Global Climate Change, Small Islands Developing States, etc.).

Considering their imminent submergence (e.g., in Funafuti, the capital of Tuvalu, a tidal range on the main atoll suggests the sea level is rising by 5-6mm per year, which represents twice the average global rate predicted by the IPCC), the publication will also conclusively note several solutions and alternatives for the Sinking Islands, like adaption plans or strategies. Those are, however, regarded as temporary by climate scientists (e.g., sea walls, sand banks, etc.).

THE ENVIRONMENTAL PERSPECTIVE

In the first part of this book, the Sinking Islands case is presented through the environmental law approach, albeit the present study is not strictly environmentally oriented. It will focus on the scientifically demonstrated facts of climate change, with specific data and scientific statistics, as well as international

---

3   *Global Warming Fast Facts*, National Geographic (June 14, 2007),
     http://news.nationalgeographic.com/news/2004/12/1206_041206_global_warming.html.

4   Maynard Roger, "Internet domain riches fail to arrive in Tuvalu," *The Independent*, last modified July 7, 2015, http://www.independent.co.uk/news/world/australasia/internet-domain-riches-fail-to-arrive-in-tuvalu-2029221.html

documentation, with direct implications for the environment in general and the Pacific Islands in particular.

In December 2006, an inhabited island in the Bay of Bengal, India, disappeared underwater as a result of climate change.[5] Two-thirds of the populated islands of Ghoramara in the same Bengal Bay have been permanently inundated. This is not an isolated incident; other inhabitants face the risk of submersion due to rising sea levels, including island nations in the Indian Ocean (Maldives Islands), the Central Pacific and the South Pacific, as well as large tracts of land from South East Asia to Western Africa. At the other end of the globe, Inuit communities in North America and Greenland fear displacement due to melting ice.

In a report released in February 2007, the scientists of the IPCC, Nobel Prize winners, admitted for the first time that most of the global warming over the past 50 years is "very likely" to be a result of human activity.[6] The panel's conclusions, drafted by representatives of 113 nations in Paris, were based on scientific studies over the past eight years.[7] In 2001, the IPCC report said human blame was "likely," a 66 percent probability.[8] In contrast, the 2007 IPCC report said "very likely," which means that there is a 90 percent certainty that climate change is caused by people.[9] Finally, the 2014 IPCC report stated that human influence on climate change is "clear."[10]

The observed widespread warming of the atmosphere and ocean, together with ice-mass loss, support the conclusion that it is extremely unlikely that

---

5   "Global warming sinks disputed island in Bay of Bengal," *Asian News International*, Mar. 26, 2010,
     http://0-search.proquest.com.bianca.penlib.du.edu/docview/436085583?accountid=14608

6   *Intergovernmental Panel on Climate Change, Climate Change 2007: The Physical Science Basis.* Contribution of Working Group I to the Fourth Assessment Report of the Intergovernmental Panel on Climate Change 72 (Lenny Bernstein et al. eds. 2007), https://www.ipcc.ch/pdf/assessment-report/ar4/syr/ar4_syr_full_report.pdf

7   Lenny Bernsyein et al., *Intergovernmental Panel on Climate Change*, p. 23

8   *U.N. Panel Blames Humans for Warming*, Climate Arc (Feb. 1, 2007),
     http://www.climateark.org/shared/reader/welcome.aspx?linkid=68328

9   *Synthesis Report, supra* note five at 27.

10   Pachauri, R.K, Meyer, L.A. et al., *IPCC, 2014: Climate Change 2014: Synthesis Report.* The contribution of Working Groups I, II and III to the Fifth Assessment Report of the Intergovernmental Panel on Climate Change, p.151. Geneva, Switzerland, http://www.ipcc.ch/pdf/assessment-report/ar5/syr/AR5_SYR_FINAL_SPM.pdf

global climate change of the past 50 years can be explained without external forcing and very likely that is not due to known natural causes alone.[11]

Additionally, in the 2014 report of the IPCC,[12] Scientists argued that increases in temperature and global sea levels caused by human activity would continue for centuries, even if greenhouse gas concentrations were to be stabilized.[13] Most of the observed increases in temperatures since the mid-twentieth century (average temperatures have risen by about 1.5°C) are very likely due to greenhouse gas emissions from the burning of fossil fuels such as oil, coal and natural gas from automobiles, power plants, and factories. It is also projected that an increase in sea levels of 7-23 inches will take place by the end of the century.[14]

At the United Nations Climate Summit in Doha, in November 2012, governmental representatives from 192 countries gathered in order to discuss how to reduce GHG emissions after the current Kyoto Protocol targets expired in 2012.[15]Talks centered on whether a further set of binding targets is needed. Although it was the first meeting of this sort since the recent IPCC, the evidence presented for climate change was "unequivocal." The meeting's initial goal was also to debate how to help less developed nations cope in a warming world. Unfortunately, the Doha Conference of Parties, organized by the United Nations Framework Convention on Climate Change (UNFCCC), remains nothing but a declarative meeting, blocked by the countries which continue to refuse to engage in the fight against climate change. This produces no results regarding an eventual new global agreement on ways to cut rising GHG emissions. Moreover, with Canada legally withdrawing from the Kyoto Protocol in December 2011, the situation became alarming for any future negotiations.

The climate change process leads to rising waters, including around the Pacific islands, which are being covered by the ocean every year, inch by inch. Several Pacific Islands, like Kiribati, are already struggling with human rights violations due to the sinking process and the humanitarian problems (e.g.: in Micronesia). The neighboring countries, particularly the developed ones (e.g.,

---

11 Susan Solomon, et al., *Technical Summary*, in CLIMATE CHANGE 2007: THE PHYSICAL SCIENCE BASIS (Susan Solomon, et al. eds., 2007), *available at* http://www.ipcc.ch/pdf/assessment-report/ar4/wg1/ar4_wg1_full_report.pdf

12 Pachauri, R.K, Meyer, L.A. et al., *Intergovernmental Panel on Climate Change*, p. 23

13 Ibid., p.2

14 Ibid.

15 *Doha Climate Change Conference – November 2012*, UNITED NATIONS FRAMEWORK CONVENTION ON CLIMATE CHANGE (2013), http://unfccc.int/meetings/doha_nov_2012/meeting/6815.php

New Zealand, Australia) are also facing tides of refugees, which is directly affecting the labor market and creating severe social inclusion issues. Moreover, historical and cultural inheritance (e.g., Polynesian, Malaysian, and Micronesian) might disappear together with the land itself as a result of the assimilation process of the ancestors' representatives (e.g., indigenous peoples) by the new Western host societies.

Accurate reports regarding glacial melting and ocean level rise could support the predictions made by scientists and could emphasize the direct and indubitable connection between the effects of climate change and the low-lying islands of the Pacific. The already expected sea level rises, in conjunction with a slow or non-existent decrease of the GHGs as well as the unexpected and less predictable weather patterns (tsunamis, cyclones, hurricanes, floods, etc.), will reveal the submerging process that the Sinking Islands are facing at this time. This process will have even more dramatic implications soon, a reality that has been recently accepted by the United Nations body, like the IPCC.[16]

A brief presentation of the existing international environmental law documents will be introduced afterward to establish the progress of environmental law through its international mechanisms, such as the United Nations Framework Convention on Climate Change[17], the 1992 Rio Declaration on Environment and Development (the principles), and the Kyoto Protocol. Together with environmental law, as one of the principal instruments in the fight against climate change, the political and economic factors will also be part of the debate, presenting the inconsistency of international law regarding its institutions.

In the second part of the environmental section, the discussion will focus on the Pacific community and its recent international actions related to environmental law. Specifically, the discourse will center on several programs and partnerships the Pacific islands were able to initiate, regardless of the non-participatory reactions coming from the developed and industrialized countries/identities (e.g. the United States of America, Australia, countries in the European Union, India, and China). The research will absorb each and every applicable

---

16 The IPCC was established by the United Nations Environmental Programme [UNEP] and the World Meteorological Organization [WMO] in 1988 to assess the scientific, technical and socio-economic information relevant for the understanding of human-induced climate change, its potential impacts, and options for mitigation and adaptation. Currently, it includes a network of more than 2,500 scientists.

17 United Nations Framework Convention on Climate Change, June 12, 1992, 1771 U.N.T.S. 107, *available at*

http://unfccc.int/resource/docs/convkp/conveng.pdf.

principle of international environmental law, the main recent developments of the international environmental agreements, as well as the complete environmental regional activities, which might influence directly or indirectly the problem of the Sinking Islands and their inhabitants. Nevertheless, the environmental analysis found in the first chapter of this work should be regarded as a component of the hybrid study proposed by this book, along with the refugee and human rights law presented in the following chapters.

THE REFUGEE PERSPECTIVE

According to the United Nations High Commissioner for Refugees, the leading international authority in the refugee field, the period of the next 10-20 years is considered to be "sufficient" to prepare the future life of predicted refugees.[18] Concurrently with their position, the studies conducted by the Jadavpur University in Calcutta, India (based on the unprecedented disappearance of the Lohachara Island in the Bay of Bengal, which displaced 10,000 people) estimate that a total of 70,000 people would need to be evacuated in the next five to ten years, only in the Bay of Bengal.[19] Worthy of note is that people of the Bay of Bengal were not considered by the scientists when they placed the figure of the predicted displaced people at somewhere between 50 and 250 million in the next 50 years.[20] However, the precise number of those likely to be displaced is still impossible to determine.

"Yet, people forced to move as a result of climate change do not fit the international legal definition of 'refugee,' which requires individuals already outside their country of origin to show that they have a well-founded fear of being persecuted because of their race, religion, nationality, political opinion

---

18 "Refugee Law in the Era of Globalization," *Human Security in the Pacific: The Climate Refugees of the Sinking Islands*. 2 (1): 12-19, http://conference.unitar.org/yale2014/sites/conference.unitar.org.yale2014/files/2014%20UNITAR-Yale%20Conference-Corendea.pdf

19 John Vidal, *Migration is the Only Escape from Rising Tides of Climate Change in Bangladesh*, THE GUARDIAN (DEC. 4, 2009), HTTP://WWW.GUARDIAN.CO.UK/ENVIRONMENT/2009/DEC/04/BANGLADESH-CLIMATE-REFUGEES.

20 *Id.*

or membership of a particular social group."[21] "As a result, the rights, entitlements and protection options (arising from the status of refugee) for people displaced by climate change are uncertain in international law, and there is no international agency with a mandate to assist them, such as the United Nations High Commissioner for Refugees."[22] Supplementary to this, maybe it should be added that, in general, terms, the United Nations High Commissioner for Refugees already faces "sufficient" difficulties with the refugees in the world. At this very moment, many scholars and international analysts are starting to question their efficiency and policy development. For example, the registration with the United Nations High Commissioner for Refugees offices, as part of the refugee status acquirement, does not represent an issue the refugees want to deal with, the actual trend being of rejecting the refugees' status and accordingly the social inclusion (e.g., the Iraqi refugees from Syria and Jordan) or they prefer to represent second humanitarian states instead of refugees, as in the case of the United Kingdom. There is also an acute crisis with the protracted refugees from the camps (although not all refugees are in camps), who represent a target of the military guerillas for recruitment (Sudan) or they are exposed to become involved in terrorism activities. The number of Internally Displaced People (IDP) is, alarmingly, increasingly becoming the core problem of the agency (IDPs 90 percent, refugees 10 percent) and also the balance between North and South is no longer equal, with the refugees' cases occurring mostly in the South.

This book will not disregard the present situation of the refugees in the international context, but it will observe and analyze the attributions of the United Nations High Commissioner for Refugees in the Pacific context, arguing the inevitability of "renewing" the refugee concept, the 1951 concept of refugees— "refugees as heroes of the Cold War," and not addressing anymore the needs of the world's geopolitical context. The center point of the research will be represented by a detailed and precise characterization of the Nonrefoulement

---

21 Jane McAdam, *Climate Change Refugee and International Law,* ABC (Sep. 17, 2007),

http://www.abc.net.au/radionational/programs/perspective/jane-mcadam/3220076; *See* Convention Relating to the Status of Refugees art 1, July 28, 1951, 189 U.N.T.S. 150, *available at* http://www.unhcr.org/3b66c2aa10.html

22 Jane McAdam, *Climate Change Refugee and International Law,* ABC (Sep. 17, 2007),

http://www.abc.net.au/radionational/programs/perspective/jane-mcadam/3220076

Principle,[23] as the main protective argument in the case of Climate Refugees. In particular, due to a restrictive application of refugee law, in general, this principle that no one should be sent back to persecution or other forms of serious harm, represents the essential element of the Climate Refugees case.

CLIMATE REFUGEES: TIME FOR RECOGNITION

In the refugee chapter, the book will focus on two new definitions attributed to refugees, or more specifically two categories of refugees: the "Climate Refugees" and the "Economic Refugees." It should be mentioned from the beginning that the two respective notions are equally regarded as being "legally incorrect" and "inexistent" by the United Nations High Commissioner for Refugees, the main authority, and mechanism in the field of refugee law.[24]

This book will dispute, supported by strong argumentation, that the two above categories of refugees are imperative to be recognized by the United Nations and must be urgently introduced to all the international law instruments, as an individual and independent *sui generis* typology of refugees.

The "Climate Refugee" (in French, Réfugiés Climatiques) classification was used for the first time by the photographers/journalists from the Collectif ARGOS, an organization based in Paris, who started their investigations on the subject in 2002.[25] Since 2002, concomitantly with a larger recognition of the climate change process, the term has been used increasingly by scholars, international institutions (others than the United Nations), and international non-governmental organizations (NGOs), generating an objective perspective on the facts of the problem.

---

23 Bonnie Docherty & Tyler Giannini, *Confronting a Rising Tide: A Proposal for a Convention on Climate Change Refugees*, 33 HARV. ENVTL. L. REV. 349, 377 (2009), *available at*

   http://www.law.harvard.edu/students/orgs/elr/vol33_2/Docherty%20Giannini.pdf (explaining that the principle of nonrefoulement is a fundamental rule of refugee law that "prohibits host states from forcibly returning a refugee to his or her home state when the refugee's 'life or freedom would be threatened on account of his race, religion, nationality, membership of a particular social group or political opinion'").

24 Antonio Guterres, "Migration, Displacement and Planned Relocation" *The UN Refugee Agency* (2012),

   http://www.unhcr.org/print/55535d6a9.html

25 Collectif Argos, *Climate Refugees* (Switzerland: In folio editions, 2007).

The reasoning will proceed methodically through the complete history of refugees' classification, the 1951 Refugee Convention, and its 1967 Protocol, as well as the entire refugee existing documentation and practice. Specifically, it will emphasize the exaggerated conservationism of the United Nations in this regard and the inevitability of a newly revised definition. Essentially, the analysis conducted in this book will argue the restricted present application of the refugee definition considering the political framework of the 1951 Convention (after World War II, Cold War period), as well the evolution of the present environmental case situations, which are not covered by the relevant refugee records.

In general terms, the Climate Refugee would be a person displaced due to climate change causes, notably land loss and degradation, facing a well-founded fear, different from the fear of persecution or fear of her/his country, as the actual refugee definition only mentions.

The rationale will also attempt to stress the difference in meaning between "Climate Refugee" and "Environmental Refugee," terms that are often confused mainly due to a nonexistent "official" definition of climate refugee. This serves as an additional argument for the importance of recognizing the term.[26] In the opinion of the author, "Environmental Refugee" has a wider meaning, including all of the following except climate change: the causes of natural disasters, floods, earthquakes, strong impact storms or any other environmental phenomenon that later leads to a migration process. The term "Climate Refugee" narrows these sources to a single main origin, which is evidently climate change, including the specific effects produced by climate change only. For example, the 2004 refugees from the Asian tsunami would be characterized as "Environmental Refugees," while the people of the Sinking Islands would be considered "Climate Refugees." The key differences lie in these two events. The former has as its main cause a natural disaster, an already known phenomenon, which in time if ameliorated, will allow the refugees to return to their respective lands.[27] The latter is caused by an unprecedented and unknown environmental phenomenon, climate change, and as a direct effect, the refugees will not have the alternative (option) of later returning, as their lands will become permanently submerged.

---

26 Bonnie Docherty, "Confronting A Rising Tide: A Proposal For A Convention On Climate Change Refugees," *Harvard Law School* (2009): 367, http://www.law.harvard.edu/students/orgs/elr/vol33_2/Docherty%20Giannini.pdf

27 Jessica B. Cooper, *Environmental Refugees: Meeting the Requirements of the Refugee Definition*, 6 N.Y.U. Envtl. L.J. 480, 483-4 (1998).

Albeit, the study will produce answers to questions inquiring how the international bodies should define the Climate Refugees or why it is important for this definition to be rapidly elaborated by the United Nations. In addition, this innovative study will focus *de stricto* on the "Climate Refugees" of the Sinking Islands as the result of climate change. However, the analyzes will advocate (as a minimum) for including the environmental causes among the already regulated classifications founded in the 1951 Refugee Convention as well as all of its ulterior related documentation.

Conclusively, this book will advocate for a broad acknowledgment of the new refugee classifications and for establishing a conceptual approach to overcome the misuse and recognition of Climate and Economic Refugee notions. Moreover, it will argue for the perception of refugees as a legal definition requiring an adoption, in particular, to the experiences that humanity presently is confronted with, and a renovated form within the international law, in general.

THE HUMAN RIGHTS PERSPECTIVE

The human rights perspective represents the third and last piece of the hybrid mechanism used by this book in order to analyze and evaluate the complex problem of the Sinking Islands.

Actions and statements from international bodies continue to shape the emerging customary international right to a clean and healthy environment. Explicit and implicit evidence of such actions and statements can be found in international court decisions, treaties, resolutions and reports from commissions, committees, secretariats, specialized agencies and similar entities. A review of these materials demonstrates increasing recognition that environmental harms adversely affect various individual and community rights, such as the rights to life, health, water, food, work, culture, development, information, and participation. It also shows that a human rights-based approach to environmental protection (e.g., right to a clean and healthy environment, the right to water, the right to natural protection, and other basic procedural and democratic rights) can provide an effective framework for addressing these issues. Whether explicit or implicit, the practice of upholding and encouraging respect for the right to a clean and healthy environment is important and should be recognized and strengthened. The following is a description of several recognized human rights affected by environmental harms such as in the case of the Sinking Islands.

These findings are based on the Earthjustice Environmental Rights Report from 2008,[28] (to which the author of this book contributed), which will be further discussed in the human rights chapter.

The right to life, perhaps the most basic human right, has extensive environmental links. The most obvious connections manifest themselves in situations such as the Chernobyl nuclear disaster and the Bhopal gas leak, each of which fouled the environment in ways that directly contributed to the loss of many lives. Less obvious, but equally devastating, are extractive industries such as mining, logging and oil development, which deprive indigenous peoples of the physical basis for their cultures and subsistence, and thereby threaten their lives.

The right to health, closely linked to the right to life, is implicated when environmental degradation pollutes air, land or water. For example, a poorly regulated aluminum smelter in the community of La Oroya, Peru, is causing severe lead contamination among local children, resulting in a slew of physical problems and endangering the health of residents.

The right to water is intrinsically linked to the rights to life and health. Without access to clean drinking, cooking and bathing water in adequate quantities, individuals and communities worldwide suffer serious illnesses. For example, toxic oil-water dumped in the Ecuadorian Amazon between 1971 and 1992 has contaminated the groundwater that residents of the Oriente region of Ecuador rely on, interfering with their right to water.

Along with deprivation of natural resources often comes denial of the right to work. When mangroves are destroyed due to poor shrimp farming practices in Brazil, for example, it devastates the marine environment and damages fish stocks, putting local fishermen out of work.

Environmental degradation also implicates the right to culture. Some of the most glaring examples of cultural deprivations involve indigenous peoples whose lifestyles often depend on their relationship with the natural environment. The impacts of climate change on the Arctic environment, for example, have disproportionate effects on Inuit culture, as the Inuit way of life is closely

---

28   Ding, Y, Anderson, K. et al., *Earthjustice Environmental Rights Report, 2008*, p.7. Oakland, California. http://earthjustice.org/sites/default/files/library/reports/2008-environmental-rights-report.pdf

linked to environmental conditions (e.g., The Arctic Petition at the American Human Rights Commission, 2007).[29]

The right to development and the right to a healthy environment share considerable common ground. Although purely economic development activities often have negative environmental effects, a holistic model of sustainable development recognizes that environmentally destructive economic progress does not produce long-term societal progress. Thus, for example, oil development in Ecuador might bring a short-term influx of capital, but depletion of the country's natural resources ultimately interferes with the ability of the population, particularly indigenous peoples who live off the land, to develop.

The right to information in the environmental context has, at least, two components: the right to obtain government-held information on request, and the government's affirmative duty to apprise the people of environmental dangers and emergencies. For instance, information about a chemical spill in the city of Harbin, China, was kept from residents in communities downstream, threatening their health and lives through a violation of the right to information.

The right to information is itself a component of the right to public participation, which includes everything from suffrage to direct involvement in the planning of development activities. This right comes into play whenever a government makes an environmentally significant decision without providing meaningful opportunities for affected parties to participate. Andean citizens, for example, have been denied their right to participate in negotiations over the Andean Free Trade Agreement, which will have broad environmental impacts that may threaten their lives and well-being.

The right to shelter and adequate housing is necessarily implicated when environmental degradation displaces individuals and communities or compels them to live in unhealthy, hazardous conditions. The European Court of Human Rights, for example, confirmed the states' obligation to relocate persons whose homes had been fouled by environmental pollution.[30]

The examples of environmental aspects of recognized human rights described here reflect only a part of the multiple connections between human rights and environmental protection, most of which are relevant for the Pacific Islanders.

---

29 Jessica Gordon, "Inter-American Commission on Human Rights to Hold Hearing after Rejecting Inuit Climate Change Petition," *Sustainable Development Law and Policy 2*, no.7 (2007): 55

http://digitalcommons.wcl.american.edu/cgi/viewcontent.cgi?article=1239&context=sdlp

30 Ding, Y, Anderson, K. et al., *Earthjustice Environmental Rights Report, 2008*, p.7.

Supported by the international human rights law and other substantive areas that combine human rights and environmental considerations (such as humanitarian law and the effects of development projects funded by multilateral development banks), this part of the book will establish the place of the Sinking Islands in the human rights context. Moreover, it will also illustrate the consequences of the climate experience over the Pacific peoples' rights and, ultimately, lives.

INTRODUCTION TO A NEW CONCEPT: THE INTERNATIONAL HYBRID LAW

In 2007, when the author of this book extended his research regarding the impact of climate change in international law, focusing on specific cases like the one in the Pacific Islands, a legal necessity emerged to simplify the analyzes of these cases, focusing on the core of the problem and not necessary on the form.

In most cases, when the phenomenon of climate change is legally analyzed, there is always a cause found within the environmental law, like violation of the principles or the case of the Kyoto Protocol. Consequently, the main effects of the "legal" climate change are mostly found in the human rights law, due to its unavoidable first impact upon the target society. Secondary, as a subsidiary effect, there is the refugee law, also present due to its strong impact, but mostly as a human alternative to this impact, regardless of the type of response: immediate, intermediate or long-term. For example, when a society is affected by a climate change related event,[31]Human rights are the first to be affected (e.g. violations of one's right to life, right to a clean environment, the right to work,

---

31   Sea level rise, drought, desertification, natural disasters or other meteorological phenomena due to climate change.

etc.). Soon after the impact, since the process in most cases is not reversible, people of the respective society try to find alternatives to improve their affected human rights by adapting or migrating. Most societies choose an instinctive and rapid response, which is migration. This does not mean that human mobility represents a failure of adaptation; only that people tend to react with immediate solutions to an oppressive situation.[32]

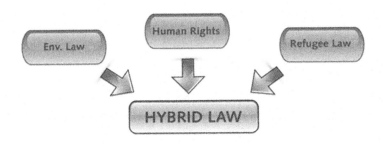

Therefore, having the primary legal cause in environmental law and the significant effects in human rights law and refugee law (subsidiary), a case study should be analyzed and researched from these three perspectives concurrently, indivisibly, interdependently, and interrelated, to complete the purpose of Hybrid Law. Hence, the research is simplified, using a single lens as a replacement for a three-way analysis.

There are two major advantages of using Hybrid Law as a legal research tool: in addition to a basic and clearer picture, if used concurrently under the umbrella of international law, the case study benefits from all principles and rights emerging from all three branches, regardless of the source.[33] Thus, if the case requires an influential argument, this could be easily found in one of the three branches and used accordingly, not necessarily considering the power (soft versus binding) of the law; the same theory of using all three branches of law also applies in the case of the signatory (or not) states of interest.

32   Janos Bogardi & Koko Warner, *Here Comes the Flood*. NATURE REPORTS CLIMATE CHANGE (DEC. 11, 2008), http://www.nature.com/climate/2009/0901/full/climate.2008.138.html

33   Example: the principles of environmental law do have a stronger resonance in international law compared with the right to a clean environment from the human rights law.

The second benefit of using Hybrid Law as a research tool stands for the increased protection of the case. The case is guarded simultaneously by three combined branches of international law, and, therefore, human security increases exponentially. One of the results of such protection is seen via Climate Refugees, who are not recognized under refugee law, but who gain more protection from human rights law and also the environmental law. Nevertheless, even though refugee law "would not apply" in the case of Climate Refugees, there are principles under the 1951 Convention that could easily be used under Hybrid Law,[34] According to the Office of the United Nations High Commissioner for Refugees (UNHCR).

Initially, the Hybrid Law research tool was intended to be used in the case of the Pacific islands only. However, since 2007 it has been also applied to other geographical regions affected by climate change like South Asia, Northern Africa or the North Pole.[35] The perspectives of the Hybrid Law could go deeper into the core of international law, at the abstract and philosophical level, if the research tool would be regarded as a concept of international law, and naturally as the progressive interpretation of law:[36] What if the main cause identified by the Hybrid Law in the field of environmental law could become the effect (or subsidiary effect) of human rights or refugee law violations, in a reverse analysis? Could climate change be considered an effect of these violations?

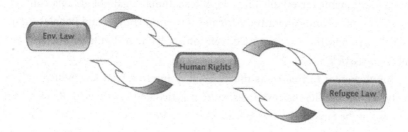

---

34 Such as the principle of "non-refoulment," which could be extracted from the refugee law and be valid in the case of climate-induced migrants, although 1951 Convention does not apply.

35 Petition to the Inter-Am. Comm'n H.R. Seeking Relief from Violations Resulting from Global Warming Caused by Acts and Omissions of the U.S. (2005), http://earthjustice.org/sites/default/files/library/legal_docs/petition-to-the-inter-american-commission-on-human-rights-on-behalf-of-the-inuit-circumpolar-conference.pdf.

36 Arsanjani Reisman et al., INTERNATIONAL LAW IN CONTEMPORARY PERSPECTIVE (2d ed. 2004).

This part of the book will explore the sources of international law in an attempt to create a clear image of the Sinking Islands in the international law context, with the related positive and negative aspects of the case. It will also try to recognize the right to a clean environment of the Sinking Islands, viewed as member states of the international community.

In this respect, the study will focus on the states' responsibility for climate change, evaluating the international legal obligations under the sources of international law (e.g., Article 38.1 of the International Court of Justice: international conventions, whether general or particular, recognized by states; international custom, as evidence of a general practice accepted as law; the general principles of law, recognized by civilized nations, and the judicial decisions and the teachings of the most highly qualified publicists from various countries as subsidiary means for the determination of rules of law) or under any other soft sources of international law, relevant in particular to the Sinking Islands.

Regarding the international conventions that could positively lead to the establishment of international legal obligations, the study will analyze the United Nations Covenant on Economic, Social and Cultural Rights, Article 24, and the United Nations Covenant on Civil and Political Rights, Article 2.1. Regionally, it will emphasize the importance of the right to a clean environment, the key argument for establishing the international legal obligations concerning the Pacific Islands under the African Charter on Human and Peoples Rights (Article 24), and the American Convention on Human Rights Protocol of San Salvador (Article 11).

Supplemental to treaties is the customary international law, which will be analyzed through its main sources: state practice and *opinio juris*. Relevant for the case of the Sinking Islands are the Trail Smelter Case[37] or the Corfu Channel Case,[38] in which it was held that states should not allow their territory to be used in such a way as to harm territory outside its jurisdiction. Judicial decisions in international law[39] concerning the right to the environment or the assessment

---

37   Trail Smelter Case (U.S. v. Canada), Arbitral Tribunal, 3 R. Int'l Arb. Awards 1905 (1949).

38   Corfu Channel Case (The United Kingdom v. Albania), 1949 I.C.J. 4 (Apr. 9).

39   E.g., Gabcikovo-Nagymaros Project, (Hungary/Slovakia) 1997 I.C.J 92, available at http://www.icj-cij.org/docket/files/92/7375.pdf

of the jurisdiction[40] will emphasize the applicability of the right to environment and right to self-identity in the case of the Sinking Islands.[41]

After setting up international legal obligations, the book will demonstrate an international obligation for states to consider additional legal arguments. This will be done to uncover a breach of this obligation under international law and establish a causal link between the respective breach and the damage suffered (in process) by the Sinking Islands. The following are former policies as related to these international obligations: *Sic utere tuo ut alienum non laedas*[42] (the United Nations Conference on Human Development since 1972, did not create law, but generally considered existing law); The Precautionary Principle (Maastricht Treaty, Barcelona Convention, International Court of Justice, avoided environmental damage through planning and blocking the flow of potentially damaging activities); The Principle of Sustainable Development, Principle 3 of the Rio Declaration, the most significant damage to the environment has happened as a result of states' pursuit of development policies; The Polluter Pays Principle (endorsed by the Organisation for Economic Cooperation and Development [OECD] in 1972, Principle 16 of the Rio Declaration); *Erga Omnes* Obligations (Barcelona Traction Case, the International Court of Justice [ICJ Reports, 1950]).

The study will argue for citizens of the Sinking Islands being able to bring a claim under the Kyoto Protocol against the responsible countries for breaching the convention as well as against countries that not a party to the Protocol, as the United States.[43] Regarding the United States, the second highest emitter of GHG and carbon, the research will demonstrate that although the US is not bound by the emissions reductions targets contained by the Kyoto Protocol, the country is a signatory (not ratified) to the 1992 United Nations Framework Convention

---

40   E.g., Bankovic v. Belgium, App. No. 52207/99, Eur. H.R. (2001), available at http://www.iilj.org/courses/documents/Bankovicv.Belgiumetal.pdf.

41   *See* Petition to the Inter-Am. Comm'n H.R. Seeking Relief from Violations Resulting from Global Warming Caused by Acts of Omission of the U.S. (2005), available at http://www.inuitcircumpolar.com/files/uploads/icc-files/FINALPetitionICC.pdf.

42   Which means "use your own property in such a way that you do not injure others."

43   Keely Boom, *See you in Court: The Rising Tide of International Climate Litigation*, THE CONVERSATION (Sept. 28, 2011), http://www.climatelaw.org/cases/country/intl/icj/palau (explaining that the Pacific Island State of Palau is seeking an Advisory Opinion to determine how the 'no harm rule' and the United Nations' Law of the Sea Convention apply to damage, such as the State becoming uninhabitable, caused by climate change. It will be the "world's first international climate change case").

on Climate Change.[44] Under Article 18 of the Vienna Convention on the Law of Treaties, as a signatory, it is under the obligation not to do anything that would defeat the object and the purpose of the treaty, pending ratification.[45] The object and purpose of the United Nations Framework Convention on Climate Change are stabilizing the greenhouse gas emissions at a level that would prevent dangerous anthropogenic (human-induced) interference with the climate system.[46] This is not an exemption *inter alia* for the United States, and it is determined that the government did not put in place the necessary regulations to cap and reduce the levels of emissions that are constant with the climate change mitigation under the United Nations Framework Convention on Climate Change.

This study will now shift to the Sinking Islands and the actual status of the Pacific Islands under international law. It will focus on the international experience in creating artificial islands, as an alternative to the submerging lands (e.g., Japan, Hong Kong). It will also center on the role of several international and regional institutions, such as churches or non-governmental organizations. The examples of different international projects for environmental protection (e.g., Venice, Italy) and the Hulhumale, the artificial island construction within Maldives Islands, will reveal opposite applications of the same concepts, under the same international development policies, but in different regions (for example, the Hulhumale Project had to be stopped due to a lack of international financial aid over $70 million). Later, the right to self-identity of the Pacific Islands' population, as well as the Pacific peoples' right to national identity, along with all the rights of a defined state, will be uncovered under customary international law. In addition, implicit consequences will be analyzed, as these people's social, political, religious and cultural rights could be directly affected by new host societies.

Centered on the anticipated submerging scenarios *vis-a-vis* the Pacific Islands, multiple fissures of international law will be demonstrated, asking for mandatory immediate international actions in this regard. If the course of sinking, as it already started, continues as predicted, it will be the first time in the history of humankind that a country loses its territory without the use of military

---

44   *Status of Ratification of the Convention*, UNITED NATIONS FRAMEWORK CONVENTION ON CLIMATE CHANGE (last visited June 17, 2013), *available at* http://unfccc.int/essential_background/convention/status_of_ratification/items/2631.php.

45   Vienna Convention on the Law of Treaties art. 18, May 23, 1969, 1155 U.N.T.S. 331.

46   United Nations Framework Convention on Climate Change, art. 2, June 12, 1992, 1771 U.N.T.S. 107, http://unfccc.int/resource/docs/convkp/conveng.pdf.

force. Moreover, under international *jurisprudence*, the definition of a State, as a person of international law, should possess the following qualifications to existence: a permanent population, a defined land, called territory, a government, and the capacity to enter into relations with other states. A nation's "territorial integrity" is one of the paramount legal principles of international law and international law does not offer a definition for a country without land. Considering *de facto* circumstances, how will international law define the citizens of the Sinking Islands, if these people will not have a territory to define their States? By all means, all the Pacific Islanders would become Stateless Persons. This perspective corroborated with the fact that those who are already emigrating are not considered refugees, may lead to the conclusion that the experiences and alternatives offered by the international community are limited and incomplete for such a scenario.[47] The 1954 United Nations Convention relating to the Status of Stateless Persons or The Hague Draft Convention of 1931 are not sufficient to protect citizens of the Sinking Islands. The Pacific Islanders may not become the object of any *opinio necessitasis juris* case, simply because their naturalization process is mandatory for the Contracting States, with no option out. The "Genuine Link" theory is inapplicable (e.g., Nottebohm Case, Liechtenstein versus Guatemala, the International Court of Justice, ICJ, 1955) with no future reference in the International Court of Justice jurisprudences. The question is: Are the Sinking Islands becoming virtual countries?

The last part of the international law approach will analyze the current activities of the main decisional factors in the case of the Sinking Islands. It should be noted that the Pacific Access Category Program of New Zealand (PAC) represents the only program so far elaborated by the countries with an important role in this problem. The PAC represents a scheme developed by the New Zealand government for the citizens of Kiribati, Tuvalu or Tonga.[48] The number of people accepted by the program is limited (75 documented immigrants per year) and the conditions are strict, referring to those able to rapidly integrate and able to work. Based on an existing offer of employment, the program is only available to citizens between the ages of 18 to 45 at the registration period closing

---

47 It is important to note that there is no basic right to a sound environment, and under the Geneva Convention climate change is not a basis for humanitarian asylum.

48 *See Pacific Access Category*, IMMIGRATION NEW ZEALAND (April 2, 2013), http://www.immigration.govt.nz/migrant/stream/live/pacificaccess/

date, with good language skills and health, and "good character" requirements.[49] Although it is a slow process and with understandable (not humanitarian) social protection, the program is unique, as Australia is not offering a response at this time on the same issue. However, "Australia's efforts do not extend beyond the AusAID-funded South Pacific Sea Level and Climate Monitoring Project," which includes 12 island nations.[50] "The project's brief is not to provide relocation funding, or even to progress the unchartered legal territory of Climate Refugees; it rather aims to help the islands 'better manage their environments and achieve sustainable development.'"[51]Moreover, other international actors that have demonstrated their humanitarian capacities in the past (e.g., Sweden, Norway, Vietnam) will most likely react when the Pacific crisis will escalate to a maximum. Canada and France have been integral in providing limited funding for relocations, in response to expert predictions. So far, no international assistance or accountability projects have been developed by the principal polluters mentioned earlier in the research.

CONCLUSION AND *DE LEGE FERENDA* PROPOSALS

The conclusion of this book will reflect on the results obtained by the research, regarding each approach the study used. Accordingly, the findings will be structured in environmental, refugee and human rights sections, all analyzed under international law, each element being presented in general (international) perspectives and particular views (Pacific, regional). Nevertheless, the conclusions expressed within this part of the dissertation will reveal different solutions, as a direct result of the conducted study, but a certain common outcome regardless of the point of view is that a galvanized world action is needed to stop (and reverse) climate change, damage to our planet which must be stopped under all circumstances.

---

49   *Who Can Register for the 2013 Pacific Access Category*, IMMIGRATION NEW ZEALAND (March 20, 2013), http://www.immigration.govt.nz/migrant/stream/live/pacificaccess/registration.htm

50   *That Sinking Feeling*, THE SYDNEY MORNING HERALD (April 22, 2007), http://www.smh.com.au/news/environment/that-sinking-feeling/2007/04/21/1176697138927.html?page=fullpage

51   *Id.*

CHAPTER ONE

HISTORICAL & LEGAL BACKGROUND

1.1. GLOBAL CLIMATE CHANGE

1.1.1. Historical evolution of the process: causes & effects

For decades, humans have been trying to understand the interactive processes in the Earth's system that governs the climate and climate change.[52] With the proliferation of modern tools and technology, combined with the cumulative nature of science, we are gaining a deeper understanding and quantification of climate processes. As a result, climate change science is becoming a new interdisciplinary approach to making sense of our environment.

The climate system consists of the atmosphere, land surface, oceans, snow and ice, and living things.[53] Over time, the "system evolves under the influence of its own internal dynamics," such as orbital forcing and the relative positions of continents and oceans,[54] and due to external factors, such as volcanic eruptions and human-induced changes.[55]

---

52 Herve Le Treut, et al., *Historical Overview of Climate Change, in* CLIMATE CHANGE 2007: THE PHYSICAL SCIENCE BASIS 95 (Susan Solomon, et al. eds., 2007), https://www.ipcc-wg1.unibe.ch/publications/wg1-ar4/ar4-wg1-chapter1.pdf

53 *Id.* at 96.

54 UNITED NATIONS ENVIRONMENT PROGRAMME, CLIMATE CHANGE SCIENCE COMPENDIUM 4 (2009), http://www.unep.org/pdf/ccScienceCompendium2009/cc_ScienceCompendium2009_full_highres_en.pdf.

55 Treut, *Physical Science Basis, supra* note 54, at 96.

Solar power radiation powers the climate system and approximately 30 percent of this energy is reflected back into space due to the presence of clouds, small particles like aerosols, and small light-colored areas of the Earth's surface such as snow, deserts, and ice.[56] The remaining energy is absorbed by the Earth's surface as a result of GHGs: water vapor, carbon dioxide (CO_2), methane (CH_4) and nitrous oxide (N_2O), which warm the earth in a process termed the "natural greenhouse effect."[57] The climate also responds indirectly to changes in solar radiation through a serious of feedback mechanisms, which can either amplify or diminish the greenhouse effect.[58] For instance, as the GHG concentration increases in the Earth's atmosphere, snow and ice begin to melt. This reveals the dark surface of the Earth, previously covered by ice, which works to absorb more of the Sun's heat, creating a warmer climate, causing more ice to melt, and resulting in a "self-reinforcing" cycle.[59]

A great deal of research has shown that, since pre-industrial times, human activity has altered the chemical composition of our atmosphere and intensified the natural greenhouse effect by releasing GHGs into the atmosphere through the combustion of fossil fuels and removal of forests (to name a few).[60] Between 1970 and 2004, global emissions of CO_2, CH_4, N_2O and other GHGs, have increased by 70 percent (24 percent between 1990 and 2004), from 28.7 to

---

[56] A.P.M. Baede, et al., *The Climate System: an Overview, in* Climate Change 2001: The Scientific Basis 89 (J.T. Houghton, et al. eds., 2001), *available at* http://www.grida.no/climate/ipcc_tar/wg1/pdf/WG1_TAR-FRONT.pdf [hereinafter Baede, *Scientific Basis*]; Treut, *Physical Science Basis, supra* note 54.

[57] *Id.*

[58] *Id.* at 96.

[59] Brian Dawson and Matt Spannagle, *The Complete Guide to Climate Change* (New York: Routledge, 2009).

[60] Treut, *Physical Science Basis, supra* note 54, at 96; *Atmospheric Conce, in* Greenhouse Gasses 14 (June 7, 2012), http://www.epa.gov/climatechange/pdfs/CI-greenhouse-gases.pdf; Baede, Scientific Basis, supra note 58, at 92("The amount of carbon dioxide ... has increased by more than 30% since pre-industrial times and is still increasing at an unprecedented rate of on average 0.4% per year.").

49 Gigatons of carbon dioxide equivalents (GtCO2-eq.).[61] While some scientists still struggle with attributing the causes of climate change to human activity (with some defined level of confidence)[62] the advancement of science has, nevertheless, allowed the climate community to make increasingly more definitive statements about human impacts on climate change.[63]

1.1.2. Scientific facts and comparative data/statistics

The primary characteristic (and limitation) of Earth science is that we are unable to perform controlled experiments on the whole system and then observe the results. However, system-scale experiments are precisely what we need to fully verify or falsify climate change hypotheses.[64] Nevertheless, more than a decade of laboratory measurements, observational experiments, and theoretical analyzes has strengthened our understanding of climate science as described below.

Detecting global surface temperatures

Efforts to quantify and record the weather started in the early 1600s, with the invention of the thermometer,[65] and continue today with the proliferation of international organizations that engage in standardized meteorological observations (e.g., International Meteorological Organization, World Meteorological Organization, and Global Observing System). Additionally, there are over 11,000

---

61 *Greenhouse Gas Emissions*, UNITED NATIONS STATISTICS DIVISION,

    http://unstats.un.org/unsd/environment/air_greenhouse_emissions.htm (last updated July 2010) (containing GHG emissions estimates for a various countries); Richard B. Alley, et al., *Summary for Policymakers, in* CLIMATE CHANGE 2007: THE PHYSICAL SCIENCE BASIS 141 (Susan Solomon, et al. eds., 2007), *available at* http://www.ipcc.ch/pdf/assessment-report/ar4/wg1/ar4_wg1_full_report.pdf; The definition of carbon dioxide equivalents (CO_2-eq) is the amount of CO_2 emission that would cause the same radiative forcing as an emitted amount of a well-mixed greenhouse gas or a mixture of well-mixed greenhouse gases, all multiplied with their respective GWPs to take into account the differing times they remain in the atmosphere.

62 Unequivocal attribution (i.e., stating explicitly that x is the cause of y) would require controlled experimentation with our climate system, but there is no "spare" Earth with which to experiment.

63 *See Reports*, INTERGOVERNMENTAL PANEL ON CLIMATE CHANGE,

    http://www.ipcc.ch/publications_and_data/publications_and_data_reports.shtml#1 (last visited on June 10, 2013) (containing various assessment reports).

64 Hans Schellnuber, et. al., EARTH SYSTEM ANALYSIS FOR SUSTAINABILITY, in Dahlem Workshop Reports (Boston: Massachusets Institute of Technology, 2004) 352.

65 Treut, *Physical Science Basis, supra* note 54, at 100.

weather stations worldwide, which measure sea, land and air temperatures along with ships, aircrafts and satellites also dedicated to the task.[66] All these work to detect global aspects of climate change.

In 2010, "the global average temperatures were estimated to be 0.53°C ± 0.09°C above the 1961-1990 annual average of 14°C."[67] "This makes 2010 tied for the warmest year in records dating back to 1880."[68] "The 2010 nominal value of +0.53°C ranks just ahead of those of 2005 (+0.52°C) and 1998 (+0.51°C), although the differences between the three years are not statistically significant, due to uncertainties mainly associated with sampling the Earth's land and sea surface temperatures using only a finite number of observation sites."[69]

As the science of climate progresses, climate change patterns are no longer reliant on a single variable (temperature), but use multiple variables (such as precipitation and global pressure patterns), along with detecting changes in ocean and atmosphere temperatures.[70] Such studies "make it easier to address attribution issues."[71]

Examples of progress in understanding climate process

To get insights into the Earth's past climate, a wide range of geomorphology and paleontology studies have also been conducted. For instance, bubbles found in the ice cores provide essential information on past surface temperatures and atmospheric chemical composition of carbon dioxide.[72] While insights on the past climate do not provide an analogy for the future, they help us to understand better the climatic process. Thus, it contributes to separate anthropogenic from

---

66   *See Climate Observation Networks and Systems*, WORLD METEOROLOGICAL ORGANIZATION,
       http://www.wmo.int/pages/themes/climate/climate_observation_networks_systems.php (last viewed June 10, 2013).

67   WORLD METEOROLOGICAL ORGANIZATION, WMO STATEMENT ON THE STATUS OF THE GLOBAL CLIMATE IN 2010 2 (2010),
       available at http://www.wmo.int/pages/prog/wcp/wcdmp/statement/documents/1074_en.pdf

68   *Id.*

69   *Id.* The data here is taken from the latest publication on the Status of Global Climate. WMO, working with UNEP, is responsible for the periodic assessments of climate change issued by the IPCC and for the publication of the biennial reviews of the Global Climate System.

70   Treut, *Physical Science Basis, supra* note 54, at 103.

71   *Id.* at 103.

72   *Id.* at 106.

natural variability, "improving the ability to detect and attribute anthropogenic climate change."[73] This is also done through improvements in numerical models.

With the advent of supercomputer speeds, climate models have grown in complexity, spatial resolution, and length of simulations.[74] Today, these models not only project time-dependent scenarios of climate evolution but can also be coupled to ocean-atmospheric models to give more accurate climate predictions.[75] By using this coupling mechanism, the National Academy of Science was the first to report on a possible "range of global mean equilibrium surface temperature increase of between 1.5°C and 4.5°C"[76] for the doubling of carbon dioxide emissions.[77]

Carbon dioxide

Without underestimating the impact of other compounds, it has been noted that the Earth's net radiation depends largely on emissions of carbon dioxide. This is not only because it is the leading cause of the increased greenhouse effect, but also because carbon dioxide remains in the atmosphere for a long time.[78] Taking account of all the GHGs, economists have suggested different future scenarios by 2100.[79] For the lowest emissions scenario, the average warming is expected to reach approximately 1.8°C; this figure would rise to 4°C in the highest emission scenario.[80] Despite the fact that detection and attribution

---

73   *Id.* at 112.

74   *Id.*

75   *Id.* at 113.

76   Treut, *Physical Science Basis, supra* note 54, at 117; *Carbon Dioxide and Climate: A Scientific Assessment,* National Academy of Sciences 16 (July 23-27, 1979), *available at* http://www.atmos.ucla.edu/~brianpm/download/charney_report.pdf

77   This range remained part of the conventional wisdom at least since IPCC's Third Assessment report in 2001.

78   William D. Collins, et al., *Global Climate Projections, in* CLIMATE CHANGE 2007: THE PHYSICAL SCIENCE BASIS 824 (Susan Solomon, et al. eds., 2007), *available at* http://www.ipcc.ch/pdf/assessment-report/ar4/wg1/ar4_wg1_full_report.pdf ("some fraction (about 20%) of emitted CO2 remains in the atmosphere for many millennia. Because of slow removal processes, atmospheric CO2 will continue to increase in the long term even if its emission is substantially reduced from present levels.").

79   *IPCC Special Reports on Climate Change,* INTERGOVERNMENTAL PANEL ON CLIMATE CHANGE (2000), *available at* http://www.ipcc.ch/ipccreports/sres/emission/index.php?idp=0

80   *Id.* Emission scenarios were developed in order to explore the uncertainties behind potential trends in global developments and GHG emissions, as well as the key drivers that influence these.

research ventured into more sophisticated observational data and modeling, the research still does not provide a perfect depiction of reality. Thus, over the decades, there has been a growing focus on the formal treatment of uncertainty.

Treating Uncertainty

When working with climate records and data, attention has been placed on identifying errors or unintended bias arising from data sampling, methods of analysis and/or data combination. To promote consistency in how such uncertainty is treated, the IPCC came up with two metrics on how to communicate confidence in climate findings:

(a) Qualitatively: "confidence in the validity of a finding, the type, amount, quality, and consistency of evidence" (understanding of theory, data, models), along with the degree of agreement.[81]

(b) Quantitatively: findings are "expressed probabilistically" based on model results, statistical analysis of observations, or judgment.[82]

In addition to this, the IPCC has set forth specific language guidelines and provided critical steps necessary to evaluate and communicate the degree of certainty in key findings.[83] Thus, by ensuring uncertainties are consistent across the science community, our ability to project the various aspects of climate change increases.

1.1.2.i. Glacial melt and sea level rise

Glaciers and ice caps that are not adjacent to the large ice sheets of Greenland and Antarctica cover an area of between 512×10^3 and 546×10^3 km², which

---

81   Michael D. Mastrandrea, et al., *Guidance Note for Lead Authors of the IPCC Fifth Assessment Report on Consistent Treatment of Uncertainties,* INTERGOVERNMENTAL PANEL ON CLIMATE CHANGE 1 (July 6-7, 2010), *available at* http://www.ipcc.ch/pdf/supporting-material/uncertainty-guidance-note.pdf.

82   *Id.*

83   *See Id.*at 38 (Explaining the likelihood terminology and the associated probability level).

represents a sea level rise equivalent to between 0.15 and 0.37 m.[84] Since the 1980s, new and improved observation techniques show a global-scale decline of snow and ice, despite growth in some places. For instance, most mountain glaciers are getting smaller, snow cover is retreating earlier, Greenland and West Antarctica's ice sheets are thinning, and sea ice is shrinking in the Arctic across all seasons.[85] Reports on individual glaciers or limited glacier areas support the global picture of ongoing strong ice shrinkage in almost all regions including notable examples in Scandinavia, the European Alps, the Asian high mountains and tropical glaciers. The most probable cause appears to be widespread warming;[86] although changes in the atmospheric moisture level in the tropics[87] and iceberg calving[88] might also be contributing.

During the twentieth century alone the rate of sea-level rise was, and still is, increasing, from a few tenths of a millimeter per year to 1.7 mm per year.[89] Many different physical processes will contribute to future sea level rise, but none will produce uniform results. For instance, based on recent observations, future projections suggest that the following process will lead to a 1m sea level rise by 2100[90]:

- Ice sheets will contribute to a 13-56 cm rise.
- Mountain glaciers will constitute 12 cm rise.
- Thermal expansion will equate to 15-40 cm.

---

84 Peter Lemke, et al., *Observations: Changes in Snow, Ice and Frozen Ground, in* CLIMATE CHANGE 2007: THE PHYSICAL SCIENCE BASIS (Susan Solomon, et al. eds., 2007), *available at* http://www.ipcc.ch/pdf/ assessment-report/ar4/wg1/ar4_wg1_full_report.pdf.

85 Atsumu Ohmura, *Cryosphere During the Twentieth Century, in* THE STATE OF THE PLANET: FRONTIERS AND CHALLENGES IN GEOPHYSICS 239 (Robert S.J. Sparks & Christopher J. Hawkesworth eds. 2004); International Union of Geodesy and Geophysics, Washington, DC, p. 257; Mark B. Dyurgerov & Mark F. Meier, *Glaciers and the Changing Earth System: A 2004 Snapshot,* INST. OF ARCTIC AND ALPINE RES., 2005, at 117, http://instaar.colorado.edu/uploads/occasional-papers/OP58_dyurgerov_meier.pdf; *Global Warming Fast Facts,* National Geographic (June 14, 2007), http://news.national-geographic.com/news/2004/12/1206_041206_global_warming.html (explaining that the by the year 2040, the Artic might have an ice-free summer).

86 Lemke, *supra* note 85 at 375.

87 Solomon, *supra* note 9 at 40.

88 Lemke, *supra* note 85 at 356.

89 UNESCO INTERGOVERNMENTAL OCEANOGRAPHIC COMM'N., SEA LEVEL RISE, AND VARIABILITY: A SUMMARY FOR POLICY MAKERS 2 (T. Aarup et al. eds., 2010), *available at* http://unesdoc.unesco.org/ images/0018/001893/189369e.pdf.

90 Bill Hare et al., "Presentation for Western Pacific Islands Durban: Future Sea Level Rise and its Implications for SIDS and LDCs," *Climate Analytics,* (2011) available at http://climateanalytics.org/ publications/2011/future-sea-level-rise-and-its-implications-for-sids-and-ldcs

- Instability of the West Antarctic ice sheet can cause up to a 3m rise, but the rate is unknown.

Overall, the glaciers and ice caps have undergone significant changes and will continue to play a fundamental role in sea level rise. Despite this, precautions have to be taken when using these trends as indicators of climate change and when reporting on future scenarios.

Issues in measuring and reporting

In an attempt to link glacial retreat to climate change, one difficulty is the sparse historical database.[91] "Although the 'extent' of ice (sea ice and glacier margins, for example) has been observed for a long time at a few locations, the 'amount' of ice (thickness or depth) is difficult to measure."[92] This makes it impossible to reconstruct past mass balance.[93] Global monitoring of ice thickness is impossible, and it becomes necessary to extrapolate findings from local measurements.[94] This can lead to issues in reporting, as was the recent case in the IPCC's Fourth Assessment Report. Specifically, IPCC's claim, made in 2007, that "Glaciers in the Himalaya are receding faster than in any other part of the world and, if the present rate continues, the likelihood of them disappearing by the year 2035 and perhaps sooner is very high if the Earth keeps warming at the current rate,"[95] was unfounded.[96] Sources revealed that this claim was not peer-reviewed scientific literature, but rather a media interview with a scientist conducted in 1999.[97] Several senior scientists have now said the claim

---

91 Lemke, *supra* note 85 at 374.

92 *Id.*

93 *Id.*

94 *Id.* at 375.

95 Rex V. Cruz, et al., *Asia, in* CLIMATE CHANGE 2007: IMPACTS, ADAPTATION AND VULNERABILITY 493 (Martin Parry, et al. eds., 2007), *available at* http://www.ipcc.ch/pdf/assessment-report/ar4/wg2/ar4_wg2_full_report.pdf

96 Damian Carrington, "IPCC Officials Admit Mistake Over Melting Himalayan Glaciers," THE GUARD-IAN (2010), http://www.guardian.co.uk/environment/2010/jan/20/ipcc-himalayan-glaciers-mistake; *See* Pallava Bagle, *Himalayan Glaciers Melting Deadline 'A Mistake,'* BBC NEWS (Dec. 5, 2009), http://news.bbc.co.uk/2/hi/south_asia/8387737.stm.

97 *Id.*

was unrealistic and that the large Himalayan glaciers could not melt in a few decades.[98] While IPCC maintained that the broader conclusion of the report is unaffected (that glaciers have melted and will affect the supply of water), some chose to publish their papers on glaciers.[99]

1.1.2.ii. Climate extreme events

There has been growing evidence on how changes in climate can lead to changes in frequency, intensity, spatial extent and duration of extreme weather and climate events ("climate extremes")[100] and can lead to unprecedented climate extremes.[101] As Bradbury and DeConcini stated, "Recent climate science assessment reports by the U.S. National Academy of Sciences and the U.S. Global Change Research Program find that several types of extreme weather are on the rise, that man-made climate change is likely responsible, and that these trends are expected to continue."[102] The confidence in changes in extreme events depends on the quantity and quality of the data available and varies across regions and the different

---

98   *Id.*("IPCC officials admit mistake over melting Himalayan glaciers: Senior members of the United Nation's climate science body admit a claim that Himalayan glaciers could melt away by 2035 was unfounded.").

99   *See* V.K. Raina, "Himalayan Glaciers: A State-of-the-Art Review of Glacial Studies, Glacial Retreat, and Climate Change," Science and Public Policy Institute, 2009, *available at*

    http://scienceandpublicpolicy.org/reprint/himalayan_review_of_glacial_studies.html

100   Simon K. Allen, et al., *Managing the Risks of Extreme Events and Disasters to Advance Climate Change Adaptation: Summary for Policy Makers*, IPCC, 2012, at 2, *available at* http://www.ipcc-wg2.gov/SREX/images/uploads/SREX-SPMbrochure_FINAL.pdf. For simplicity, this paper uses the Climate Change Adaptation Community's terminology (CCA Community), which refers to extreme events primarily based on its statistical occurrence (rare). This is contrary to the Disaster Risk Reduction community's definition, which mainly focuses on different hazard and disaster types (including non-meteorological phenomena such as earthquakes). Increasingly, there has been a call for the international community to bridge the gap between these two disciplines. *See* John Birkmann, et al., *Addressing the Challenge: Recommendations and Quality Criteria for Linking Disaster Risk Reduction and Adaptation to Climate Change*, German Committee for Disaster Reduction, 2009, at 6, *available at* http://www.preventionweb.net/files/10193_DKKVreport.pdf.

101   "Global Warming Fast Facts," *National Geographic*, 2007,

    http://news.nationalgeographic.com/news/2004/12/1206_041206_global_warming.html (describing some extremes as wildfires, heat waves, and tropical storms).

102   *See* James Bradbury and Christina Deconcini, "The Connection Between Climate Change and Recent Extreme Weather Events," World Resources Institute, 2012, *available at* http://www.wri.org/publication/fact-sheet-connection-between-climate-change-and-recent-extreme-weather-events

extremes.[103] To summarize the latest findings on extreme events since 1950, the IPCC's latest Special Report on climate change concludes[104]:

- Warm days and nights: *Very likely* that there has been an overall increase in some warm days and nights, and a decrease in the number of cold days and nights (particular to North America, Europe, and Australia).

- Daily temperatures: *Medium confidence* that Asia has experienced a warming trend in daily temperature extremes, with *low to medium confidence* for all of Africa and South America. In many (but not all) regions of the globe, there is *medium confidence* that the length or number of warm spells or heat waves has increased.

- Heavy precipitation: The number of heavy precipitation events in some regions has increased (statistically significant) and a majority of regions *likely* experienced increases rather than decreases.

- Tropical cyclones: After accounting for past changes in climate observations, there is *low confidence* that tropical cyclone activity has increased in the long term.

- Storms: In Northern and Southern Hemisphere, it is *likely* that there has been a poleward shift in extra-tropical storm tracks.

- Droughts: *Medium confidence* that some regions have experienced more intense and longer droughts such as in West Africa and southern Europe; while central North America and northwestern Australia has experienced less frequent and less severe droughts.

---

103 Simon K. Allen, et al., *Managing the Risks of Extreme Events and Disasters to Advance Climate Change Adaptation: Summary for Policy Makers*, IPCC, 2012, at 7, *available at* http://www.ipcc-wg2.gov/SREX/images/uploads/SREX-SPMbrochure_FINAL.pdf.

104 Simon K. Allen, et al., *Managing the Risks of Extreme Events and Disasters to Advance Climate Change Adaptation: Summary for Policy Makers*, IPCC, 2012, at 7, *available at* http://www.ipcc-wg2.gov/SREX/images/uploads/SREX-SPMbrochure_FINAL.pdf.

- Floods: Difficult to generalize a statement on floods due to limited available instrumental records of floods at gauge stations.

While it is challenging to attribute a single extreme event to anthropogenic climate change, the authors of the IPCC report have tried to assign a level of confidence to each specific event with some variation.[105]

1.1.3. Impacts, Vulnerabilities, and Adaptation

Currently, the planet is not on track to limit dangerous climate change; in fact, it is rapidly heading towards a world 4 to 6°C warmer by the end of this century, as compared to pre-industrial levels.[106] Not accounting for climate change mitigation and enhanced climate policy, the IPCC's Fifth Assessment Report projects impacts of climate change on the various socio-economic sectors[107]:

- Freshwater resources and their management: Decrease in the water volume stored in glaciers, salinization of groundwater and estuaries, increased risk of flood and drought due to rain variability, water shortage in certain areas (specifically in the Mediterranean Basin, western USA, and Australia) and water pollution, all indicate an overall net negative impact of climate change on future water resources and freshwater ecosystems.

- Food products: Even small increases in temperature will decrease yields in seasonally dry and tropical regions. Thus, the number of people at risk of food insecurity is projected to increase. Particularly, smallholder and subsistence farmers are the least likely to respond

---

105 For example, there is low confidence in the attribution of any detectable changes in tropical cyclones to anthropogenic influences, and medium confidence for the intensification of precipitation. The difference in confidence level is a result of the incomplete understanding of the physical mechanisms linking tropical cyclone metrics to climate change. See IPCC 2012, Section 3.

106 *Turn Down the Heat: Why a 4°C Warmer World Must be Avoided*, The World Bank, Nov. 2012, at xiii, http://climatechange.worldbank.org/sites/default/files/Turn_Down_the_heat_Why_a_4_degree_centrigrade_warmer_world_must_be_avoided.pdf (explaining that by the year 2100, there is a 20% chance that the world could warm more than 4°C.

107 Thomas Stocker, et al., *Technical Summary*, in Climate Change 2013, *available at* http://www.ipcc.ch/pdf/assessment-report/ar5/wg1/WG1AR5_TS_FINAL.pdf

to these changes as they are usually constrained by other factors such as poverty and other climate-related processes.[108]

- Coastal systems and low-lying areas: Analysis shows that in developing countries, even with only moderate changes in sea levels, inundation of agricultural land in coastal areas would double the coastal populations at risk.[109] To make matters worse, some of the largest cities (with five million or more inhabitants) have on average one-fifth of their population and one-sixth of their land area within the coastal zone. With the rise in sea levels and greater storm intensity, coastal settlements will be put under a significant amount of risk, especially in low-income countries.[110]

- Infrastructure: Vulnerability of infrastructure to climate change is generally greater in high-risk zones such as coastal and riverine areas and whose economies are closely linked to climate-sensitive resources.[111]

- Health: The projected impacts of climate change on human health tend to vary with country. For instance, expected trends in warming are projected to increase malnutrition, hunger, and subsequent disorders most notably in Africa, where warming is projected to decrease further crop availability. For Europe, the tick-borne

---

108 The effects of climate change will increase the likelihood of crop failure, increase diseases, and mortality among livestock, impact livelihoods by forcing households to sell their assets, cut health and educational expenditure and migration, and increase the likelihood of indebtedness and dependency on external help. John Morton, *The Impact of Climate Change on Smallholder and Subsistence Agriculture*, 104 PROC. OF THE NAT'L ACAD. OF SCI. 19680, 19685 (2007).

109 Susmita Dasgupta et al., "Exposure of Developing Countries to Sea Level Rise and Storm Surges," CLIMATE CHANGE 106 (2008): 567, HTTP://LINK.SPRINGER.COM/ARTICLE/10.1007%2Fs10584-010-9959-6#page-2

110 For instance, low-lying atoll communities, such as the Maldives and Kiribati, are especially vulnerable, as 80 percent of the islands lie one meter or less above sea level. Recent studies predict that sea levels could rise by up to two meters by 2100. In such a scenario, there will be devastating impacts on many low-lying countries, coastal regions, and cities. *See* William Hare et al., "Climate Hotspots: Key Vulnerable Regions, Climate Change, and Limits to Warming," 11 REGIONAL ENVTL. CHANGE 1, (2011), http://rd.springer.com/article/10.1007/s10113-010-0195-4

111 Tourism is a major economic factor, especially for small island developing states. It is likely that sea-level rise coupled with storms can damage the tourism infrastructure at coasts, thereby putting the economy and population at risk.

encephalitis is expected to move further north-eastward. For low-income countries, it is estimated that diarrheal diseases will increase by 2030, with an annual increase of 5-18 percent by 2050 for Aboriginal communities in Australia.

In sum, climate change is projected to have profound impacts on humans and our environment. Without adequate adaptation measures in place, it is probable that we might reach some of these anticipated changes.

Vulnerability

Vulnerability as a concept has evolved out of the social sciences and was first introduced to respond to the purely hazard-oriented perception of disasters.[112] Some authors have chosen to separate the term into biophysical vulnerabilities[113]and social vulnerabilities.[114] Although there is no universal definition of vulnerability,[115] we will focus on IPCC Fourth Assessment Report's definition of vulnerability in the context of climate change: "vulnerability to climate change is the degree to which geophysical, biological and socio-economic system are susceptible to and unable to cope with, adverse impacts of climate change."[116] In turn, IPCC conceptualizes vulnerability as an outcome of susceptibility, exposure and adaptive capacity for any given impact. Adding to this, the IPCC developed

---

112 *See* Jorn Birkmann, *Measuring Vulnerability to Promote Disaster-Resilient Societies: Conceptual Frameworks and Definitions, in* MEASURING VULNERABILITY TO NATURAL HAZARDS: TOWARDS DISASTER RESILIENT SOCIETIES 9 (Jorn Birkmann ed., 2006) (exploring how "vulnerability" has been defined by the various disciplines).

113 Looking at the system as a whole and measuring the extent by which it is vulnerable to the impacts of climate change. *See* GERMAN ADVISORY COUNCIL ON GLOBAL CHANGE, WORLD IN TRANSITION 4 (2005): FIGHTING POVERTY THROUGH ENVIRONMENTAL POLICY

114 Understood with a specific focus on the social features of a social-environmental system, such as social inequalities regarding income, age or gender, as well as characteristics of communities and the built environment. *See* Alexander Fekete, "Assessment of Social Vulnerability to Rover Floods in Germany" (Ph.D. dissertation, United Nations University), available at http://www.ehs.unu.edu/file/get/8069. Also Susmita Dasgupta et al., "Exposure of Developing Countries to Sea Level Rise and Storm Surges," CLIMATE CHANGE 106 (2008): 567, http://link.springer.com/article/10.1007%2Fs10584-010-9959-6#page-2

115 Janos J. Bogardi, *Introduction, in* MEASURING VULNERABILITY TO NATURAL HAZARDS: TOWARDS DISASTER RESILIENT SOCIETIES (2006): 1-2

116 Stephen H. Schneider, et al., *Assessing Key Vulnerabilities and the Risk from Climate Change, in* CLIMATE CHANGE 2007: IMPACTS, ADAPTATION AND VULNERABILITY 783 (Martin Parry, et al. eds., 2007), *available at* http://www.ipcc.ch/pdf/assessment-report/ar4/wg2/ar4_wg2_full_report.pdf

a specific criterion by which policymaker can identify which climate change impacts can be characterized as "key" vulnerabilities.[117] The criteria include[118]:

1. The magnitude of impacts: The scale (area and/or number of people affected) and intensity (degree of damage) of the impact.

2. Timing: Will the impact happen now or in the distant future?

3. Persistence and reversibility: A harmful effect is one that persists and is not reversible (e.g., near-permanent drought conditions in semi-arid regions in Africa).

4. Likelihood and confidence: The probability an outcome has/will occur and the subjective assessment that any statement on the findings will prove correct.

5. Potential for adaptation: The lower the ability of an individual/group/society to adapt to the adverse impacts of climate change, the more likely the consequences can be characterized as 'key' vulnerability.

6. Distribution: The disproportionate effects of climate change on the most vulnerable communities have been emphasized extensively by both the academic world and in international policies.[119] As the United Nations Global Report on Human Settlements *Cities and Climate Change* (2011) reiterates, "the more affluent in our society are less vulnerable, with the impacts of climate change felt most by the most marginalized groups which include (but are not limited to), the urban poor, children, women and the elderly."[120] Thus,

---

117 *Id.* at 785.

118 *Id.* at 785-6.

119 Bicknell, J., Dodman, D., and Satterthwaite, D, eds. 2009. *Adapting cities to climate change: Understanding and addressing the development challenges.* Sterling: Earthscan.

120 Wendy Steele & Nidhi Mittal, *Building 'Equitable' Urban Resilience: The Challenge for Cities, in* Resilient Cities 2: Cities and Adaptation to Climate Change – Proceedings of the Global Forum 2011 187, 188 (Konrad Otto-Zimmermann ed., (2012).

vulnerability is not a homogenous term, but rather includes regional variation, income, age and gender differences.[121]

7. The importance of vulnerable systems: Various societies and people may value the impacts of climate change on human and natural systems differently. For instance, if a community relies on a particular system for its livelihoods, this system may be regarded more important than an isolated system in a remote area.

Critical vulnerabilities can serve as a useful concept for informing the dialogue on dangerous anthropogenic interference. In particular, the criteria described above can be used to define levels of climate change that would constitute dangerous anthropogenic interference with the climate system under Article 2 of the UNFCCC. As IPCC puts it, "Interpreting Article 2 (ultimately the obligation of the Conference of the Parties to the UNFCCC) involves a scientific assessment of what impacts might be associated with different levels of greenhouse gas concentrations or climate change; and a normative evaluation by policy-makers of which potential impacts and associated likelihoods are significant enough to constitute, individually or in combination. This assessment is informed by the magnitude and timing of climate impacts as well as by their distribution across regions, sectors and population groups."[122]

The question of what is dangerous and "key" clearly relates to values and judgments about risk and, therefore, does not rely on pure science.[123] Thus, when it comes to vulnerability and climate change impacts, decisions are often made under uncertainty and based on personal judgments and perception.[124] Furthermore, the term "vulnerability" requires a highly interdisciplinary approach that looks at both the socio-economic and bio-geographical processes. Furthermore, we cannot look at this term in isolation from adaptation.

---

121 *Id.* at 189.

122 Schneider, *supra* note 118 at 784.

123 *Id.* at 73.

124 Schneider, supra note 118; Hare, *supra* note 93. Also Susmita Dasgupta et al., "Exposure of Developing Countries to Sea Level Rise and Storm Surges," CLIMATE CHANGE 106 (2008): 567, http://link.springer.com/article/10.1007%2Fs10584-010-9959-6#page-2

Adaptation

Adaptation is closely linked to the concept of vulnerability, and it also features a number of different definitions and understandings in natural and social sciences. These range from viewing adaptation as the development of genetic or behavioral characteristics to cope with changing environment, to purely cultural practices allowing societies to survive climate-induced changes.[125] The most widely used definition refers to adaptation as the "adjustment in natural or human systems in response to actual or expected climatic stimuli or their effects, which moderates harm or exploits beneficial opportunities"[126]

Adaptation and the Role of Intergovernmental Panel on Climate Change and United Nations Framework Convention on Climate Change

While mitigation was clearly defined in the original UNFCCC negotiations at the Rio Summit in 1992, adaptation has only recently come into the spotlight. This can be mainly attributed to IPCC and UNFCCC's procedures and agendas, as well as the policy on climate change adaptation. For instance, it was IPCCC's Second Assessment Report that shed international light on the socioeconomic impacts of climate change and stressed potential measures necessary for effective adaptation.[127] However, the firm focus on adaptation was the result of the recognition that, despite substantial mitigation efforts, many adverse climate effects will likely occur, and human suffering and economic losses can and should be reduced via adaptation measures. This was done in part through IPCC's Fourth Assessment Report (2007) which acknowledged that "even the

125 Barry Smit and Johanna Wantel, "Adaptation, Adaptive Capacity and Vulnerability" GLOBAL CLIMATE CHANGE 282 (2006) available at http://www.uio.no/studier/emner/annet/sum/SUM4015/h08/Smit.pdf

126 Richard J.T. Klein, et al., *Interrelationships Between Adaptation and Mitigation, in* CLIMATE CHANGE 2007: IMPACTS, ADAPTATION AND VULNERABILITY 750 (Martin Parry, et al. eds., 2007), *available at* http://www.ipcc.ch/pdf/assessment-report/ar4/wg2/ar4_wg2_full_report.pdf.

127 Terry Barker, et al., *Technical Summary, in* CLIMATE CHANGE 2007: MITIGATION OF CLIMATE CHANGE 27 (Bert Metz, et al. eds., 2007), *available at* http://www.ipcc.ch/pdf/assessment-report/ar4/wg3/ar4_wg3_full_report.pdf

most stringent mitigation efforts cannot avoid further impacts of climate change in the next few decades, making adaptation unavoidable."[128]

Since 2007, adaptation has gained increasing recognition and has become a key priority within climate change negotiations at international and national level. For instance, measures for adaptation to climate change are receiving increasing financial support (e.g., ad hoc Working Group on Long-Term Cooperative Action under the Convention 2009;[129] also the Adaptation Fund for developing countries struggling with climate change).[130] Additionally, options and limits to dealing with extreme events are increasingly seen as a major challenge to climate change adaptation.[131] Moreover, the Cancun Adaptation Framework explicitly stated that: "Adaptation must be addressed with the same priority as mitigation and requires appropriate institutional arrangements to enhance adaptation action and support."[132]

Not surprisingly, adaptation strategies have been designed and initiated, in particular for the least developed countries (LDCs), under the umbrella of the National Adaptation Programmes (NAPAs) supported by UNFCCC.[133] Additionally, as part of the Cancun Adaptation Framework, Parties established the Adaptation Committee to promote the implementation of enhanced action

---

128 Richard J.T. Klein, et al., *Interrelationships Between Adaptation and Mitigation, in* CLIMATE CHANGE 2007: IMPACTS, ADAPTATION AND VULNERABILITY 750 (Martin Parry, et al. eds., 2007), *available at* http://www.ipcc.ch/pdf/assessment-report/ar4/wg2/ar4_wg2_full_report.pdf.

129 *Ad hoc Working Group on Long-Term Cooperative Action under the Convention.* 2009a. "Contact group on enhanced action on adaptation and its means of implementation." Non-paper No. 31, Resumed seventh session, 2–6 Nov 2009, Barcelona. http://unfccc.int/files/meetings/ad_hoc_working_groups/lca/application/pdf/mitigationnp28091009.pdf.

130 *About the Adaption Fund,* Adaption Fund (last visited June 17, 2013), *available at* https://www.adaptation-fund.org/about (providing further information about the Adaptation Fund).

131 IPCC. 2012. Op. cit.

132 *The outcome of the Work of the Ad Hoc Working Group on Long-term Cooperative Action Under the Convention,* Draft Decision -/CP.16, http://unfccc.int/files/meetings/cop_16/application/pdf/cop16_lca.pdf; *see: Adaptation: Adapting to the Impacts of Climate Change,* UNFCCC THE CANCUN AGREEMENTS (last visited June 17, 2013),

   http://cancun.unfccc.int/adaptation/ (providing users with updates on the progress of adaptation and UN-FCCC's commitment to adaptation, particularly in the least developed countries),

133 *See National Adaptation Programmes of Action (NAPAs),* UNITED NATIONS FRAMEWORK CONVENTION ON CLIMATE CHANGE (last visited June 18, 2013), *available at* http://unfccc.int/national_reports/napa/items/2719.php.

on adaptation in a coherent manner under the Convention, inter alia, through technical support, information sharing, and recommendations to the Parties.[134]

Coming out of this, a growing number of European and North American countries are implementing national adaptation strategies and programs as a response to actual and potential climate change impacts.[135] Germany, for instance, has developed a national adaptation strategy named the German Adaptation Strategy (DAS), focusing on different sectors and cross-sectoral themes.[136] Likewise, the UK Adaptation Strategy formulates first principles of effective adaptation, which encompass—among other issues—the aspect of addressing the risk associated with today's climate variability and extremes as well as the effect of using adaptive management strategies to cope with uncertainty.[137]

Aside from these notable positive examples, there are several challenges when approaching climate change adaptation including:

- Physical limits: Some "physical impacts and changes due to hazards and climate change can be so extreme that either the ecosystem and environmental service basis is destroyed or it is physically impossible to reduce losses and adjust communities to these levels and magnitude of stress;"[138]

- Financial limits: These can be key "barriers when the response and adjustment to the actual and potential impacts would be too costly

---

134   *See Adaptation Committee*, UNITED NATIONS FRAMEWORK CONVENTION ON CLIMATE CHANGE (last visited June 18, 2013), *available at* http://unfccc.int/adaptation/cancun_adaptation_framework/adaptation_committee/items/6053.php.

135   *National Adaptation Strategies*, EUROPEAN ENVIRONMENT AGENCY (2012), http://www.eea.europa.eu/themes/climate/national-adaptation-strategies (containing a list of countries showing progress towards national adaptation strategies).

136   *Combating Climate Change: The German Adaptation Strategy*, FED. MINISTRY FOR THE ENV'T, NATURE CONSERVATION AND NUCLEAR SAFETY (March 2009),

      https://secure.bmu.de/fileadmin/bmu-import/files/english/pdf/application/pdf/broschuere_dem_klimawandel_begegnen_en.pdf.

137   *UKCIP: Supporting Adaptation*, UKCIP (last visited June 18, 2013), www.ukcip.org.uk/index.php.

138   Susmita Dasgupta et al., "Exposure of Developing Countries to Sea Level Rise and Storm Surges," CLIMATE CHANGE 106 (2008): 567, http://link.springer.com/article/10.1007%2Fs10584-010-9959-6#page-2

      Jorn Birkmann, "First- and Second-Order Adaptation to Natural Hazards and Extreme Events in the Context of Climate Change," NATURAL HAZARDS 58 (2011): 811.

and would by far exceed the capacity of a household, province, country, state, or region;"[139]

- Scale: There is an agreement that it is easier to adapt to smaller magnitudes of global mean temperature change than to larger ones.[140]

- Political, social and institutional limits: These "imply that political systems, social networks, and structures as well as institutional/ organizational capacities are too limited to deal with the potential adaptation to climate change impacts effectively."[141] These also imply "that political will and priorities may themselves constitute a barrier of their own for setting and giving priorities to long-term adaptation goals that might be beneficial for [the] future."[142]

In turn, despite the fact that adaptation has been practiced for centuries by both human and natural systems, we have to be cautious in how adaptation strategies are used and how effective they are. We need a better understanding of not only how adaptation works and under what context, but also the practical, institutional and technical obstacles in implementing adaptation strategies in diverse settings and regions.

Climate Change and the Pacific

The majority of Pacific Island countries are located in tropical and sub-tropical regions with year-round warm temperatures and high to moderate rainfall. Extremes of rainfall, temperature and tropical storms pose significant risks to Pacific Island countries. The key climate related hazard risks in the Pacific

---

139 *Id.* For instance, it can be very costly to plan adaptation strategies for some key vulnerabilities, such as loss of biodiversity and melting of glaciers. *See* Tom Wilbanks, et al., *Industry, Settlement and Society, in* CLIMATE CHANGE 2007: IMPACTS, ADAPTATION AND VULNERABILITY 376-78 (Martin Parry, et al. eds., 2007), *available at* http://www.ipcc.ch/pdf/assessment-report/ar4/wg2/ar4_wg2_full_report.pdf.

140 *Id.* at 383 (explaining that it is also easier to adapt to gradual temperature changes rather than abrupt changes).

141 Birkmann, *supra* note 144 at 814.

142 *Id.*

include flooding, drought and wind/storm surges from tropical cyclones.[143] It is estimated that on average, between seven and eight cyclones per year occur in the Pacific region.[144] Disaster losses can seriously impede economic and social development, representing a major portion of GDP for small island developing states (SIDS).[145] For instance, in 1990, a tropical cyclone, Ofa, transformed Niue from a country that thrived on exporting food to one that was dependent on imports for at least two years.[146] In 2004, Niue was hit again by another cyclone, Heta, which had an, even more, profound impact on the country's agricultural production.[147] Despite the impact of disasters on the Pacific region's economy, the economic effects of climate change and the costs to adapt have not yet been assessed at both the regional and national level to help inform investment decisions and national adaptation strategies.[148]

The vulnerability to climate change impacts of Pacific Island countries and their ability to respond is inextricably linked to broader development, geographical and cultural challenges. Specifically, the region's limited resources, a concentration of population and infrastructure in coastal areas, susceptibility to natural disasters such as cyclones,[149] The sensitivity of freshwater supplies, along with isolation, and limited financial, technical and institutional capacities all exacerbate their vulnerability and limit their ability to respond to climate impacts (i.e. adaptive capacity).[150] Another major disadvantage derives from

---

143 M.C. Simpson, et al., "An Overview of Modeling Climate Change Impacts in the Caribbean Region with contribution from the Pacific Islands," United Nations Development Programme (UNDP) 170 (2010), *available at*

http://www.caribsave.org/assets/files/UNDP%20Final%20Report.pdf.

144 Simpson, *supra* note 149 at 170; *See Pacific Island Overview,* World Bank (last viewed June 18, 2013), http://www.worldbank.org/en/country/pacificislands/overview.

145 Simpson, *supra* note 149 at 170.

146 *Id.*

147 *Id.*

148 *Id.*

149 Bettencourt, *supra* note 3 at 1 (explaining that between 1950 and 2004, Cyclones accounted for 76 percent of the reported disasters).

150 Simpson, *supra* note 149 at 181.

their small size, which narrows their range of resources,[151] and increases the pressure on the relatively small watersheds and threatened supplies of fresh water. Moreover, due to the coastal zone concentration in a limited land area, the adverse effects of climate change and sea-level rise present significant risks to the sustainable development of SIDS.[152] Adding to this, religious factors, such as the "do nothing" beliefs that preach to the people that destruction is inevitable, make believers more likely to nothing about "inescapable" events.[153]

Despite the Pacific Island countries' large disadvantages, communities have a long history of resilience to volatile climate conditions.[154] However, changes in sea level, temperature and rainfall, and intensity of tropical storms[155] increase the severity of climate change impacts, making it harder for vulnerable countries to recover after a change.[156] To provide a better depiction of climate change impacts in the Pacific, the Report on Adaptation Challenges in Pacific Island Countries[157][158] summarizes the following:

---

151 *Id.* ("Small economies are generally more exposed to external shocks, such as extreme events and climate change, than larger countries, because many of them rely on one or few economic activities such as tourism and fisheries. The cost of adaptation about gross the domestic product can be very high. The World Bank, Mimura et al., (2007) estimated that by 2050, in the absence of adaptation, a high island such as Fiji could experience damages of up to US \$52 million (equivalent to two to three percent of Fiji's GDP in 1998).").

152 Poh P. Wong, "Small Island Developing States," CLIMATE CHANGE 2 (2011): 1.

153 *Asia Pacific Human Development Report on Climate Change: Pacific Stakeholder Consultations Report,* UNITED NATIONS DEVELOPMENT PROGRAMME 4 (2009),
     http://hdru.aprc.undp.org/ext/HDRU/pdf/Pacific_APHDR_CC_Stakeholder_Consultation_Report.pdf

154 Bettencourt, *supra* note 3 at 4 (explaining that although the number of disasters in the Pacific Islands is rising, the number of fatalities per disaster is actually declining, showing how resilient Pacific Islanders are to these disasters).

155 *Id.* at 5 ("Hurricane-strength cyclones have increased systematically in the southwest Pacific, a trend that has also been observed at the global level over the past 30 years.").

156 Jon Barnett and John Campbell, CLIMATE CHANGE AND SMALL ISLAND STATES: POWER, KNOWLEDGE, AND THE SOUTH PACIFIC 12 (2010).

157 *Report on Adaptation Challenges in Pacific Island Countries,* SREP, at 10-11 (2013), http://www.sprep.org/attachments/Publications/Adaptation_challenge_PICs_13.pdf.

158 John Hay, "Climate Change and Small Island States," TIEMPO (2010),
     http://www.tiempocyberclimate.org/portal/archive/issue3637/t3637a1.htm.

- Land use changes,[159] including settlement and use of marginal lands for agriculture, are decreasing the natural resilience of environmental systems, and hence their ability to accommodate the added stresses arising from changes in climate and sea level.

- Given the limited area and low elevation of the inhabitable lands, the most direct and severe effects of climate and sea-level changes will be increasing risks of coastal erosion, flooding and inundation; these effects are exacerbated by the combination of seasonal storms, high tides and storm surges.

- Other direct consequences of anticipated climate and sea level changes would probably include: reduction in subsistence and commercial agricultural production of such crops as taro and coconut; decreased the security of potable and other water supplies; increased risk of dengue fever, malaria, cholera and diarrhoeal diseases; and decreased human comfort.

- Groundwater resources of the lowlands of high islands and atolls may be affected by flooding and inundation from sea level rise; water catchments of smaller, low-lying islands will be at risk from any changes in the frequency of extreme events.

- The overall impact of changes in climate and sea level will likely be cumulative and determined by the interactions and synergies between the stresses and their effects.[160]

---

159 The United Nations Development Programme (UNDP) in their Consultation Report highlights that the Pacific should examine the issues in land ownership, which is a significant barrier to climate change adaptation. They gave the example of Tonga squatter communities resettling from outer islands to an unregulated coastal area, which posed serious health problems, but yet was largely ignored by the government.

160 *Report on Adaptation Challenges in Pacific Island Countries*, SREP, at 10-11 (2013), http://www.sprep.org/attachments/Publications/Adaptation_challenge_PICs_13.pdf.

Apart from environmental impacts, the quality of the environment itself has strong implications for the full enjoyment of human rights.[161]

In response to these challenges, both donor organizations and governments have taken some notable steps toward climate change in the Pacific.

The island nations of the Pacific Islands Forum have been active participants in international negotiations through the UNFCCC, as members of the Alliance of Small Islands States (AOSIS).[162] In addition, a significant amount of policies and multilateral agreements have been done to manage the impacts of climate change in the Pacific, including:

- The Pacific Catastrophe Risk Assessment and Financing Initiative (PCRAFI), which was developed by the World Bank in 2010 to help provide countries with the necessary tools and financial mechanisms to reduce and mitigate the countries' vulnerability to climate change.[163]

- The Pacific Islands Framework for Action on Climate Change was developed to improve and upgrade policies, tools, institutional capacity and governance, to monitoring climate change processes.[164]

---

161 *Human Rights and Climate Change*, MINISTRY OF FOREIGN AFFAIRS: REPUBLIC OF MALDIVES (last visited June 18, 2013), http://www.foreign.gov.mv/v3/?p=menu_item&sub_id=50&submenu=Human%20 Rights%20and%20Climate%20Change (explaining that the Maldives hosted a "Small Island States Conference on the Human Dimension of Global Climate Change" on November 13-14, 2007. "During the conference, the world's Small Island States, discussed the impact of global warming on individual people in their countries and also, for the first time, asked the question: how does climate change affect the human rights of our citizens. The outcome of the conference was the Male' Declaration on the Human Dimension of Global Climate Change, which for the first time in an international agreement explicitly stated that "climate change has clear and immediate implications for the full enjoyment of human rights").

162 AOSIS, formed in 1990, is an organization of 43 islands states from the Caribbean, Indian, Atlantic and Pacific Oceans that has taken a vocal role in the UNFCCC process. For a detailed study on AOSIS policy, see Tuiloma Neroni Slade and Jacob Werksman, *An examination of the Kyoto Protocol from a small islands perspective*, CLIMATE CHANGE AND DEVELOPMENT 63 (2000), http://environment. research.yale.edu/documents/downloads/o-u/Slade.pdf.

163 "Pacific Islands: Disaster Risk Reduction and Financing in the Pacific," THE WORLD BANK (2012) http://go.worldbank.org/19SGQ75120.

164 *Pacific Islands Framework for Action on Climate Change* 2006-2015, SEREP (June 12, 2005), http://www.sprep.org/att/publication/000438_PI_Framework_for_Action_on_Climate_ Change_2006_2015_FINAL.pdf.

- The Pacific Adaptation to Climate Change Project (PACC) was initiated in 13 participating countries in efforts to promote climate change adaptation as a prerequisite for sustainable development in the Pacific. The project focuses on building capacity of the participating countries to adapt to climate change in key development sectors including coastal zone management, food security, and water resource management.[165]

Thus, while, on one hand the Pacific is extremely vulnerable to climate change impacts, on the other hand, a significant amount of donor/government work on climate change in the Pacific is being conducted to help communities to cope better with the effects of climate change in the near future. The international community has also implemented and developed measures and policies, not just for the Pacific but worldwide as will be demonstrated in the following discussion on climate change and international law.

1.2 EVOLUTION OF THE REFUGEE LAW

1.2.1. Protecting Climate Refugees

"In August 2006, the government of the Maldives organized a meeting of representatives from governments, environmental and humanitarian organizations, and United Nations agencies on an issue that had until then been largely outside the climate policy debate: the protection and resettlement of 'climate refugees'"[166] For a small island nation like the Maldives, located only a few meters above sea level, this question is surely at the heart of its national security, if not national survival. Such low-lying island nations are likely to be the first to suffer from

---

165 "PACC Overview," *Secretariat of the Pacific Regional Environment Programme* (2013), http://www.sprep.org/Pacific-Adaptation-to-Climate-Change/about-pacc.

166 Frank Biermann & Ingrid Boas, *Protecting Climate Refugees: The Case for a Global Protocol*, ENVIRONMENT (Nov.-Dec. 2008) (explaining that at the meeting, delegates "proposed an amendment to the 1951 Geneva Convention Relating to the Status of Refugees that would extend the mandate of the UN refugee regime to include climate refugees"); David Keane, *The Environmental Causes and Consequences of Migration: A Search for the Meaning of 'Environmental Refugees*, 16 GEO. INT'L ENVTL. L. REV.209 (2004).

global climate change, and many atolls may disappear or become uninhabitable over the course of the century.

Yet climate-related migration could also evolve into a larger, global crisis far beyond threats to a few island nations. According to some estimates, more than 200 million people might have to give up their homes due to climate change by 2050.[167] Such estimates have a large margin of error[168] and depend on underlying assumptions about population growth, economic development, temperature increase, or the degree and timing of climate change impacts such as sea-level rise. And yet most scenarios agree on a general trend: in this century, global warming may force millions of people—mainly in Asia and Africa—to leave their homes and migrate to other places.

The Intergovernmental Panel on Climate Change's 2007 assessment indicates that climate change will likely include regional increases in the severity and frequency of extreme weather events.[169] In some worst-case scenarios, by 2080, with a global temperature increase of merely 1–2 degrees, storm surges could affect approximately 103 million people each year.[170] Gradual sea-level rise, another major effect of climate change, will threaten low-lying coasts and further increase the damage caused by storm surges.[171] Thousands of small islands

---

167 N. Myers, "Environmental Refugees: A Growing Phenomenon of the 21st Century," *Philosophical Transactions: Biological Sciences 357,* no. 1420 (2002): 609 and 611

168 A. Suhrke, "Environmental Degradation and Population Flows," *Journal of International Affairs 47,* no. 2 (1994): 478; S. Castles, "Environmental Change and Forced Migration: Making Sense of the Debate," New Issues in Refugee Research Working Paper 70 (Geneva: United Nations High Commissioner for Refugees, 2002), 2–3; and R. Black, "Environmental Refugees: Myth or Reality?" New Issues in Refugee Research Working Paper 34 (Geneva: United Nations High Commissioner for Refugees (UNHCR), 2002), 2–8.

169 Intergovernmental Panel on Climate Change, *Climate Change Impacts, Adaptation and Vulnerability, Contribution of Working Group II to the Fourth Assessment Report of the Intergovernmental Panel on Climate Change,* M. L. Parry, O. F. Canziani, J. P. Palutikof, P. J. van der Linden, and C. E. Hanson, eds. Cambridge, UK: Cambridge University Press, 2007, chapters 9, 10, 13 and 16. For the effects of climate change on sea-level rise, the severity of tropical cyclones, and the severity and frequency of storm surges, see also German Advisory Council on Global Change, *The Future Oceans: Warming Up, Rising High, Turning Sour,* Berlin: German Advisory Council on Global Change, 2006, 38–39 and 40–43; *see Global Warming Fast Facts,* National Geographic (June 14, 2007),

   http://news.nationalgeographic.com/news/2004/12/1206_041206_global_warming.html.

170 Rachel Warren, "Understanding the Regional Impacts of Climate Change," TYNDALL CENTRE FOR CLIMATE CHANGE RESEARCH 67 (2006), http://www.tyndall.ac.uk/sites/default/files/wp90.pdf.

171 Robert Nicholls, et al., "Increasing Flood Risk and Wetland Losses Due to Global Sea-Level Rise: Regional and Global Analyses," GLOBAL ENVIRONMENTAL CHANGE 72 (1999).

will be at risk, and many possibly flooded.[172] If sea levels rise by 1m, storm surges could make island nations such as the Maldives, the Marshall Islands, Kiribati, or Tuvalu mostly uninhabitable.[173] In addition, droughts and water scarcity may increase because of global warming. Some studies predict that even under the lowest growth rate assumptions, a world 1–2 degrees warmer could lead to water shortages for 700–1,500 million people.[174] Hundreds of millions of people who depend for their water supply on glacier melt could experience severe water stress. Asia, Africa, Latin America, and the small island states have the largest populations at risk of becoming climate refugees. Asia is vulnerable because of its highly populated, low-lying coastal regions and high vulnerability to tropical cyclones.[175] A temperature increase of 2–3 degrees could result in 39–812 million South Asians at risk of water stress.

Climate refugees just from Bangladesh might outnumber all current refugees worldwide. Water scarcity and drought will also affect millions of Africans.[176] Fourteen African countries experience water scarcity currently. This may increase to 25 countries by 2030. Africa is also highly vulnerable to sea-level rise, notably in the river deltas of Egypt and Nigeria. In Latin America, thousands of people in Venezuela and Uruguay live in areas where the risk of flooding is high while millions of Guatemalans and Mexicans may face increasing droughts. Water scarcity due to glacier melts in the South American Andes may affect 37 million people in 2010 and 50 million people in 2050, including larger cities such as Quito, Ecuador and La Paz, Bolivia.[177]

Most climate refugees are expected to remain within their home countries, especially when only parts of the country will be affected by climate change. Yet some studies suggest that climate refugees could potentially also cross international borders. For example, the Development, Concepts and Doctrine Centre Global Strategic Trend Programme of the United Kingdom's Ministry

---

172 Ibid, p. 81; and N. W. Arnell et al., "The Consequences of CO_2 Stabilization for the Impacts of Climate Change," *Climatic Change* 53 (2002): 432.

173 See German Advisory Council on Global Change, note 4, pages 46 and 50.

174 Warren, Arnell, Nicholls, Levy, and Price, note 30, page 20.

175 Munich Re Group, *Megacities—Megarisks: Trends and Challenges for Insurance and Risk Management*, Munich: Münchner Rückversicherungs- Gesellschaft (2004) 76.

176 See, for example, Warren, Arnell, Nicholls, Levy, and Price, note 30, page 18.

177 L. Bijlsma et al., "Coastal Zones and Small Islands." In *Climate Change 1995—Impacts, Adaptations and Mitigation of Climate Change: Scientific-Technical Analyses*, R. T. Watson, M. C. Zinyowera, and R.H. Moss, eds. Cambridge, (UK: Cambridge University Press, 1996), 289–324.

of Defense foresee significant migration flows from sub-Saharan Africa toward the Mediterranean, the Middle East and Europe between 2007 and 2036.[178] The German Advisory Council on Global Change predicts mass migration to the United States from the Caribbean islands and Central America and many migration flows within Central America.

In light of this looming climate migration crisis, the current refugee protection regime of the United Nations seems poorly prepared. At present, the UNHCR deals with around 14 million refugees.[179] It is doubtful, without major reforms, whether this institution can protect and support a stream of refugees that is possibly 20 times larger. Moreover, its current mandate covers only individual political refugees who flee their countries because of state-led persecution based on race, religion, political opinion or ethnicity.[180]

As a result, delegates at the Maldives meeting in 2006 proposed an amendment to the 1951 Geneva Convention Relating to the Status of Refugees that would extend the mandate of the United Nations refugee regime to include climate refugees.[181] Yet such an amendment does not promise to effectively resolve the emerging climate refugee crisis. Indeed, it is highly uncertain such a proposal is even politically feasible. The United Nations refugee regime is already under constant pressure from industrialized countries that seek restrictive interpretations of its provisions; it is highly unlikely these governments will agree to extend the same level of protection to a new group 20 times larger than those currently under United Nations oversight and equal to half the population of the European Union.[182] More importantly, the proposal of extending the United Nations refugee regime misses the core characteristics of the climate refugee

---

178 UK Development, Concepts and Doctrine Centre (DCDC), *The DCDC Global Strategic Trends Programme 2007–2036*, 3rd edition, Swindon, (UK: Crown Copyright/MOD, 2007), 29.

179 UNHCR, *2012 Global Trends: Refugees, Asylum-seekers, Returnees, Internally Displaced and Stateless Persons* (Geneva: UNHCR, 2012), 4–5.

180 J. McGregor, "Climate Change and Involuntary Migration: Implications for Food Security," *Food Policy* 19, no. 2 (1994): 126; and D. Keane, "The Environmental Causes and Consequences of Migration: A Search for the Meaning of 'Environmental Refugees,'" *Georgetown International Environmental Law Review* 16, no. 2 (2004): 214–15.

181 See Republic of the Maldives Ministry of Environment, Energy and Water, *Report on the First Meeting on Protocol on Environmental Refugees: Recognition of Environmental Refugees in the 1951 Convention and 1967 Protocol Relating to the Status of Refugees* (Male, Maldives, 14–15 August 2006, on file with authors).

182 N. Myers, "Environmental Refugees: A Growing Phenomenon of the 21st Century," *Philosophical Transactions: Biological Sciences* 357 (2002) 1420.

crisis. Climate refugees do not have to leave their countries because of a totalitarian government. In principle, they still enjoy the protection of their home country's government. The protection of climate refugees is therefore essentially a development issue that requires large-scale, long-term planned resettlement programs for groups of affected people, mostly within their country. Often this will be in concert with adaptation programs for other people who are not evacuated but can still be protected, for instance, through strengthened coastal defenses. From this standpoint, then, international agencies such as the United Nations Development Programme (UNDP) and the World Bank are better equipped than the UNHCR to deal with the emerging problem of climate refugees.

Scenarios of streams of millions of climate refugees have conjured up the risk of violent conflict, both within affected countries and internationally once refugees try to cross borders.[183] Climate migration could thus turn into a "threat to the peace" and international security, a phrase that is at the center of Article 39 of the United Nations Charter that mandates the Security Council to request all types of measures to respond to such threats, including the use of force.[184] Indeed, in April 2007, the council addressed the impacts of climate change on international peace and security. British Foreign Secretary Margaret Beckett, who chaired the session; Papua New Guinea United Nations Ambassador Robert G. Aisi, who spoke on behalf of the Pacific Islands Forum; and United Nations Secretary-General Ban Ki-Moon named climate change-induced mass migration as a possible factor that could lead to major conflict and instability in the world.[185]

Representatives from most developing countries, however, forcefully maintained that the United Nations Security Council is the wrong institution to deal with climate policy. One concern is that most climate-related migration will occur in Africa, Asia and Latin America. Allowing the Security Council to exert a strong mandate will thus extend its sway over the internal affairs of developing nations. Yet the Council lacks legitimacy in many developing countries because of the exclusive voting power of its five permanent members (China,

---

183 German Advisory Council on Global Change, note 19, page 174; and DCDC, note 20, pages 78–79.

184 United Nations, *Charter of the United Nations* (New York: United Nations, 1945).

185 United Nations Security Council, "Security Council Holds First-Ever Debate on Impact of Climate Change on Peace, Security, Hearing over 50 Speakers," 5,663rd Meeting of 17 April 2007, United Nations Department of Public Information News and Media Division. For a review of the debate, see F. Sindico, "Climate Change: A Security (Council) Issue?" *Climate Change Law Review* 1 (2007): 29–34.

France, Russia, the United Kingdom and the United States)—many of which are, at the same time, the largest emitters of GHGs. Moreover, it is dubious what the Security Council could initiate that could not be done by other institutions such as the UNFCCC or intergovernmental agencies such as the UNDP and the United Nations Environment Programme (UNEP). The core function of the Security Council is the preservation of international peace, mainly through mandating United Nations member States to take forceful action against countries whose governments pose a threat to international security and do not comply with international rules and requests from the council. The emerging climate refugee crisis is clearly different in character, so it remains unclear whether a stronger role of the council is needed and what its added benefits would be. Moreover, given that developing countries— including India and China—have explicit objections toward any role of the Security Council in climate policy,[186] a stronger involvement seems rather unlikely in any case, at least for their plans.

For these reasons, dealing with the climate refugee issue calls for a different approach: a separate, independent legal and political regime created under a Protocol on the Recognition, Protection, and Resettlement of Climate Refugees to the United Nations Framework Convention on Climate Change. Such a protocol could build the political support from almost all countries as parties to the climate convention. It could draw on widely agreed principles such as common but differentiated responsibilities and the reimbursement of full incremental costs. It could aid climate refugees by linking their protection with the overall climate regime, including future advances in climate science in defining risks for people in certain regions. Given the increasing pressure from developed nations to integrate advanced developing countries in a global mitigation regime of quantified reduction and limitation objectives, a protocol on the protection of climate refugees could become for developing countries a major bargaining chip in negotiations. Such an agreement would operate under five principles. First, at the core of the agreement must be the objective of a planned and voluntary resettlement and reintegration of affected populations over periods of many years and decades, as opposed to mere emergency response and disaster relief.[187] Spontaneous flights, often unavoidable during political turmoil or war, can then be prevented for climate change-driven events such as floods.

---

186 Idem.

187 B. Müller and C. Hepburn, *IATAL—An Outline Proposal for an International Air Travel Adaptation Levy* (Oxford, UK: Oxford Institute for Energy Studies, 2006).

Second, climate refugees must be seen and treated as permanent immigrants to the regions or countries that accept them. Climate refugees cannot return, for purely objective reasons, to their homes as political refugees can (at least in theory, as they have nowhere to return to).

Third, the climate refugee regime must be tailored not to the needs of individually persecuted people (as in the current United Nations refugee regime) but entire groups of people, such as populations of villages, cities, provinces, or even entire nations, as in the case of small island states.

Fourth, an international regime for climate refugees will be targeted less toward the protection of persons outside their states than toward the support of governments, local communities and national agencies to protect people within their territories. Essentially, the governance challenge of protecting and resettling climate refugees involves international assistance and funding for the domestic support and resettlement programs of affected countries that have requested such support.

Fifth and finally, the protection of climate refugees must be seen as a global problem and a global responsibility.[188] In most cases, climate refugees will be poor, and their own responsibility for the past accumulation of GHGs will be small. By a large measure, the wealthy industrialized countries have caused most past and present GHG emissions, and it is thus these countries that have the greatest moral, if not legal, responsibility for the victims of global warming. This does not imply transnational migration of 200 million climate refugees into the developed world. Yet it does suggest the responsibility of the industrialized countries to do their share in financing, supporting and facilitating the protection and resettlement of climate refugees.[189]

Regarding terminology, some intergovernmental agencies—such as the International Organization for Migration and the UNHCR—reject the term climate "refugee" because of narrow legal definitions in the post-1945 system. In their view, the term "refugee" should remain limited to an individual recognized under the 1951 Geneva Convention Relating to the Status of Refugees: "a person who is outside his or her country of nationality or habitual residence" and

---

188 Myers, Norman. "Environmental Refugees: A Growing Phenomenon." *Philosophical Transactions: Biological Sciences* 357 (2002): 1420.

189 Camillo Boano, Roger Zetter, and Tim Morris, T, "Environmentally Displaced People: Understanding the linkages between environmental change, livelihoods and forced migration," *Refugee Studies Centre* (2008): 4-32.

cannot rely on the protection of his or her home state for fear of persecution.[190] As an alternative, some international agencies prefer the notion of "environmentally displaced persons", which is more in line with the UNHCR's "internally displaced persons" designation that carry with it less responsibility on the part of the international community.[191] However, because climate change will cause both transnational and internal flight, the UNHCR's traditional distinction between the two categories of involuntary migration does not seem germane; it is difficult to argue that a global governance mechanism for the protection of people who have lost their homes due to climate change should bestow a different status, and a different term, depending on whether they have crossed a border. Moreover, it does not stand to reason to reserve the stronger term, "refugee" for a category of people who earned international attention after 1945 and to invent less appropriate terms—such as "climate-related environmentally displaced persons"—for new categories of people who are forced to leave their homes now, with similar grim consequences. Why should inhabitants of some atolls in the Maldives who require resettlement for reasons of a well-founded fear of being inundated by 2050 receive less protection than others who fear political persecution? Therefore, it seems sensible to continue using the term "climate refugees" and adjust the outdated United Nations terminology accordingly by allowing for different types of refugees (for instance, political refugees that fall under the 1951 Geneva Convention and climate refugees that fall under the climate refugee protocol proposed here) as well as for different agreements on their protection.[192]

To resettle millions of people additional and, most likely, substantial funds will be required. Institutionally, the best governance mechanism would be a separate fund, which might be called the "Climate Refugee Protection and Resettlement Fund"[193] While one could link the operational aspects of this fund with existing financial mechanisms to increase efficiency, the governance of the fund should be independent and stand under the authority of the meeting of the parties to the climate refugee protocol. To generate the funds needed,

190   The 1951 Refugee Convention. *The UN Refugee Agency* (2015) http://www.unhcr.org/pages/49da0e466.html.

191   Idem.

192   Guy Goodwin-Gill. "Protocol relating to the Status of Refugees," *Audiovisual Library of International Law* (2013) http://legal.un.org/avl/ha/prsr/prsr.html

193   German Advisory Council on Global Change, which proposed an Environmental Migration Fund, note 19, page 211.

the Climate Refugee Protection and Resettlement Fund could be coupled with currently proposed, novel income-raising mechanisms, such as an international air-travel levy.[194] A fundamental question for this new facility will be the amount of funding required by the international community and the funding principle underlying the climate refugees' protection. For mitigation programs under the climate convention, industrialized countries have committed to reimbursing developing countries the agreed full incremental costs, a concept originally developed in the 1990 London amendments to the Montreal Protocol on the protection of the ozone layer.[195] Similar provisions apply to adaptation.[196] In addition, the climate convention obliges industrialized countries to assist the most vulnerable countries in meeting adaptation costs (Article 4.4) and gives exclusive rights to the least developed countries (Article 4.9). This suggests applying the principle of reimbursement of full incremental costs to the protection and resettlement of climate refugees, at least in situations where the causal link with climate change—namely sea-level rise—is undisputed. For other situations in which climate change is only one factor to account for environmental degradation—for example, in the case of water scarcity—a principle of additional funding instead of full reimbursement may be more appropriate. In any case, the costs of the voluntary resettlement and reintegration of millions of people who have to leave their islands, coastal plains, or arid areas will be substantial— probably in the order of billions of Euros over the coming decades. Even if novel mechanisms are introduced, the final responsibility for funding will rest with the governments of industrialized countries and possibly wealthier developing countries.

---

194 B. Müller and C. Hepburn, *IATAL—An Outline Proposal for an International Air Travel Adaptation Levy* (Oxford, UK: Oxford Institute for Energy Studies, 2006).

195 F. Biermann, "Financing Environmental Policies in the South: Experiences from the Multilateral Ozone Fund," *International Environmental Affairs* 9, no. 3 (1997): 179–218.

196 Article 4, paragraph 3 of the climate convention reads: "The developed country Parties and other developed Parties included in Annex II shall provide new and additional financial resources . . . including for the transfer of technology, needed by the developing country Parties to meet the agreed full incremental costs of implementing measures that are covered by paragraph 1 of [Article 4] and that are agreed between a developing country Party and the international entity or entities referred to in Article 11, in accordance with that Article." Paragraph 1 of Article 4 includes in section (e) the commitment of developing countries to "cooperate in preparing for adaptation to the impacts of climate change and develop and elaborate appropriate and integrated plans for coastal zone management, water resources and agriculture, and for the protection and rehabilitation of areas, particularly in Africa, affected by drought and desertification, as well as floods." United Nations Framework Convention on Climate Change, art. 4, June 12, 1992, 1771 U.N.T.S. 107, *available at* http://unfccc.int/resource/docs/convkp/conveng.pdf.

Implementation through existing United Nations Agencies—a climate refugee protocol should not create new international bureaucracies; the resettlement of millions of climate refugees over the course of the century should be the task of existing agencies. Given the complexity of climate-related flight, the best model will be to mandate not one single agency but rather a network of agencies as implementing agencies of the protocol. A crucial role lies with the UNDP and the World Bank, both of which could serve as implementing agencies for the climate refugee protocol in the planned voluntary resettlement of affected populations. Although it lacks a strong operational mandate, the UNEP may provide further assistance in terms of scientific research and synthesis, information dissemination, legal and political advice, and other core functions of this program. A small coordinating secretariat to the climate refugee protocol would be needed, possibly as a subdivision of the climate secretariat in Bonn.[197] In addition, although it is unlikely to be the primary agency given the special characteristics of the climate refugee crisis, the UNHCR should play a role; its expertise in view of emergencies, as well as its legal and technical expertise in dealing with refugee crises, will be indispensable for the protection of climate refugees.

1.3. HUMAN RIGHTS GENERALITIES AND APPLICABILITY

1.3.1. Alien Tort Claims Act

The Alien Tort Claims Act is a 200-year-old statute that grants United States district courts "original jurisdiction of any civil action by an alien for a tort only, committed in the violation of the law of nations or a treaty of the United States."[198] The statute was little used until 20 years ago when the Filartiga versus Pena-Irala[199] Decision resurrected it as a tool for aliens to seek redress for human rights violations. Filartiga v. Pena-Irala allowed the parent of a Paraguayan torture victim to sue a former Paraguayan official for harms inflicted while the

---

197 F. Biermann, "'Earth System Governance' as a Crosscutting Theme of Global Change Research," *Global Environmental Change* 17, 3–4 (2007).

198 28 U.S.C. § 1350 (1996).

199 Filartiga v. Pena-Irala, 630 F.2d 876 (2d Cir. 1980).

son was in police custody.[200] Thus began the modern use of the ATCA, which has included suits for torture, summary execution, disappearances, war crimes, genocide, prolonged arbitrary detention, and in some cases cruel, inhumane, and degrading treatment.[201] A successful claim under the ATCA must satisfy three essential elements: (1) an alien sues (2) for a tort (3) that was committed in violation of the law of nations.[202] Given that "alien" is defined rather clearly in United States courts, this element has not been the subject of any litigation.[203] The second element has been the subject of judicial and academic discussion as to how it should be interpreted,[204] but by far the most troublesome aspect is the third element.[205] Because there is no authoritative definition of everything encompassed in "international law," determining what constitutes the "law of nations" has proven to be a difficult task for the courts.

Because the ATCA lay dormant for much of its existence, courts still struggle with defining the sources of the law of nations or violations of this body of law. Additionally, the question remains open because the United States Supreme Court has yet to rule on this issue.[206] Filartiga instructed courts to look at the norms of international law to identify a rule enforceable under the ATCA in United States courts. A norm will fall within the law of nations if it is universal or widely accepted by the global community, definable, or specific so that the court can determine when a violation has occurred, and obligatory or binding.[207] Notably, courts have rejected the idea that the law of nations is a static principle. Rather, courts have embraced it as dynamic and changing as the international community recognizes new rights and duties.[208]

---

200   Idem.

201   Hari M. Osofsky, Environmental Human Rights under the Alien Tort Statute: Redress for Indigenous Victims of Multinational Corporations, *Suffolk Transnat'l L. Rev.* 20 (1998): 335, 342

202   28 U.S.C. § 1350 (1996).

203   Saman Zia-Zarifi, Suing Multinational Corporations in the U.S. for Violating International Law, 4 UCLA J. Int'l L & For. Aff. (1999): 81, 90.

204   Idem.

205   Ibidem.

206   Hari M. Osofsky, Environmental Human Rights under the Alien Tort Statute: Redress for Indigenous Victims of Multinational Corporations, 20 Suffolk Transnat'l L. Rev (1998).

207   Filartiga v. Pena-Irala, 630 F.2d 876, 881 (2d Cir. 1980).

208   Beanal v. Freeport-McMoRan, Inc., 969 F. Supp. 362, 370 (E.D. La. 1997).

When the ATCA began to be used in the 1970s, there was debate as to whether it could be applied only to state actors. In Filartiga, the defendant was a former state official, and thus state action was not at issue. But, the issue was squarely addressed in Kadic v. Karadzic, where the court found that non-state actors were within the reach of the ATCA.[209] Specifically, the court said: We do not agree that the law of nations, as understood in the modern era, confines its reach to state action. Instead, we hold that certain forms of conduct violate the law of nations whether undertaken by those acting under the auspices of a state or only as private individuals.[210]

The court gave torture, piracy, slave trading, genocide, war crimes and violations of international humanitarian law as examples of such conduct for which there is individual, as opposed to state, responsibility.[211] In addition, there is a well-settled principle that non-state actors acting in close concert or cooperation with a state are held to be acting as a state and therefore subject to the same standards of conduct as a state. In Beanal v. Freeport-McMoRan, Inc., the court set forth a four-part test to determine if a private actor is in such close concert with a government as to be considered a "state actor."[212] The court found that only one of the following needs to be satisfied: (a) the existence of a substantial nexus between the State's and the defendant's conduct, (b) the state and the defendant operate interdependently, (c) the defendant participated jointly with the state or its agents, or (d) the defendant performed a function traditionally carried out by the public sector.[213] Thus, where the international law imposes a duty upon non-state actors, causes of action for breaches of this duty can be brought under the ATCA. It is still unclear whether the ATCA can be used to enforce violations of environmental human rights. No court has squarely addressed this issue, but if environmental human rights can be shown to be an international norm and part of the law of nations, then such claims could be brought in United States district courts.

While it may not seem obvious at first, genocide could be a result of severe environmental destruction, and thus a violation of international and environmental law. In Beanal, the plaintiff urged that destruction of one's homeland was

---

209   See Kadic v. Karadzic, 70 F.3d 232, 239 (2d Cir. 1995).

210   Idem.

211   Ibidem.

212   See Beanal, 969 F. Supp. at 377-79.

213   Idem.

a form of genocide because it deprived the people of their ability to survive in their traditional way.[214] Specifically, Beanal alleged the defendant was guilty of cultural genocide by destroying the native lands of the Amungme tribe, which resulted in their forced relocation to foreign areas.[215] While the court found that genocide was clearly a violation of international law, it said Beanal's claim of cultural genocide was unconvincing. But the court did grant him leave to amend his complaint to make his claims of actual or cultural genocide more clear.[216]

The human right to a healthy environment is supported implicitly and explicitly in numerous international, regional, and national legal works. It is important to detail these rights because it is a violation of these rights that will form the foundation of the ATCA claim.

Several international human rights instruments have been interpreted as supporting environmental human rights. The UDHR contains several sections applicable to the right to a healthy environment, including sections focusing on the right to a standard of living, housing, food and free development of peoples.[217] Similarly, the International Covenant on Economic, Social, and Cultural Rights recognizes the right to an adequate standard of living, right to health, including improvements to the environment and the right to dispose of one's natural resources.[218] Additionally, the International Covenant on Civil and Political Rights supports these same rights in several of its provisions.[219] Although the United Nations General Assembly has yet to adopt a resolution expressly recognizing the human right to a healthy environment, it has recognized the connection between environmental protection and the advancement of human rights.[220] Most importantly, in 1990, the General Assembly recognized "that all individuals are entitled to live in an environment adequate for their health and well-being."[221] In the same year, the United Nations commissioned a report on

---

214 See Beanal v. Freeport McMoRan, Inc., 969 F.Supp. 362, 372 (E.D. La. 1997).

215 Idem.

216 Ibidem.

217 Universal Declaration of Human Rights, G.A. Res 217A, arts. 3, 22, 25, 28, U.N. Doc. A/810 (1948).

218 International Covenant on Economic, Social and Cultural Rights, G.A. Res. 2200A, arts. 1, 7, 11, 12, 15, U.N. DocA/6546, (1966).

219 International Covenant on Civil and Political Rights, Dec. 19, 1966, art. 1, 999 U.N. T.S. 171.

220 Luis E. Rodriguez-Rivera, Is the Human Right to Environment Recognized Under International Law? It Depends on the Source, 12 Colo. J. Int'l Envt'l L. & Pol'y 1 (2001): 24.

221 G.A. Res 45/94, U.N. GAOR, 45th Sess., Supp. No. 49A, at 178, U.N. Doc. A/45/749 (1990).

the preservation of the environment and the promotion of human rights. In 1994, the results of the study were published in the Ksentini Final Report, which incorporated the Draft Principles on Human Rights and the Environment.[222] This report includes an extensive survey of environmental human rights sources and concludes that there is "universal acceptance of the environmental rights recognized at the national, regional and international level."[223] The Draft Declaration incorporated into the Ksentini Report also recognizes that "all persons have the right to a secure, healthy, and ecologically sound environment"[224] More recently, the Bizkaia Declaration, a product of the International Seminar of Experts on the Right to the Environment and organized by the United Nations, declared the explicit right to a healthy environment.[225] Under Article 1, "Everyone has the right, individually or in association with others, to enjoy a healthy and ecologically balanced environment . . . which may be exercised before public bodies and private entities, whatever their legal status under national and international law."[226] These international sources are clear evidence of the acceptance of the right of all individuals to a healthy environment.

In addition to these sources supporting environmental human rights, international law recognizes a general duty not to damage the environment, particularly the environment of others. The Stockholm Declaration, adopted by the Stockholm Convention in 1972, established standards for environmental protection.[227] Specifically, Principle 21 said nations have "the sovereign right to exploit their own natural resources pursuant to their own environmental policies, and the responsibility to ensure that activities within their jurisdiction or control do not cause damage to the environment of other States or areas beyond the limits of national jurisdiction."[228] In 1992, the Rio Declaration was adopted by 176 nations and reiterated the standards in the Stockholm Declaration. Principle

---

222 Final Report prepared by Mrs. Fatma Zohra Ksentini, Special Rapporteur, U.N. ESCOR Commission on Human Rights, Sub-Commission on Prevention of Discrimination and Protection of Minorities, 46th Sess., U.N. Doc. E/CN.4/Sub.2/1994/9 (1994).

223 Idem.

224 Draft Principles on Human Rights and the Environment, in Ksentini Report, Annex I at 75.

225 Declaration of Bizkaia on the Right to the Environment, U.N. Educational, Social, and Cultural Organization, U.N. Doc. 30C/INF.11, art. 1 (1999).

226 Idem.

227 See Report of the U.N. Conference on the Human Environment, U.N. Doc.A/CONF. 48/14/rev/1, U.N. Sales No. E.73.1.A.14 (1972), reprinted in 11 I.L.M. 1416.

228 Idem.

2 of the Rio Declaration adopted Principle 21 of the Stockholm Declaration and added that states have the right to pursue "their own environmental and development policies."

The right to a healthy environment is also recognized by several regional and national instruments. Both the African Charter on Human and People's Rights and the San Salvador Protocol state that people have the right to live in a healthy environment.[229] Over 70 countries endorse these two agreements and pledge adherence to the principles set forth. Additionally, the over 60 national constitutions have specific provisions relating to the environment, and many national legislatures have enacted provisions to help people realize and enforce the right to a healthy environment.[230]

Courts have supported the right to a healthy environment in many opinions. Successful suits against private polluters have demonstrated that if the plaintiff can meet the many qualifications, United States courts are willing to recognize and remedy environmental degradation. In other countries, there have been successful suits against governmental entities charged with protecting the environment. Of note is the opinion by the Philippines Supreme Court in Minors Oposa v. Factoran.[231] In this case minors, represented by their parents, sued the Philippine Secretary of the Department of Environment and Natural Resources to compel the cancelation of timber contracts. In supporting the constitutional right to a healthy environment, the court was particularly concerned with the rights of future generations.[232] Courts in Colombia, Chile, Ecuador, and Peru, have also recognized the right to a healthy environment. Some courts have gone even further and granted environmental protections more expansive than those provided by their constitution. There is extensive recognition of the right to a healthy environment both explicitly and implicitly at the international, regional, and national levels. This support is supplemented by the general recognition of the necessity of a healthy environment and the right of a state, or of individuals, to have such an environment. In Filartiga, the court found an international norm

---

229 African Charter on Human and People's Rights, 1520 U.N.T.S. 217, 250, art. 24 (1982). Additional Protocol to the American Convention on Human Rights in the Area of Economic, Social and Cultural Rights (Protocol of San Salvador), 28 I.L.M. 161 (1989).

230 John Lee, "The Underlying Legal Theory to Support a Well-Defined Human Right to a Healthy Environment as a Principle of Customary International Law," *J. Envtl. L.* 283 (2000): 306-07.

231 See Minors Oposa v. Factoran, G.R. No. 101083, 30 July 1993 (Phil.), reprinted in 33 I.L.M. 173 (1994).

232 Idem.

existed because the United Nations charter created general human rights.[233] These rights were then expanded to include a ban on torture on the basis of non-binding United Nations resolutions, as well as international and regional agreements, national constitutions and the United States State Department.

As demonstrated above, there is extensive support for recognizing environmental human rights as an international norm. First, there is the general declaration of human rights in the United Nations Charter.[234] This can be expanded to include environmental human rights through other United Nations resolutions, namely, the UDHR and The International Covenant on Economic, Social, and Civil Rights. Second, there is recognition of the right by the General Assembly in 1990, the Ksentini Report, and the Draft Principles on Human Rights and the Environment. This right has additional support in international and regional agreements, such as the African Charter and San Salvador Protocol. Lastly, environmental human rights are recognized in judicial opinions from many countries and in many nations' Constitutions. In sum, the nature and quality of these sources overlap with the sources cited in Filartiga, and thus should be sufficient for a court to recognize the right to a healthy environment as part of the law of nations.

1.3.2. Alien Tort Claim Act and Pacific Island Nations

If the nations frame their complaint as an environmental human rights violation, they may need to prove state involvement. Unlike cases such as Aguinda, where the local government and Texaco were acting in concert in Ecuador, no such claim can be made here. The GHG emissions that are leading to rising sea levels are not being produced in island nations, nor are they result of corporate activity on the island.[235] Rather, the largest source of GHG emissions lies far away in the United States.[236] Because judicial interpretation of the ATCA has not yet included human rights violations as one of the harms that do not require a state action, the nations will have to make a claim that GHG emission by corporations

---

233 See Filartiga v. Pena-Irala, 630 F.2d 876, 881 (2d. Cir. 1980).

234 See generally U.N. Charter, available at http:// www.un.org/overview/charter/contents.html.

235 Intergovernmental Panel on Climate Change, Climate Change 2001: Impacts, Adaptation, and Vulnerability, at 17.3.4 (Feb. 2001) ("[T]he Pacific Islands region as whole accounts for 0.03% of the global emissions of CO2 from fuel combustion."), http://www.ipcc.ch/pub/tar/wg2/637.htm#1734

236 See UNFCCC Greenhouse Gas Inventory Database.

in the United States is done under color of state law. Such a claim is daunting, but not insurmountable. First, major corporations in coal, oil, gas and energy production industries do extensive lobbying of Congress.[237] This influence is reflected in national policies regarding emission and pollution standards set by the national government. This close relationship could be enough to satisfy the "strong nexus" test. These corporations not only influence national policy, but they are also guided by it and, this may be enough to satisfy a court that these actions are occurring under the color of state action.[238] While courts have determined in the past that carrying out state policy alone is not enough to satisfy the "strong nexus" test, this moves one step beyond. Through their hefty campaign contributions, the oil and gas industry is essentially setting state policy. This combination of creation and implementation of state policy could potentially satisfy the state actor test. In contrast, if the Pacific island nations choose to frame the claim in terms of genocide, the state actor dilemma goes away. Under Kadic, genocide does not require state action when pursuing an ATCA claim.[239] Similarly, the court in Beanal indicated that cultural genocide would not require state action under the ATCA.[240] Therefore, while the claim of genocide may be more difficult based on the facts it removes the potential hurdle of trying to prove state involvement. There are advantages and disadvantages to either approach. On the one hand, while a claim for violation of environmental human rights best suits the factual scenario presented here, this is an emerging area of law, only newly recognized under international law, and United States district courts may be hesitant to see it as part of the "law of nations." Additionally, as courts have not yet determined whether environmental human rights violations require state action, the plaintiffs would need to be prepared to make such a proffer. On the other hand, a claim for cultural genocide or traditional genocide is not as factually on point; however, genocide is clearly recognized as a violation of the law of nations and does not require a showing of state action.

Two common barriers often occur in ATCA actions, but may not be an issue here. The first is forum nonconveniens ("FNC"). Previously, ATCA actions have

---

237 William Gibson, Industry Bets Big on Energy Policy Ads, *Orlando Sentinel,* last modified Aug. 19, 2001, http://articles.orlandosentinel.com/2001-08-19/news/0108190309_1_energy-policy-bush-energy-energy-and-economic

238 Idem.

239 Kadic v. Karadzic, 70 F.3d 232, 239 (2d Cir. 1995).

240 Beanal v. Freeport-McMoRan, Inc., 969 F. Supp. 362, 372-73 (E.D. La. 1997).

pursued corporations that are not cited in the United States and forcing the corporations to defend in a foreign forum. But here, if the defendants were US entities, getting a dismissal based on FNC would be very challenging for the defendants. Even non-US entities were named as defendants; they could be pursued under the ATCA, provided they have sufficient contacts with the United States. If Pacific island nations are to be successful with an ATCA claim seeking redress for harms inflicted upon them from global warming and rising sea levels, they will have to meet several criteria. These criteria are set forth in the text of the ATCA and by judicial interpretation of the ATCA. First, the suit must be brought by an alien.[241] While it is possible for a single individual or nation to bring this action, it may be even more powerful if several nations band together to form a class action and litigate this issue once. Because the money award from such an action would likely be big, it could be beneficial for the nations to get involved in the litigation as early as possible before the funds were depleted. Second, the claim must be in tort. Third, the tort must be a violation of the law of nations. This will be challenging because there is no precedent, but as this Comment suggests, the tools to make this claim exist. Finally, depending on how the nations' frame their claims, they may have to address whether state actors are involved. As with all tort claims, several elements must be satisfied. The claim could allege intentional or negligent harm.

Potential defendants fall into two categories: private corporations or government. Private corporations could be sued either en masse in one action or individually. Suing the government for failing to set lower GHG emission levels, pulling out of the Kyoto Protocol, and failing to force corporations to comply with the current emission standards is another option. Under a negligence theory, the negligent act would be releasing high levels of GHGs, when it is avoidable. The duty arises from international law, and the many sources discussed previously, which proscribe actions having significant, negative, transboundary environmental impacts. There is also the issue of causation, both actual and legal. Actual causation could be shown that but for the high levels of GHGs released by the defendant; there would not have been an excessive rise in global temperatures and sea levels. Proximate cause, using the foreseeability test, can also be satisfied since credible science has forecast for years that GHG emission would have significant consequences including rising sea levels.[242] In

---

241 28 U.S.C. § 1350 (1996).

242 See Intergovernmental Panel on Climate Change.

addition, the Pacific island nations' pleas for help have put the rest of the world on notice. The damages sought would clearly be compensatory, either for the cost of relocating to a new island or for modifying their current home to continue to sustain life in the face of rising seas. The plaintiff nations could also seek punitive damages if the court allowed. Finally, although the defendants are likely to raise procedural and jurisdictional defenses discussed previously,[243] the defendants have few of the traditional tort cases as available here. This is simply not a case where contributory negligence, consent or privilege can be claimed. Thus, regarding classic tort law analysis, the plaintiffs can establish all the necessary elements for a successful tort action. As outlined above, Pacific island nations could frame an ATCA claim as cultural, and possibly literal, genocide or as a violation of the environmental human rights of indigenous peoples.

1.3.3. Environmental Human Rights in the Context of Indigenous Peoples

The greatest impediment facing Pacific island nations in making a claim under the ATCA is establishing a violation of international norms. As outlined above, because there is greater international recognition for human rights, an environmental human rights claim may be more successful than a strict environmental law claim. Such a claim is bolstered by the facts that not only are environmental human rights at issue, but also the rights of indigenous peoples. Indigenous peoples are broadly defined as the living descendants of pre-invasion inhabitants of a land now dominated by others.[244] While not all of the threatened Pacific island nations have populations that would qualify as indigenous, some do. For example, the Marshall Islands were occupied by the Spanish, Germans and Japanese before ultimately coming under the control of the United States.[245] The United States proceeded to use the islands to test nuclear bombs, evacuating or relocating inhabitants as necessary.[246] While the island nation has since gained its freedom, it is still highly influenced by these invasions and is making legisla-

---

243 Idem.

244 S. James Anaya, *Indigenous Peoples in International Law* (New York: Oxford University Press, 2004).

245 Brief Historical Chronology of the Marshall Islands (2001), Republic of the Marshall Islands Embassy,

http://www.rmiembassyus.org/about/history.html

246 Idem.

tive efforts to preserve its native culture and history.[247] If the native culture is to be maintained, it must be in the face of this Western presence. International recognition of the importance of preserving native culture favors making a claim under the ATCA. The following section outlines the international community's strong support for the rights of indigenous people.

The special right of indigenous peoples to a healthy environment is supported in several international conventions. The Rio Declaration not only sets forth standards to protect the environment, but also acknowledges the unique position of indigenous people. Specifically, states should support indigenous peoples and their quest for sustainable development. The 1994 Draft Declaration of Principles on Human Rights and the Environment also provides clear and explicit protection to indigenous peoples. Similarly, the Universal Declaration of Human Rights supports the human right to culture. Lastly, the International Covenant on Civil and Political Rights also implicitly supports these same rights.[248]

There are many regional covenants and national constitutions that recognize the special right of an indigenous population to a healthy and sustainable environment. In the Declaration of Principles of Indigenous Rights by the Fourth General Assembly of the World Council of Indigenous Peoples, Principle 13 states that "no action or course of conduct may be undertaken which, directly or indirectly, may result in the destruction of land, air, water, sea, ice, wildlife, habitat or natural resource without the free and informed consent of the indigenous peoples affected."[249] Under the Inter-American Declaration on the Rights of Indigenous Peoples, indigenous people are entitled to the human right of a "healthy environment." Additionally, as of 1998, 50 nations have explicitly recognized a right to a healthy environment in their constitutions, and an additional 33 have recognized a duty to protect or defend the environment. Thus, the aggregation of international, transnational and regional documents that support

---

247 Dirk H.R. Spennemann, Historic Preservation Legislation in the Republic of Marshall Islands (2000), Republic of the Marshall Islands Embassy, http://life.csu.edu.au/marshall/html/RMILAW/Historic_Overview.html.

248 1994 Draft Declaration of Principles on Human Rights, arts. 5, 8, 20, reprinted in 3 RECIEL 259 (1994). Part II (14) states; "Indigenous peoples have the right to protection against any action or course of conduct that may result in the destruction or degradation of their territories, including land, air, water, sea-ice, wildlife or other resources." Id. See UDHR, supra note 116, arts. 3, 22, 25, 28. International Covenant on Civil and Political Rights, supra note 118, art. 1.

249 World Council of Indigenous Peoples, Declaration of Principles (2008)
    http://www.cwis.org/fwdp/Resolutions/WCIP/wcip.txt

indigenous peoples' environmental human rights makes a compelling case that they are universal, definable and obligatory, and are thus international norms within the "law of nations."

In addition to the rights recognized in international conventions and agreements, indigenous peoples have found a special position in judicial opinions addressing environmental questions. This may be because humans existing in a degraded environment are exposed to such risks as diminished health, economic hardship and loss of culture. These risks are particularly profound for indigenous peoples who tend to be the most directly tied to the damaged land. Both international human rights tribunals and national courts have acknowledged indigenous peoples' special relationship to the land and the needs that arise out of that relationship. For example, the Inter-American Commission on Human Rights found that the rights of the Yanomami of Brazil were violated when a road was built through their territory causing extensive environmental damage.[250] The Commission found their rights to life, liberty, personal security and preservation of health and well-being were violated. Similarly, in Lubicon Lake Band v. Canada,[251] the United Nations Human Rights Committee found that the Lubicon Lake Band had a fundamental right to culture, and its ability to control its natural resources was directly tied to this right. The committee relied upon the International Covenant on Civil and Political Rights and its provision protecting the cultural rights of minorities.[252] Lastly, several Latin American courts "have stated without reserve that the right to a healthy environment is a fundamental human right." Taken together, these opinions demonstrate the special status of indigenous peoples and the courts' recognition of their environmental human rights.

---

250 Resolution N 12/185, Case No. 7615 (Brazil), Mar. 5, 1985.

251 See United Nations Doc. CCPR/C/38/D/167/1984, Annex II (1990).

252 Idem.

1.4.1. Pacific Cultures: Polynesian, Malaysian & Micronesian

In making a claim of genocide, cultural genocide is most plausible. While there is no specific definition of cultural genocide, statements by the United Nations are informative.[253] The Draft United Nations Declaration on the Rights of Indigenous Peoples claims a right for indigenous people not to be subjected to cultural genocide, including the prevention of and redress for: (a) any act which has the aim or effect of depriving them of their integrity as distinct societies, or of their cultural or ethnic characteristics or identities; (b) any form of forced assimilation or integration or; (c) dispossession of their lands, territories or resources.[254] Under Kadic, there is an international binding prohibition on genocide.[255] Cultural genocide, while grounded in the same roots as genocide, is more of an emerging legal claim and courts have not had an opportunity to rule particularly on this issue.[256] But, as the United Nations has made clear, there is a need for both prevention of and redress for harms caused as a result of cultural genocide. Now is the time for the courts to take the next step and make a legally binding prohibition on cultural genocide, a step the Beanal court suggested it was ready to do.

If the indigenous people of these Pacific island nations are to survive they will most likely have to abandon their homelands.[257] This will mean leaving behind not only their traditional ways, traditional lands, cultural icons and relics, but also the environment that has sustained them for generations.

This forced immigration forms the basis of the cultural genocide claim. First, cultural genocide can be the deprivation of cultural or ethnic characteristics. By leaving behind all their cultural icons, relics and traditional way

---

253 Draft United Nations Declaration on the Rights of Indigenous Peoples, U.N. Doc. E/CN.4/1995/2, (1994), reprinted in 34 I.L.M. 541 (1995).

254 Idem, art.7.

255 See Kadic v. Karadzic, 70 F.3d 232, 242 (2d Cir. 1995).

256 In Beanal, the only case to deal with cultural genocide, the court recognized that cultural genocide may exist as part of international law, but the plaintiff had failed to provide the court with the sources necessary to establish this fact.

Beanal v. Freeport-McMoRan, Inc., 969 F. Supp. 362, 373 (E.D. La. 1997).

257 See Beanal v. Freeport -McMoRan, Inc., 197 F.3d 161, 168 (5th Cir. 1999).

of life, the Islanders are deprived of cultural characteristics. Second, cultural genocide can be forced assimilation or integration.[258] By being forced to move to new lands, the Pacific Islanders will most certainly experience some degree of forced integration. Third, cultural genocide can be dispossession of lands.[259] This clearly is already happening and, if these islands are ultimately submerged, will result in the complete dispossession of native lands. As the islands' indigenous peoples' claim is grounded in all three possible definitions of cultural genocide, a claim on this basis is far from frivolous. Claims of true genocide, the extinguishing of an entire race or culture, are more tenuous, but still not absurd. Genocide can be "deliberately inflicting on the group conditions of life calculated to bring about its physical destruction in whole or in part."[260] In the absence of foreign assistance for relocation, these people will die. Their islands are like sinking ships, and it is only a matter of time before the inhabitants can no longer survive. Therefore, if they do not get assistance in the form of decreased GHG emissions and financial support, the island inhabitants could suffer complete physical destruction. The real genocide claim would be quite challenging to make because of the intentionality requirements of "deliberate" and "calculated." A court is not likely to accept that GHG emitters are intentionally trying to submerge Pacific island nations. Nevertheless, such a claim could be strengthened by analogizing to the law of toxic torts. Specifically, if the act of excessive GHG emissions is intentional, then the consequences of the act are also intentional.[261] Given the petitions of Pacific island nations to the United Nations and the United States, the world is aware of their plight. Because polluters cannot claim ignorance, their actions are calculated recklessness at best. Continuing production of excessive GHGs with knowledge of the consequences may be enough to sway a court that a defendant acted intentionally.

Framing a claim as an environmental human rights violation is the most appropriate to the factual scenario. The facts of this case demonstrate that these nations face both immediate and future environmental destruction that

---

258 See Draft United Nations Declaration on the Rights of Indigenous Peoples, supra note 188, art. 7.

259 Idem.

260 Convention on the Prevention and Punishment of the Crime of Genocide, Jan. 12, 1951, art. 2(c), 78 U.N.T.S. 277.

261 Restatement (Second) of Torts §8A cmt. b, (1965) ("Intent is not, however, limited to consequences that are desired. If the actor knows that consequences are certain, or substantially certain, to result from his act, and still goes ahead, he is treated by the law as if he had in fact desired to produce the result").

rises to the level of a human rights violation. First, as the seas rise, the islands become more susceptible to erosion from the forces of the ocean. Second, they are in danger of losing their primary protein food source: fish, which live in and depend upon the coral reefs. Last, their freshwater sources are threatened. While in cases like Aguinda, the primary environmental harm was toxic pollution, destruction in the absence of pollution could still be an environmental harm.[262] Both pollution and destruction make the environment inaccessible and unusable. Destruction of the environment, inflicted by another is a violation of the human right to a healthy environment. Breach of this right is even clearer in this case, where not only will the indigenous people be deprived of a clean environment, but they will eventually be deprived of an environment altogether when the islands are submerged.

Pacific island nations find themselves in a very vulnerable position and must take action if they are to have any hope of survival. This Comment suggests how these nations might pursue an action under the ATCA against the United States, the major source of GHG emissions. While such a claim would cover new ground legally, the foundation in international human rights law is sufficient to make the claim. A claim like this would certainly gather significant media attention. Thus, even if the claim were not legally successful, it could still be a success by bringing the world's attention to the problem.

---

262 For example, ozone depletion and loss of species due to habitat loss are environmental problems addressed in environmental law. David Hunter et al., *International Environmental Law and Policy* 1-6 (1998).

CHAPTER TWO

THE ENVIRONMENTAL PERSPECTIVE

2.1. CLIMATE CHANGE UNDER THE INTERNATIONAL ENVIRONMENTAL LAW

2.1.1. Brief evolution of the process

Climate change impacts are already affecting the planet and its people, and science shows that it will get far worse. In his paper, Klaus Topfer argues that the most severe impacts will be on the lives and livelihoods of the poor and developing countries, especially small island states. And the biggest culprits are the rich and the developed countries.[263]

Although progress has been made (e.g. we have international agreements, more resources for scientific research leading to stronger evidence, policy advances, a change in industry rhetoric, a definite increase in public awareness), it all falls far short of what is needed. At the heart of the problem is the production and use of fossil fuel—particularly the emissions of carbon dioxide from the burning of coal, oil, and gas. Developed countries have accepted legally binding emissions targets in the Kyoto Protocol, thestill widely recognized to be seriously inadequate.[264]

Over the last few years, different legal actions have been taken across the world to implement a law to combat climate change. Multiple stakeholders and

---

263 Klaus Topfer, "Climate Justice: Enforcing Climate Change Law," CLIMATE JUSTICE (2002).

264 Ibid.

organizations (e.g. human rights law, emission control regulations, endangered species protection, freedom of information and international legal obligations) have proposed a variety of national and international legal theories. Judgments and administrative decisions have begun to come through.[265]

The field of law has been weak in the worldwide effort to deliver a "cleaner, healthier and ultimately a more just world."[266] There are over 1000 international and regional agreements, addressing a variety of environmental issues beginning with the protection of the species and ending with conservation of seas and oceans. Most countries also have environmental laws. And yet, unless these laws are complied with, they are nothing more than symbols. This is an issue affecting billions of people who are being denied their rights. Furthermore, it presents not only a national, but also a regional and global concern.[267]

In his paper "Climate Change, Conflict and Security: International Law Challenges," Ben Saul brings up predictions that have been made about the potential for climate change to fuel war and other forms of violent conflict.[268] "At the extreme end, it has been suggested that the uncontrolled effects of climate change could generate conflicts on the scale of the world wars, but lasting for centuries."[269]

Another study suggests that 46 countries with 2.7 billion people are at high risk of violent conflict due to climate change interacting with existing underlying causes of conflict; while a further 56 countries with 1.2 billion people are at high risk of political instability, possibly leading to violent conflict in the longer term.[270]

Growing concern about the security risks posed by climate change has emerged in the leading global institutions such as the United Nations Security Council and the European Union. National militaries have increasingly begun to conceptualize climate change as a national security threat while proponents of

---

265 Ibid.

266 Ibid.

267 Ibid.

268 Ben Saul, *Climate Change, Conflict and Security: International Law Challenges*, SYDNEY LAW SCHOOL Oct. 2009, at 1, *available at* http://ssrn.com/abstract=1485175.

269 Ibid.

270 Ibid.

the "human security" approach have sought to recast climate change as a critical source of global insecurity.[271]

While there has been much consideration of the political and strategic implications of climate change as a critical security risk, to date, far less attention has been devoted to thinking about whether and how the general international law is relevant to addressing the risks posed by climate change to international security.

Paradoxically, that threat may be aggravated by certain measures taken in response to climate change. Any post-Kyoto global compact for reducing carbon emissions and mitigating climate change would already come too late to neutralize all of the security risks flowing from the level of climate change that has already occurred or is underway and irreversible over the coming decades.[272]While such an agreement would be a significant role in containing the risks, it is also necessary to consider how existing specialized branches of international law might assist (or be unable to assist), or be modified, to further manage security threats.[273]

At the level of the general law, the principles of state responsibility appear ill-equipped to deal with the harm caused by one state to another through carbon emissions. Even assuming that a relevant primary rule can be identified as in the prohibition of transboundary environmental harm, or the nebulous precautionary principle—the secondary standards of state responsibility would require considerable adaptation to address the peculiar problems of causation associated with carbon emissions. Carbon emitters are numerous, and their effects are diffuse and widespread, rendering it difficult to demonstrate the kind of causal responsibility which is typical in classic transboundary cases such as the pollution of a river by an upstream factory, or toxic plumes blown on the wind from a particular facility to a particular cross-border town.[274]

It is in the specialized branches of public international law that there may be more promising scope for measures designed to avert the security risks related to climate change. In international economic law and the law of development,

---

271 Ibid.

272 International Alert, op. cit., 4.

273 Ben Saul, *Climate Change, Conflict and Security: International Law Challenges*, SYDNEY LAW SCHOOL OCT. 2009, at 7, *available at* http://ssrn.com/abstract=1485175.u

274 *Id.* at 7.

there is a clear need for stronger global or multilateral governance and management of resource scarcity and distribution.

In the field of global migration, international law is currently poorly equipped to respond to the challenge of climate-induced displacement and the potential security risks it may bring. Mobility as a whole is generally left to national legal discretion rather than being subject to comprehensive international legal control. The climate-induced displaced are very unlikely to meet the legal definition of a refugee and therefore generally fall outside of the parameters of international legal protection, and complementary human rights-based protection is currently underdeveloped beyond agreed areas (such as non-return to torture). They are likely to be seen as another manifestation of mere 'economic migrants' — much maligned and seldom admitted to developed countries, particularly given increasing restrictions on migration in the wake of the global financial crisis of 2008-09.[275]

For pragmatic reasons, a comprehensive mobility strategy need not necessarily involve the formulation of a new international treaty covering, for instance, environmental migration, but it would require a commitment by developed states to actively managing the problem, including by providing development assistance for internal relocation where appropriate.

The previous survey of some of the specialized branches of international law illustrates how averting conflict risks associated with climate change requires a system-wide, preventive approach. It is vital, therefore, to consider the range of ways in which public international law can be marshaled to prevent, contain and remedy the consistent security threats. Engaging the specialized branches of international law enables a thicker, more systemic response to the security risks attending climate change and is likely to prove more effective than relying on individual institutions (such as the Security Council) or normative frameworks (such as a new global climate deal). The costs of modifying the international law in these ways are undoubtedly less than the human and financial costs, which will likely ensue from resource conflicts and sovereign competition aggravated by unmitigated climate change.[276]

---

275 *Id.*

276 *Id.*

2.1.2. United Nations Framework Convention on Climate Change

"The UNFCCC is an international environmental treaty produced at the United Nations Conference on Environment and Development (UNCED), informally known as the Earth Summit, held in Rio de Janeiro from 3 to 14 June 1992."[277] The objective of the treaty is to stabilize GHG concentrations in the atmosphere at a level that would prevent dangerous anthropogenic interference with the climate system."[278]

"The treaty is considered legally non-binding."[279] "Instead, it provides for updates (called "protocols") that would set mandatory emission limits. The main update is the Kyoto Protocol, which has become much better known than the UNFCCC itself."[280]

"One of its first tasks was to establish national GHG inventories of GHG emissions and removals, which were used to create the 1990 benchmark levels for the accession of Annex I countries to the Kyoto Protocol and the commitment of those countries to GHG reductions."[281] "Updated inventories must be regularly submitted by Annex I countries."[282]

The fourth chapter of the UNFCCC[283] "highlights the impacts of and the vulnerabilities to climate change in the four regions: Africa, Asia, Latin America and Small Island Developing States.[284]

"Information is scarce about the scale of potential future impacts, and is, even more, scant for the costs of avoiding them by adaptation; a point stressed in the UNFCCC report."[285] "Some sectors such as mining and manufacturing,

---

277 United Nations Framework Convention on Climate Change, Environment (last viewed June 24, 2013), *available at* http://www.environment.gen.tr/climate-change/599-united-nations-framework-convention-on-climate-change.html.

278 *Id.*.

279 *Id.*

280 *Id.*

281 *Id.*

282 *Id.*

283 *See* Climate Change: Impacts, Vulnerabilities and Adaptation in Developing Countries, UNFCCC 18 (2007), http://unfccc.int/resource/docs/publications/impacts.pdf

284 "Climate Change: Impacts, Vulnerabilities and Adaptation in Developing Countries, UNFCCC 18 (2007), http://unfccc.int/resource/docs/publications/impacts.pdf

285 Parry, *supra* note 313, at 11.

energy, retailing and tourism, were not included in the UNFCCC report."[286] Within some sectors that were examined, the funding needs estimated were clearly only partial. In health, for example, just three areas of impact, where there were sufficient views, were considered: the effect of climate change on diarrheal diseases, malaria, and malnutrition in lowland middle-income countries. Adaptation costs for health effects in high-income countries were not estimated. A major problem is the absence of case studies to test the top-down form of UNFCCC analysis. The few national figures available tend to suggest costs more than the UNFCCC estimates. For example, agencies responsible for flood management in England and Wales have determined a need to spend (due to climate change) an additional $30 million annually in 2011, growing to $720 million by 2035 (Environment Agency, 2009).

In most cases, the UNFCCC estimation of funding needs was derived from applying an increase in cost to those areas of investment that are deemed to be climate-sensitive. In agriculture, for example, two percent of investment on infrastructure is taken to be climate-sensitive. In some sectors, particularly the built environment, the investment flows are so large that even small changes in this markup can change estimates significantly.

In particular, applying a "climate markup" is not appropriate when current investment flows are well below what they should be. In several parts of the world, current levels of investment are considered far from adequate and lead to current high vulnerability to climate, including its variability and extremes, the latter case being termed a current "adaptation deficit" (Burton, 2004). This partly explains why impacts from climate change are expected to be greatest in lowland middle-income countries (IPCC, 2007). To avoid these effects, the adaptation deficit (which is largely a development deficit) will need to be made good. For good reason, these costs were not included in the UNFCCC estimate, which was aimed at identifying the additional cost of climate change, but it needs to be stressed that without the adaptation deficit being made good, the enhanced investment for adaptation will not be sufficient to avoid serious damage from climate impacts. Dlugolecki (2007), in a background paper for the UNFCCC study, estimated (at $200 billion per year) the costs of damage from present-day extreme weather and took this as a reflection of the current scale of inadequate adaptation. The Millennium Development Goals represent an attempt to make right some, but probably not all, of the adaptation deficit, and have been

---

[286] *Id.*

estimated around $200 billion by 2015 (Sachs and McArthur, 2005). To make good, the entire development deficit probably requires enhancing official development assistance to 0.7 percent of GDP of OECD countries. Hence, the issues of development and adaptation costs are intimately linked, and this requires further exploration.

The UNFCCC takes the first line, but this leads to estimations of the value that are substantially lower than if one assumed a development pathway that protects the poor against vulnerability to climate change. In this report, we conclude that removing the housing and infrastructure deficit in low- and middle-income countries will cost around $315 billion per year (in today's figures) over 20 years; while adapting this upgraded infrastructure specifically to meet the challenge of climate change will cost an additional $16–63 billion per year.[287]

It is not clear what proportion of expected damage would be avoided by the proposed UNFCCC investment levels. Most impacts are projected to increase non-linearly with climate change, and adaptation costs similarly with impacts (IPCC, 2007). Therefore, it will probably be very inexpensive to avoid some impacts but prohibitively expensive to avoid others; some impacts we cannot avoid even if funds were unlimited because the technologies are not available (e.g., in connection with ocean acidification). We need to be clear, then, about how much we are willing to pay for adaptation to avoid damages. To illustrate, we might aim (on a scale of reducing cost) to adapt to: (i) all those impacts that reduce human welfare, or (ii) all those that are economically feasible (i.e., cheaper to adapt to than to be born), or (iii) all those that are affordable within a given budget constraint (for example, the size of the global Adaptation Fund).[288]

Implicit in the above is that much damage will not be adapted to over the longer term because adaptation is either not economical or not feasible. We term this 'residual damage.' In the UNFCCC report, it is not clear how much residual damage might be expected. But it is imperative that we start to consider this because the amount may be significant and is likely to increase over time. In the evaluation reported here, residual impacts are estimated at a fifth of all results in agriculture in 2030 and, over the longer term, may account for up to two-thirds of all potential effects across all sectors, depending on the amount of climate change not avoided by mitigation.[289]

---

287 Parry, *supra* note 313, at 12.

288 Parry, *supra* note 313, at 12.

289 Parry, *supra* note 313, at 13.

The UNFCCC study may have given insufficient weight to the value of "soft adaptation." It is easier analytically to cost out structural measures like the expansion of water supply systems, and the UNFCCC study focused on these. In reality, it will often be cheaper to apply "soft adaptation" options. Measures to use water more efficiently, for example, may obviate the need for expensive new infrastructure. Conversely, the human health costs do not include changes in infrastructure ("hard adaptation"), which may be considerable.[290]

The UNFCCC estimate of adaptation costs is a "snapshot" for 2030 at one point along the climate impact curve, and its authors note the importance of the question, "While the adaptation cost curve seems quite gentle between now and 2030, how steeply will it grow thereafter?" Some believe it may rise steeply, possibly quadratically in some sectors (IPCC, 2007). It is very important that this be analyzed, so we are sufficiently prepared for escalating adaptation costs beyond 2030.[291]

2.1.3. Intergovernmental Panel on Climate Change

The IPCC was established in 1988 by the United Nations Environment Programme (UNEP) and the WMO to support national policy and "provide the world with a clear scientific view on the current state of knowledge in climate change and its potential environmental and socio-economic impacts."[292] The IPCC has been referred to as the "hybrid science" policy project that is driven by both science and politics.[293]Whereby the process is scientific, the IPCC ultimately reports back to the governments and is influences by their priorities and interests.[294]

---

290 Parry, *supra* note 313, at 13.

291 Parry, *supra* note 313, at 13.

292 Organization, INTERGOVERNMENTAL PANEL ON CLIMATE CHANGE (last viewed June 17, 2013), http://www.ipcc.ch/organization/organization.shtml#.UExBgFRhPoA.

293 Reiner Grundmann, Climate Change and Knowledge Politics, 16 ENVIRONMENTAL POLITICS 414, 416 (2007); MARK PELLING, ADAPTATION TO CLIMATE CHANGE: FROM RESILIENCE TO TRANSFORMATION 9 (2011), http://talos.unicauca.edu.co/gea/sites/default/files/Adaptation%20to%20Climate%20Change%20From%20 Resilience%20to%20Transformation.pdf.

294 Reiner Grundmann, Climate Change and Knowledge Politics, 16 ENVIRONMENTAL POLITICS 414 (2007)

The most notable and widely recognized publication that the IPCC produced includes four Assessment Reports in 1990, 1995, 2001 and 2007.[295] These reports are published commercially and can be obtained from IPCC's general website.[296] They feature the latest scientific, technical and socio-economic literature on climate change. They also cover a broad and geographically balanced participation of experts from all relevant fields of knowledge.

The Assessment reports aim to have a transparent and multi-stage review process, which ultimately results in authoritative and unbiased reports. The IPCC is leading some activities such as the publication of Special Reports and hosting expert meetings to facilitate discussions of topics relevant to the assessment process and to receive new input from the scientific community.[297] Despite these efforts, some have stressed that IPCC's reports do not feature the full account of existing knowledge and/or information on climate change.

The IPCC process has several limitations that have been pointed out in both literature and the international community. For starters, some evidence on climate change and human reaction is difficult to include.[298] This is the case with limited evidence of climate change impacts and experiences in adaptation such as in the Caribbean, Latin America, Asia and Africa.[299] The knowledge is often gained/ stored by local actors and only published regionally or nationally, thus never making it to international peer review journals and IPCC Assessment reports.[300] To overcome this limitation, the Fourth Assessment Report (AR4) has tried to incorporate "gray literature produced by governments and NGOs."[301] Moreover, to foster a more inclusive scientific representation of world regions, a

---

295 See Reports, INTERGOVERNMENTAL PANEL ON CLIMATE CHANGE (last viewed June 17, 2013), http://www.ipcc.ch/publications_and_data/publications_and_data_reports.shtml#.UdBnAvm1ExE

296 See Reports, INTERGOVERNMENTAL PANEL ON CLIMATE CHANGE (last viewed June 17, 2013), http://www.ipcc.ch/publications_and_data/publications_and_data_reports.shtml#.UdBnAvm1ExE

297 IPCC Working Group III, INTERGOVERNMENTAL PANEL ON CLIMATE CHANGE (last viewed June 20, 2013),

   http://www.ipcc-wg3.de/index_html_old; See Publications and Data, INTERGOVERNMENTAL PANEL ON CLIMATE CHANGE (last viewed June 20, 2013), http://www.ipcc.ch/publications_and_data/publications_and_data.shtml#1 (giving a schematic description of the IPCC review process).

298 MARK PELLING, ADAPTATION TO CLIMATE CHANGE: FROM RESILIENCE TO TRANSFORMATION 10 (2011), http://talos.unicauca.edu.co/gea/sites/default/files/Adaptation%20to%20Climate%20Change%20From%20Resilience%20to%20Transformation.pdf.

299 Id.

300 Id.

301 Id.

quota system, and travel funds have been provided to those residing in low- and middle-income countries.[302]

Another common critique of the IPCC process relates to its credibility and the actual review process. This was particularly the case with the 2007 AR4 report, which came under scrutiny in 2010.[303] It was discovered that the 3,000-page publication contained numerous errors, including the statement it made regarding the melt rate of glaciers in the Himalayas.[304] "This led to questions being raised about the overall credibility of the report's findings, prompting United Nations Secretary-General Ban Ki-moon to ask the InterAcademy Council to convene a panel of experts to conduct an independent review."[305] "Based on this review, the IAC issued a report with recommended measures and actions to strengthen IPCC's processes and procedures so as to be better able to respond to future challenges and ensure the ongoing quality of its reports."[306]

Lastly, the IPCC process has been slow to recognize climate change debates that do not necessarily use the language of climate change or publish in climate change journals.[307] These include various disciplines such as disaster risk reduction, social and food security.[308] However, IPCC is beginning to move past this with IPCC's Special Report on *Managing the Risk of Extreme Events and Disaster to Advance Climate Change Adaptation*, which asks to bridge the gap between the climate change adaptation, development and disaster risk management community.[309] Thus, the next challenge for the IPCC will be to increasingly recog-

---

302 *Id.*

303 IPCC: Climate Impact Rick Set to Increase, BBC News (Nov. 18, 2011), http://www.bbc.co.uk/news/science-environment-15745408; Review of the IPCC, INTERACADEMY COUNCIL (Aug. 30, 2010), http://reviewipcc.interacademycouncil.net/ (explaining that the IPCC underwent an independent review by the InterAcademy Council).

304 IPCC: Climate Impact Rick Set to Increase, BBC News (Nov. 18, 2011), http://www.bbc.co.uk/news/science-environment-15745408.

305 IPCC: Climate Impact Rick Set to Increase, BBC News (Nov. 18, 2011), http://www.bbc.co.uk/news/science-environment-15745408.

306 Review of the IPCC, INTERACADEMY COUNCIL (Aug. 30, 2010), http://reviewipcc.interacademycouncil.net/; Climate Change Assessments, Review of the Processes & Procedures of the IPCC INTERACADEMY COUNCIL (Aug. 30, 2010), http://reviewipcc.interacademycouncil.net/report.html (including the complete report on the IPCC and recommendations).

307 MARK PELLING, ADAPTATION TO CLIMATE CHANGE: FROM RESILIENCE TO TRANSFORMATION 10 (2011), http://talos.unicauca.edu.co/gea/sites/default/files/Adaptation%20to%20Climate%20Change%20From%20Resilience%20to%20Transformation.pdf.

308 *Id.*

309 *Id.* at 11.

nize the parallel communities related to climate change, but also to retain its core purpose for consolidating knowledge for the policy community on climate change.[310]

2.1.4. The Kyoto Protocol

The Kyoto Protocol (Protocol)[311] is a protocol to UNFCCC[312], aimed at fighting climate change.[313] The Protocol was initially adopted on 11 December 1997 in Kyoto, Japan, and entered into force on 16 February 2005.[314] As today, 191 states have signed and ratified the protocol.[315] The only remaining signatory not to have ratified the protocol is the United States.[316] Other United Nations member states that did not ratify the protocol are Afghanistan, Andorra, and South Sudan. In December 2011, Canada denounced the Protocol.[317]

Under the Protocol, 37 countries ("Annex I countries") committed themselves to a reduction of four GHGs (carbon dioxide, methane, nitrous oxide, sulfur hexafluoride) and two groups of gases[318] (hydrofluorocarbons and perfluorocarbons) produced by them, and all member countries gave general commitments.[319] At negotiations, Annex I countries (including the US) collectively agreed to reduce

---

310 *Id.* at 11.

311 Kyoto Protocol to the United Nations Framework Convention on Climate Change art. 3, Dec. 10, 1997, 37 I.L.M. 22, *available at* http://unfccc.int/essential_background/kyoto_protocol/items/1678.php [hereinafter Kyoto Protocol]

312 The United Nations Framework Convention on Climate Change is also referred to as the FCCC.

313 *Kyoto Protocol,* UNITED NATIONS FRAMEWORK CONVENTION ON CLIMATE CHANGE (last visited June 24, 2013), *available at* http://unfccc.int/kyoto_protocol/items/2830.php.

314 *Kyoto Protocol,* UNITED NATIONS FRAMEWORK CONVENTION ON CLIMATE CHANGE (last visited June 24, 2013), *available at* http://unfccc.int/kyoto_protocol/items/2830.php.

315 *Status of Ratification of the Kyoto Protocol,* UNITED NATIONS FRAMEWORK CONVENTION ON CLIMATE CHANGE (last visited June 24, 2013), *available at* http://unfccc.int/kyoto_protocol/status_of_ratification/items/2613.php (explaining that there are currently 192 parties to the Protocol, but one party is a regional economic integration organization).

316 *Id.*

317 *Id.*

318 Kyoto Protocol, *supra* note 347, at Annex B; *What is the Kyoto Protocol?,* CARBONIFY.COM (last viewed June 28, 2013), http://www.carbonify.com/articles/kyoto-protocol.htm.

319 Kyoto Protocol, *supra* note 347, at Annex A.

their GHG emissions by 5.2 percent on average for the period 2008-2012.[320] "This reduction is relative to their annual emissions in a base year, usually 1990. Since the US has not ratified the treaty, the collective emissions reduction of Annex I Kyoto countries fell from 5.2 percent to 4.2 percent below base year."[321]

"Emission limits do not include emissions by international aviation and shipping, but are in addition to the industrial gasses, chlorofluorocarbons, or CFCs, which are dealt with under the 1987 Montreal Protocol on Substances that Deplete the Ozone Layer."[322]

The benchmark 1990-emission levels accepted by the Conference of the Parties of UNFCCC (decision 2/CP.3) were the values of 'global warming potential' calculated for the IPCC Second Assessment Report. These figures are used for converting the various GHG emissions into comparable CO_2 equivalents (CO_2-eq) when computing overall sources and sinks.[323]

The Protocol allows for [sic] several 'flexible mechanisms,' such as emissions trading, the clean development mechanism (CDM) and joint implementation (JI) to allow Annex I countries to meet their GHG emission limitations by purchasing GHG emission reductions credits from elsewhere, through financial exchanges, projects that reduce emissions in non-Annex I countries, from other Annex I countries, or from Annex I countries with excess allowances.[324]

Each Annex I country is required to submit an annual report of inventories of all anthropogenic GHG emissions from sources and removals from sinks under UNFCCC and the Kyoto Protocol. These countries nominate a person (called a "designated national authority") to create and manage its GHG inventory. Virtually all of the non-Annex I countries have also established a designated national authority to maintain its Kyoto obligations, specifically the "CDM process" that determines which GHG projects they wish to propose for accreditation by the CDM Executive Board.[325]

---

320 Kyoto Protocol, HALFMANTER.COM (last viewed June 28, 2013), http://www.halfmantr.com/koyoto-protocol.

321 Id; What is the Kyoto Protocol?, CARBONIFY.COM (last viewed June 28, 2013), http://www.carbonify.com/articles/kyoto-protocol.htm.

322 Id.

323 Id.

324 Id.

325 Id.

"The view that human activities are likely responsible for most of the observed increase in global mean temperature ("global warming") since the mid-20th century is an accurate reflection of current scientific thinking."[326] "Human-induced warming of the climate is expected to continue throughout the 21st century and beyond."[327]

IPCC has produced a range of projections of what the future increase in global mean temperature might be. IPCC's projections are 'baseline' projections, meaning that they assume no future efforts are made to reduce GHG emissions. The IPCC projections cover the period from the beginning of the 21st century to the end of the 21st century. The "likely" range (as assessed to have a greater than 66 percent probability of being correct, based on the IPCC's expert judgment) is a projected increased in global mean temperature over the 21st century of between 1.1 and 6.4°C[328]

"The range also reflects uncertainty in the response of the climate system to the past and future GHG emissions (measured by the climate sensitivity)."[329]

Most countries are Parties to the UNFCCC.[330] Article 2 of the Convention states its ultimate objective, which is to stabilize the concentration of GHGs in the atmosphere "at a level that would prevent dangerous anthropogenic (i.e., human) interference with the climate system."[331] The natural, technical, and social sciences can provide information on decisions relating to this objective,

326 International Agreement: The Kyoto Protocol, INSIDE STORY MEDIA (June 24, 2013), http://www.insidestorymedia.com/international-agreementthe-kyoto-protocol/; See What is the Kyoto Protocol?, CARBONIFY.COM (last viewed June 28, 2013), see Global Warming Fast Facts, National Geographic (June 14, 2007),

http://news.nationalgeographic.com/news/2004/12/1206_041206_global_warming.html.

327 International Agreement: The Kyoto Protocol, INSIDE STORY MEDIA (June 24, 2013),

http://www.insidestorymedia.com/international-agreementthe-kyoto-protocol/.

328 International Agreement: The Kyoto Protocol, INSIDE STORY MEDIA (June 24, 2013),

http://www.insidestorymedia.com/international-agreementthe-kyoto-protocol/.

329 Id.

330 Status of Ratification of the Convention, UNITED NATIONS FRAMEWORK CONVENTION ON CLIMATE CHANGE (last visited June 17, 2013), available at http://unfccc.int/essential_background/convention/status_of_ratification/items/2631.php; What is the UNFCCC & the COP, CLIMATE LEADERS (last viewed June 24, 2013), http://www.climate-leaders.org/climate-change-resources/india-at-cop-15/unfccc-cop.

331 United Nations Framework Convention on Climate Change, Art. 2, June 12, 1992, 1771 U.N.T.S. 107, available at

http://unfccc.int/resource/docs/convkp/conveng.pdf.

e.g., the possible magnitude and rate of future climate changes. However, the IPCC has also concluded that the decision of what constitutes "dangerous" interference requires value judgments, which will vary between different regions of the world. Factors that might affect this decision include the local consequences of climate change impacts, the ability of a particular region to adapt to climate change (adaptive capacity), and the ability of a region to reduce its GHG emissions (mitigate capacity).

The primary aim of the Kyoto Protocol is to contain emissions of the main anthropogenic (i.e., human-emitted) GHGs in ways that reflect underlying national differences in GHG emissions, wealth and capacity to make the reductions. The treaty follows the main principles agreed in the original 1992 United Nations Framework Convention. According to the treaty, in 2012, Annex I Parties who have ratified the treaty must have fulfilled their obligations of GHG emissions limitations established for the Kyoto Protocol's first commitment period (2008–2012). These emissions limitation commitments are listed in Annex B of the Protocol.[332]

The ultimate objective of the UNFCCC is the "stabilization of GHG concentrations in the atmosphere at a level that would prevent dangerous anthropogenic interference with the climate system." Even if Annex I Parties succeed in meeting their first-round commitments, much greater emission reductions will be required in future to stabilize atmospheric GHG concentrations.[333]

The five principal concepts of the Kyoto Protocol are:

• Establishing commitments for the reduction of GHGs that are legally binding for Annex I Parties. The Annex I Parties took on legally binding commitments based on the Berlin Mandate, which was a part of UNFCCC negotiations leading up to the Protocol.

• Implementing policies and measures for the reduction of GHGs by Annex 1 countries. In addition, they are required to increase the absorption of these gasses and utilize all mechanisms available, such

---

332 International Agreement: The Kyoto Protocol, INSIDE STORY MEDIA (June 24, 2013), http://www.insidestorymedia.com/international-agreementthe-kyoto-protocol/.

333 International Agreement: The Kyoto Protocol, INSIDE STORY MEDIA (June 24, 2013), http://www.insidestorymedia.com/international-agreementthe-kyoto-protocol/; *Richard Black, Climate talks a tricky business*, BBC NEWS (Nov. 18, 2006), http://news.bbc.co.uk/2/hi/science/nature/6161998.stm.

as joint implementation, the CDM, and emissions trading, in order to be rewarded with credits that would allow more GHG emissions at home.

- Minimizing Impacts on Developing Countries by establishing an adaptation fund for climate change.

- Accounting, Reporting and Reviewing in order to ensure the integrity of the Protocol.

- Establishing a Compliance Committee to enforce compliance with the commitments under the Protocol.[334]

Under the Kyoto Protocol, 37 industrialized countries, and the European Community commit themselves to binding targets for GHG emissions.[335] The targets apply to the four GHGs carbon dioxide, methane, nitrous oxide, sulfur hexafluoride, and two groups of gasses, hydrofluorocarbons, and perfluorocarbons. The six GHG are translated into CO_2 equivalents in determining reductions in emissions. These reduction targets are in addition to the industrial gasses, chlorofluorocarbons, or CFCs, which are dealt with under the 1987 Montreal Protocol on Substances that Deplete the Ozone Layer.[336]

Under the Protocol, only the Annex I Parties have committed themselves to national or joint reduction targets (formally called "quantified emission limitation and reduction objectives" (QELRO)—Article 4.1). Parties to the Kyoto Protocol not listed in Annex I of the Convention (the non-Annex I Parties) are mostly low-income developing countries and participate in the Kyoto Protocol through the CDM.[337]

---

334 International Agreement: The Kyoto Protocol, INSIDE STORY MEDIA (June 24, 2013), http://www.insidestorymedia.com/international-agreementthe-kyoto-protocol/.

335 International Agreement: The Kyoto Protocol, INSIDE STORY MEDIA (June 24, 2013), http://www.insidestorymedia.com/international-agreementthe-kyoto-protocol/.

336 Michael Grubb, The Economics of the Kyoto Protocol 4 WORLD ECONOMICS 143 (July-Sept. 2003), http://ynccf.net/pdf/CDM/The_economic_of_Kyoto_protocol.pdf.

337 Michael Grubb, The Seven Myths of Kyoto, 1 CLIMATE POLICY 269, 269 (2001), http://www.econ.cam.ac.uk/rstaff/grubb/publications/JR09.pdf.

The emissions limitations of Annex I Parties vary between different Parties. Some Parties have emissions limitations that reduce below the base year level; some have limitations at the base year level (i.e., no permitted increase above the base year level) while others have limitations above the base year level. Emission limits do not include emissions from international aviation and shipping. Although Belarus and Turkey are listed in the Convention's Annex I, they do not have emissions targets as they were not Annex I Parties when the Protocol was adopted; Kazakhstan does not have a target but has declared that it wishes to become an Annex I Party to the Convention.

Annex I Parties can use a range of sophisticated "flexibility" mechanisms (explained in the following sections) to meet their targets. Annex I Parties can achieve their goals by allocating reduced annual allowances to major operators within their borders, or by allowing these operators to exceed their allocations by offsetting any excess through a mechanism that is agreed by all the parties to the UNFCCC, such as by buying emission allowances from other operators that have excess emissions credits.

"The design of the European Union Emissions Trading Scheme (EU ETS) implicitly allows for trade of national Kyoto obligations to occur between participating countries."[338]

"One of the environmental problems with EIT is the large surplus of allowances that are available. Russia, Ukraine and the new EU-12 member states (the Kyoto Parties Annex I Economies-in-Transition, abbreviated "EIT": Belarus, Bulgaria, Croatia, Czech Republic, Estonia, Hungary, Latvia, Lithuania, Poland, Romania, Russian Federation, Slovakia, Slovenia and Ukraine) have a surplus of allowances, while many OECD countries have a deficit. Some of the EITs with a surplus regard it as potential compensation for the trauma of their economic restructuring. When the Kyoto treaty was negotiated, it was recognized that emissions targets for the EITs might lead to them having an excess number of allowances. This excess of quotas was viewed by the EITs as 'headroom' to grow their economies. The surplus has, however, also been referred to by some as 'hot air,' a term which Russia (a country with a surplus of allowances) views as 'quite offensive.'"[339]

---

338 Tom Delay, et al., *Global Carbon Mechanisms: Emerging Lessons and Implications*, CARBON TRUST 1 (March 2009), http://www.carbontrust.com/media/84904/ctc748-global-carbon-mechanisms-emerging-lessons-and-implications.pdf.

339 The layman's guide to the Kyoto Protocol.

OECD countries with a deficit could meet their Kyoto commitments by buying allowances from transition countries with a surplus. Unless other commitments were made to reduce the total surplus in allowances, such trade would not result in emissions being reduced.[340]

A Green Investment Scheme (GIS) under the Kyoto Protocol is a plan that aims to achieve environmental benefits from trading surplus allowances (AAUs). The GIS is meant to achieve greater flexibility in reaching the targets of the Kyoto Protocol, and simultaneously to sustain the environmental integrity of IET.[341]

Under the GIS, a Party to the Protocol can sell the excess of its Kyoto quota units (AAUs) to another Party. The revenue from the AAU sales should be targeted towards the development and implementation of projects either acquiring the GHGs emission reductions (hard greening) or building up the necessary framework for this process (soft greening).

Latvia was one of the front-runners of GISs. In 2011, the World Bank announced that Latvia has stopped offering AAU sales because of low AAU prices. In 2010, Estonia became the new source for AAU buyers, followed by the Czech Republic and Poland.

Japan's policy to follow its Kyoto target included the purchase of AAUs sold under GISs. In 2010, Japan and Japanese firms were the main buyers of AAUs.[342]

According to a press release from the United Nations Environment Program:

"After ten days of tough negotiations, ministers and other high-level officials from 160 countries reached agreement on a legally binding Protocol under which industrialized countries will reduce their collective emissions of GHGs by 5.2 percent. The agreement aims to lower overall emissions from a group of six GHGs by 2008–12, calculated as an average over these five years. Cuts in the three most important gases—carbon dioxide (CO_2), methane (CH_4), and nitrous oxide (N_2O)—will be measured against the base year of 1990. Cuts in three long-lived industrial gases—hydrofluorocarbons (HFCs), perfluorocarbons

---

340 "Kyoto Protocol." Climate change is coming soon. Accessed August 11, 2014. http://takeachange. weebly.com/kyoto-protocol.html

341 http://unfccc.int/files/essential_background/kyoto_protocol/application/pdf/kpstats.pdf

342 A Survey of Organizations, Providers, and Research Involved in the Effort to Understand and Deal with Climate Change (last viewed June 28, 2013), www.kyotoprotocol.com.

(PFCs), and sulfur hexafluoride (SF6)—can be measured against either a 1990 or 1995 baseline."[343]

National limitations range from eight percent reductions for the European Union and others to seven percent for the US, six percent for Japan, zero percent for Russia, and permitted increases of eight percent for Australia and ten percent for Iceland.[344]

The agreement supplements the UNFCCC adopted at the Earth Summit in Rio de Janeiro in 1992, which did not set any limitations or enforcement mechanisms. All parties to UNFCCC can sign or ratify the Kyoto Protocol, while non-parties to UNFCCC cannot. Most provisions of the Kyoto Protocol apply to developed countries, listed in Annex I to UNFCCC. These facts are based on the Earthjustice Environmental Rights Report from 2008 (to which the author of this book contributed). [345]

In addition, the report also describes Kyoto Parties' usage of land, change of lands and forestry (LULUCF) in meeting their targets. LULUCF activities are also called "sink" activities. Changes in sinks and land use can have an effect on the climate (IPCC, 2007). Particular criteria apply to the definition of forestry under the Kyoto Protocol.[346]

Forest management, cropland management, grazing land management, and revegetation are all eligible LULUCF activities under the Protocol (Dessai, 2001, p. 9). Annex I Parties use of forestry management in meeting their targets is capped.

The UNFCCC adopts a principle of "common but differentiated responsibilities." The parties agreed that:

1. The largest share of historical and current global emissions of GHGs originated in developed countries;

---

343 John Kirshon, *Kyoto Protocol Signed by 160 Nations*, SCIENCE & NATURE (March 25, 2013), http://suite101.com/article/kyoto-protocol-signed-by-160-nations-a179004.

344 A Survey of Organizations, Providers, and Research Involved in the Effort to Understand and Deal with Climate Change (last viewed June 28, 2013), www.kyotoprotocol.com.

345 Ding, Y, Anderson, K. et al., *Earthjustice Environmental Rights Report, 2008*, p.7. Oakland, California. http://earthjustice.org/sites/default/files/library/reports/2008-environmental-rights-report.pdf

346 *Id.*

2. Per capita emissions in developing countries are still relatively low, and

3. The proportion of global emissions originating in developing countries will grow to meet social and development need.[347]

According to all the agreements and the data, there were established the top-ten emitters, where 10 countries produce around 70 percent of global GHG emissions[348].

Top 10 Emitters

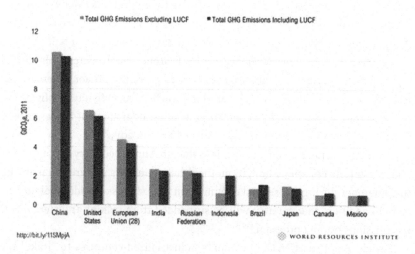

*LUCF refers to emissions stemming from land use change and forestry.

"The Protocol also reaffirms the principle that developed countries have to pay billions of dollars, and supply technology to other countries for climate-related studies and projects. The policy was initially agreed in UNFCCC."[349] One such principle is called The Adaptation Fund. It has been established by the

---

347 United Nations Framework Convention on Climate Change, June 12, 1992, 1771 U.N.T.S. 107, *available at* http://unfccc.int/resource/docs/convkp/conveng.pdf.

348 World Resources Institute http://www.wri.org/blog/2014/11/6-graphs-explain-world%E2%80%99s-top-10-emitters

349 POLLUTION: AN OVERVIEW 152 (eM Publications, Nov. 14, 2010).

Kyoto Protocol Parties of the UNFCCC to fund concrete adaptation projects in developing countries (that are also Parties to the Kyoto Protocol).

The protocol left several issues to be decided later by the sixth Conference of Parties (COP). In 2000, COP6 tried to resolve these issues at its meeting in the Hague, but could not due to disputes between the European Union that desired a tougher, more strict agreement) and the United States, Canada, Japan and Australia (all of which wanted it to to be less rigid and more flexible).[350]

In 2001, following the COP6 meeting, a second part of the meeting COP6bis happened in Bonn (where the required decisions were finally adopted). After a few deliberations, the supporters of the protocol (the European Union) managed to get Japan and Russia in as well by allowing more use of carbon dioxide sinks.[351] "The first Meeting of the Parties to the Kyoto Protocol (MOP1) was held in Montreal from 28 November to 9 December 2005. "On 3 December 2007, Australia ratified the protocol during the first day of the COP13 in Bali."[352]

Of the signatories, 36 developed Contact Group countries (plus the EU as a party in the European Union) agreed to a 10 percent emissions increase for Iceland; but, since the EU's member states each have individual obligations, much larger increases (up to 27 percent) are allowed for some of the less developed EU countries.[353]Reduction limitations expired in 2013.[354]

If the enforcement branch determines that an Annex I country is not in compliance with its emissions limitation, then that country is required to make up the difference during the second commitment period plus an additional 30 percent. In addition, that country will be suspended from making transfers under an emissions trading program.[355]

Article 4.2 of the UNFCCC commits industrialized countries to "[take] the lead" in reducing emissions (Grubb, 2003, p. 144).[356] The initial aim was for industrialized countries to stabilize their emissions at 1990 levels by the year

---

[350] POLLUTION: AN OVERVIEW 152 (eM Publications, Nov. 14, 2010).

[351] *Id.*

[352] *Id.* at 153.

[353] http://topics.nytimes.com/topics/reference/timestopics/subjects/k/kyoto_protocol/index.html

[354] POLLUTION: AN OVERVIEW 153 (eM Publications, Nov. 14, 2010).

[355] *Id.* at 153.

[356] Michael Grubb, *The Economics of the Kyoto Protocol* 4 WORLD ECONOMICS 143, 144 (July-Sept. 2003), http://ynccf.net/pdf/CDM/The_economic_of_Kyoto_protocol.pdf.

2000. The failure of key industrialized countries to move in this direction was a principal reason Kyoto moved to binding commitments.[357]

At the first UNFCCC Conference of the Parties in Berlin, the G77—a lobbying group that represents 133 developing countries, of which China is an associate—was able to push for a mandate where it was recognized that[358]

- developed nations had contributed most to the then-current concentrations of GHGs in the atmosphere;

- developing country emissions per-capita were still relatively low; and

- that the share of global emissions from developing countries would grow to meet their development needs.

This mandate was recognized in the Kyoto Protocol in that developing countries were not subject to emission reduction commitments in the first Kyoto commitment period. However, the significant potential for growth in developing country emissions made negotiations on this issue tense (Grubb, 2003, pp. 145–146).[359] In the final agreement, the CDM was designed to limit emissions in developing countries, but in such a way that developing countries do not bear the costs of limiting emissions. The general assumption was that developing countries would face quantitative commitments in later commitment periods, and at the same time, developed countries would meet their first-round commitments.[360]

In the UK, following 1990, emissions had declined because of a switch from coal to gas ("Dash for Gas"), which has lower emissions than coal. This was due to the UK's privatization of coal mining and its switch to natural gas supported by North Sea reserves. Germany benefitted from the 1990 base year because of its reunification between West and East Germany. East Germany's emissions fell

---

357 *Id.* at 153.

358 *Id.* at 153.

359 Michael Grubb, *The Economics of the Kyoto Protocol* 4 WORLD ECONOMICS 143, 145-6 (July-Sept. 2003),

http://ynccf.net/pdf/CDM/The_economic_of_Kyoto_protocol.pdf.

360 *Id.* at 153.

dramatically following the collapse of the East German industry after the fall of the Berlin Wall. Germany could, therefore, take credit for the resultant decline in emissions.[361]

Japan promoted the idea of flexible baselines and favored the base year of 1995 for HFCs. Their HFC emissions had grown in the early 1990s as a substitute for CFCs banned in the Montreal Protocol. Some of the former Soviet satellites wanted a base year to reflect their highest emissions before their industrial collapse.[362]

EIT countries are privileged by being able to choose their base-year nearly freely. However, the oldest base-year accepted is 1986.[363]

- The inclusion of carbon sinks (e.g., by including forests, that absorb CO_2 from the atmosphere).[364]

- And having current net emissions as the basis for responsibility, i.e., ignoring historical emissions.[365]

The US originally proposed for the second round of negotiations on Kyoto commitments to follow the negotiations of the first (Grubb, 2003, p. 148).[366] In the end, negotiations on the second period were set to open no later than 2005. Countries over-achieving in their first period commitments can "bank" their unused allowances for use in the subsequent period.[367]

The EU initially argued for only three GHGs to be included—CO_2, CH_4, and N_2O—with other gasses such as HFCs regulated separately (Liverman, 2008, p. 13). The EU also wanted to have a "bubble" commitment, whereby it could make a collective commitment that allowed some EU members to increase their emissions while others cut theirs. The most vulnerable nations—the Alliance of Small

---

361 *Id.* at 153.

362 *Id.* at 153.

363 A Survey of Organizations, Providers, and Research Involved in the Effort to Understand and Deal with Climate Change (last viewed June 28, 2013), www.kyotoprotocol.com.

364 POLLUTION: AN OVERVIEW 119 (eM Publications, Nov. 14, 2010).

365 *Id.*

366 Michael Grubb, *The Economics of the Kyoto Protocol* 4 WORLD ECONOMICS 143, 148 (July-Sept. 2003), http://ynccf.net/pdf/CDM/The_economic_of_Kyoto_protocol.pdf.

367 POLLUTION: AN OVERVIEW 119 (eM Publications, Nov. 14, 2010).

Island States (AOSIS)—pushed for deep uniform cuts by developed countries, with the goal of having emissions reduced to the greatest possible extent.[368]

The final days of negotiation of the Protocol saw a clash between the EU and the US and Japan.[369] The EU aimed for flat-rate reductions in the range of 10–15 percent below 1990 levels while the US and Japan supported reductions of 0–5 percent. Countries that had supported differentiation had different ideas as to how it should be calculated, and many different indicators were proposed: relating to GDP, energy intensity (energy use per unit of economic output), etc. According to Grubb,[370]The only common theme of these indicators was that each proposal suited the interests of the country making the proposal.[371]

The final commitments negotiated in the Protocol are the result of last minute political compromises (Liverman, 2008, pp. 13–14). These include an eight percent cut from the 1990 base year for the EU, seven percent for the US, six percent for Canada and Japan, no cut for Russia, and an eight percent increase for Australia. This equates to an overall cut of 5.2 percent below 1990 levels. Since Australia and the US did not ratify the treaty (although Australia has since done so), the cut is reduced from 5.2 percent to about two percent.[372]

Considering the growth of some economies and the collapse of others since 1990, the range of fixed targets is much greater (Aldy et al., 2003, p. 7). The US faced a cut of about 30 percent below "business-as-usual" (BAU) emissions (i.e., predicted emissions should there be no attempt to limit emissions) while Russia and other economies in transition faced targets that allowed substantial increases in their emissions above BAU. On the other hand, Grubb (2003, p. 151) pointed out that the US, having per-capita emissions twice that of most other OECD countries, was vulnerable to the suggestion that it had enormous potential for making reductions. From this viewpoint, the US was obliged to cut emissions back more than other countries.[373]

---

368 *Id.*

369 Michael Grubb, *The Economics of the Kyoto Protocol* 4 WORLD ECONOMICS 143, 149 (July-Sept. 2003), http://ynccf.net/pdf/CDM/The_economic_of_Kyoto_protocol.pdf.

370 *Id.*

371 POLLUTION: AN OVERVIEW 119 (eM Publications, Nov. 14, 2010).

372 POLLUTION: AN OVERVIEW 119 (eM Publications, Nov. 14, 2010).

373 http://www.climatechange.gov.au/government/initiatives/kyoto.aspx

When George W. Bush was elected US president in 2000, he was asked by US Senator Hagel what his administration's position was on climate change.[374] Bush answered that he took climate change "very seriously," but that he opposed the Kyoto treaty, because "it exempts 80 percent of the world, including major population centers such as China and India, from compliance, and would cause serious harm to the US economy" (Dessai, 2001, p. 5).[375] "Almost all world leaders (e.g., China, Japan, South Africa, and Pacific Islands) expressed their disappointment over President Bush's decision not to support the treaty."[376]

For the Protocol to enter into legal effect, it was required that the Protocol has ratified by 55 Parties including 55 percent of 1990 Annex I emissions.[377] The US accounted for 36 percent of emissions in 1990, and without US ratification, only an EU +Russia +Japan +small party coalition could place the treaty into legal effect.[378] A deal was reached in the Bonn climate talks (COP-6.5), held in 2001.[379] According to the EU, the Kyoto Protocol had been saved.[380] For the G77/China, the Bonn agreement represented the "triumph of multilateralism over unilateralism."[381]

Article 25 of the Protocol specifies that the Protocol enters into force "on the ninetieth day after the date on which not less than 55 Parties to the Convention, incorporating Parties included in Annex I which accounted in total for at least 55 percent of the total carbon dioxide emissions for 1990 of the Annex I countries, have deposited their instruments of ratification, acceptance, approval or accession."[382]

---

374 Letter from the President to Senators Hagel, Helms, Craig, and Roberts (March 13, 2001), http://georgewbush-whitehouse.archives.gov/news/releases/2001/03/20010314.html.

375 Suraje.Dessai, *The Climate Regime from The Hague to Marrakech: Saving or Sinking the Kyoto Protocol?* Tyndall Centre for Climate Change Research (2001), http://www.tyndall.ac.uk/sites/default/files/wp12.pdf; Letter from the President to Senators Hagel, Helms, Craig, and Roberts (March 13, 2001), http://georgewbush-whitehouse.archives.gov/news/releases/2001/03/20010314.html.

376 Dessai, *supra* note 441, at 6.a

377 *Id.* at 3.

378 *Id.*

379 *Id.*

380 *Id.* at 8

381 *Id.*

382 United Nations Framework Convention on Climate Change, art.25, June 12, 1992, 1771 U.N.T.S. 107, *available at* http://unfccc.int/resource/docs/convkp/conveng.pdf.

The EU and its Member States ratified the Protocol in May 2002. One of the two conditions, the "55 parties" clause, was reached on 23 May 2002 when Iceland ratified the Protocol. The ratification by Russia on 18 November 2004 satisfied the "55 percent" clause and brought the treaty into force, effective 16 February 2005, after the required lapse of 90 days.[383]

In 2010, Canada, Japan, and Russia stated that they would not take on further Kyoto targets.[384] The Canadian government invoked Canada's legal right to withdraw formally from the Kyoto Protocol on 12 December 12, 2011.[385] By signing the Protocol, Canada was bound by 2012 to a 6% cut in its greenhouse emissions, below 1990 levels.[386] However instead of decreasing, by 2009 Canada's emissions were 17% higher than its 1990 levels.[387] That contributed to Canada's decision to withdraw from the Protocol.[388] Environment Minister Peter Kent cited Canada's liability to "enormous financial penalties" under the treaty unless it withdrew.[389] Canada's move comes days after climate-change negotiators met to hammer out a global deal in Durban, South Africa. Kent explains that he recently signed Durban agreement may provide an alternative way forward.[390]

---

383 POLLUTION: AN OVERVIEW 116 (eM Publications, Nov. 14, 2010).

384 *Canada Pulls Out of, Denounces Kyoto Protocol*, CBS NEWS (Dec. 13, 2011),
     http://www.cbsnews.com/8301-202_162-57341907/canada-pulls-out-of-denounces-kyoto-protocol/.

385 *Canada Pulls Out of Kyoto Protocol*, CBC NEWS (Dec. 12, 2011), http://www.cbc.ca/news/politics/
     story/2011/12/12/pol-kent-kyoto-pullout.html.

386 David Ljunggren & Randall Palmer, *Canada to Pull out of Kyoto Protocol*, FINANCIAL POST (Nov. 12, 2013),
     http://business.financialpost.com/2011/12/13/canada-to-pull-out-of-kyoto-protocol/.

387 *Id.*.

388 *Id.*.

389 *Canada Pulls Out of, Denounces Kyoto Protocol*, CBS NEWS (Dec. 13, 2011), http://www.cbsnews.
     com/8301-202_162-57341907/canada-pulls-out-of-denounces-kyoto-protocol/ (stating that pulling
     out of the Kyoto Protocol will save Canada $14 billion in fees that it would otherwise have to pay
     when it does not meet the set targets).

390 *Id.* Canada's Environment Minister Peter Kent left after announcing that Canada will formally withdraw from the Kyoto protocol on climate change, on Parliament Hill in Ottawa, 12 December 2011.

Unfortunately, Canada's decision to withdrawal left itself open to criticism from the international community, especially other ratifying countries.[391] China is just one example of a country that openly criticized the decision made by Canada.[392] China is calling Canada's decision to withdraw from the Kyoto Protocol "regrettable" and says it goes against the efforts of the international community.[393] Further, Foreign Ministry spokesman expressed China's dismay at the news that Canada had pulled out of the Kyoto Protocol.[394] He explained that Canada's timing was particularly bad because negotiators at the just-concluded Durban conference made what he described as substantial progress on the issue of the Kyoto Protocol's second commitment period.[395] The Chinese negotiator at Durban, Xie Zhenhua, debated that "he is concerned that developed nations are reluctant to reduce their own GHG emissions, which many scientists say exacerbate global warming."[396] Zhenhau also placed responsibility on "developed countries to provide financial and technical aid to help developing nations fight against and cope with the effects of climate change."[397]

UNFCCC made projections of changes in emissions of the Annex I Parties and the effectiveness of their PaMs. It was noted that their projections should be

---

391 For example, a spokesperson for the island nation of Tuvalu, a nation that is especially at risk by rising sea levels, accused Canada of an "act of sabotage" against his country. *Canada's Kyoto Withdrawal Called an 'Act of Sabotage,'* THESTAR.COM (Dec. 13, 2011), http://www.thestar.com/news/world/2011/12/13/canadas_kyoto_withdrawal_called_an_act_of_sabotage.html. However, not all countries were disappointed in Canada's decision. Australian government minister Greg Combet defended Canada and its decision, saying that this withdrawal does not mean Canada will not "play its part in global efforts to tackle climate change." Julian Drape, *Australia Defends Canada's Kyoto Exit,* The Sydney Morning Herald (Dec. 13, 2011), http://news.smh.com.au/breaking-news-national/australia-defends-canadas-kyoto-exit-20111213-1osyd.html.

392 Michael Comte, *Canada's Kyoto Withdrawal Under Fire From China,* Google (Dec. 13, 2011),

   http://www.hostednews.com/afp/article/ALeqM5g_GgIYWBOKyBGYFE-i5e24tyVsEg?docId=CNG.29f281d349da57cf7c0165dde5cba5ae.271 ("explaining that a representative from China stated "[w]e hope Canada will face up to its responsibilities and obligations, honor its commitments and actively participate in relevant international cooperation against climate change"); China's outrage is particularly interesting because "China has always insisted that as a developing country it should be exempt from binding obligations on emissions" *Id.*

393 *Id.*

394 *Id.*

395 *China: Canada's Kyoto Protocol Withdrawal 'Regrettable,'* Voice of America (Dec. 12, 2011),

   http://m.voanews.com/a/149464.html.

396 *Id.*

397 *Id.*

interpreted with caution.[398] For the 39 Annex I Parties, UNFCCC (2011) projected that existing PaMs would lead to annual emissions in 2010 of 17.5 thousand Tg CO_2 eq, excluding LULUCF, which is a decrease of 6.7 percent from the 1990 level. Annual emissions in 2020 excluding LULUCF were projected to reach 18.9 thousand Tg CO_2 eq, which is an increase of 0.6 percent from the 1990 level.

UNFCCC made an estimate of the total effect of implemented and adopted PaMs. Projected savings were estimated about a reference (baseline) scenario where PaMs are not implemented. PaMs were projected to deliver emissions savings about baseline of about 1.5 thousand Tg CO2 eq by 2010, and 2.8 thousand Tg CO2 eq by 2020. In percentage terms, and using annual emissions in the year 1990 as a reference point, PaMs were projected to deliver at least a five percent reduction about baseline by 2010.

2.1.4.i. Targets and Mechanisms

Flexible mechanisms, also known as Kyoto Mechanisms, refer to International Emissions Trading (IET), the CDM and Joint Implementation (JI). These mechanisms are meant to lower the costs of achieving its emission targets under the Kyoto Protocol. Moreover, these mechanisms allow Parties to achieve emission reductions cost effectively in other countries. As a result, the benefit for the atmosphere is generally the same even though the cost of limiting emissions can vary considerably from region to region.[399]

For a while, there was concern that the mechanisms do not confer a "right to emit" on Annex 1 Parties or lead to exchanges of fictitious credits that would undermine the Protocol's environmental goals. Therefore, the negotiators of the Protocol and the Marrakesh Accords, therefore, tried to design a system that fulfilled the cost-effectiveness promise of the mechanisms, while at the same time addressing concerns about environmental integrity and equity.[400]

To take part in the mechanisms, Annex 1 Parties had to meet the following criteria:

---

398 http://unfccc.int/meetings/unfccc_calendar/items/2655.php?year=2011

399 Bashmakov, I., et al., "6. Policies, Measures, and Instruments," Executive summary, in IPCC TAR WG3 2001

400 United Nations Framework Convention on Climate Change, art., June 12, 1992, 1771 U.N.T.S. 107, *available at* http://unfccc.int/resource/docs/convkp/conveng.pdf;, *Kyoto Protocol Reference Manual On Accounting of Emissions and Assigned Amount*, Bonn, Germany: Climate Change Secretariat (UNFCCC), p. 55.

1. They must have ratified the Kyoto Protocol.

2. They must have calculated their assigned amount regarding tons of CO_2-equivalent emissions as referred to in Articles 3.7 and 3.8 and Annex B of the Protocol.

3. They must have in place a national system for estimating emissions and removals of GHGs within their territory.

4. They must have in place a national registry to record the creation and movement of Emission Reduction Units, Certified Emission Reductions, Assigned amount units and Removal Units (RMU)s and must annually report such information to the Secretariat.

5. They must report information on emissions and removals to the secretariat on an annual basis.

The Protocol defines three "flexibility mechanisms" that can be used by Annex I Parties in meeting their emission limitation commitments. The flexibility mechanisms are International Emissions Trading (IET), the CDM, and Joint Implementation (JI). IET allows Annex I Parties to "trade" their emissions (Assigned Amount Units, AAUs, or "allowances" for short).[401]

The economic basis for providing this flexibility is that the marginal cost of reducing (or abating) emissions differs among countries.[402] "Marginal cost" is the cost of abating the last tone of CO2-eq for an Annex I/non-Annex I Party. At the time of the original Kyoto targets, studies suggested that the flexibility mechanisms could reduce the overall (aggregate) cost of meeting the objectives. Studies also showed that national losses in Annex I gross domestic product (GDP) could be reduced by use of the flexibility mechanisms.[403]

---

401 www.kyotoprotocol.com A Survey of Organizations, Providers, and Research Involved in the Effort to Understand and Deal with Climate Change (last viewed June 28, 2013), www.kyotoprotocol.com.

402 Toth, F.L., et al., "10. Decision-making Frameworks," 10.4.4. Where Should the Response Take Place? The Relationship between Domestic Mitigation and the Use of International Mechanisms, in IPCC TAR WG3 2001.

403 Hourcade, J.-C., et al., "8. Global, Regional, and National Costs and Ancillary Benefits of Mitigation," 8.3.1 International Emissions Quota Trading Regimes, in IPCC TAR WG3 2001.

The CDM and JI are called "project-based mechanisms," in that they generate emission reductions from projects. The difference between IET and the project-based mechanisms is that IET is based on the setting of a quantitative restriction of emissions while the CDM and JI are based on the idea of "production" of emission reductions. The CDM is designed to encourage production of emission reductions in non-Annex I Parties while JI encourages production of emission reductions in Annex I Parties.

The production of emission reductions generated by the CDM and JI can be used by Annex I Parties in meeting their emission limitation commitments.[404] The emission reductions produced by the CDM and JI are both measured against a hypothetical baseline of emissions that would have occurred in the absence of a particular emission reduction project. The emission reductions produced by the CDM are called Certified Emission Reductions (CERs); reductions generated by JI are called Emission Reduction Units (ERUs). The reductions are called "credits" because they are emission reductions credited against a hypothetical baseline of emissions.

The Protocol presents two mechanisms that allow Annex I countries to meet their GHG emission reduction commitments by getting GHG "credits." The credits are acquired by an Annex I country financing projects that reduce emissions in non-Annex or Annex I countries or by purchasing credits from Annex I countries with excess credits.[405]

The project-based mechanisms allow Annex I countries with low GHG-emitting industries and high environmental standards, to purchase carbon credits on the world market instead of reducing GHG emissions within their countries. Annex I countries usually aim to buy carbon credits as cheaply as possible, while non-Annex I countries want to increase the value of carbon credits that come from their domestic GHG reducing projects.[406]

Via Joint Implementation, any Annex I country can invest in emission reduction projects in any other Annex I country as another option of reducing emissions domestically.

---

404 Bashmakov, I., et al., "6. Policies, Measures, and Instruments," 6.3.2 Project-based Mechanisms (Joint Implementation and the Clean Development Mechanism), in IPCC TAR WG3 2001

405 Carbon Trust (March 2009). "Global Carbon Mechanisms: Emerging lessons and implications (CTC748)." Carbon Trust website. Retrieved 31 March 2010.

406 World Bank (2008), *Development and Climate Change: A Strategic Framework for the World Bank Group: Technical Report*, Washington, DC, USA: The International Bank for Reconstruction and Development/ The World Bank.

Through the CDM, countries can meet their domestic emission reduction targets by buying GHG reduction units from nonAnnex I developing countries. Such countries have no GHG emission restrictions but have financial incentives to develop GHG emission reduction projects to receive Certified Emission Reductions that can then be sold to Annex I countries, encouraging sustainable development.[407]

Kyoto provides for a "cap and trade" system, a system that forces national caps on the emissions of Annex I countries. This cap makes countries lower their emissions by approximately 5.2 percent below their 1990 baseline over a four-year period (from 2008 to 2012). An example of a "cap and trade" system is the "EU ETS."[408]

The ultimate buyers of credits are often individual companies that expect emissions to exceed their quota or assigned allocation units, AAUs. So they will purchase credits directly from any other party with excess allowances, a broker or a JI/CDM developer.

Allowances and carbon credits are commonly bought by financial investors for speculation purposes, or for futures contracts. A high volume of trading in this secondary market helps price discovery and liquidity, and in this way contributes to keeping down costs and set a clear price signal in CO_2. This market has grown significantly, with banks, brokers, funds, arbitrageurs and private traders now participating in a market valued at about $60 billion in 2007.[409]

Kyoto enables a group of several Annex I countries to create a market-within-a-market together. The EU elected to be treated as such a group and created the EU Emissions Trading Scheme (ETS). The scheme went into operation on 1 January 2005, although a fresh market has existed since 2003.[410]

The sources of Kyoto credits are the CDM and Joint Implementation (JI) projects. The CDM allows the creation of new carbon credits by developing emission reduction projects in non-Annex I countries while JI allows project-specific credits to be converted from existing credits within Annex I countries. CDM

---

407 Michael Grubb, *The Economics of the Kyoto Protocol* 4 WORLD ECONOMICS 143 (July-Sept. 2003), http://ynccf.net/pdf/CDM/The_economic_of_Kyoto_protocol.pdf.

408 A Survey of Organizations, Providers, and Research Involved in the Effort to Understand and Deal with Climate Change (last viewed June 28, 2013), www.kyotoprotocol.com.

409 Stern, N. 2007. *Stern Review on the Economics of Climate Change* (pre-publication edition). Cambridge University Press, Cambridge.

410 "Govt still not serious about climate change: Labor." *ABC News Online.* 26 October 2006. Retrieved 30 October 2006.

projects produce Certified Emission Reductions (CERs), and JI projects produce Emission Reduction Units (ERUs), each equivalent to one AAU. Kyoto CERs are also accepted for meeting EU ETS obligations and ERUs will become similarly valid from 2008 for meeting ETS obligations (although individual countries may choose to limit the number and source of CER/JIs they will allow for compliance purposes starting from 2008). CERs/ERUs are overwhelmingly bought by project developers by funds or individual entities, rather than being exchange-traded like allowances.[411]

Since the creation of Kyoto is subject to a lengthy process of registration and certification by the UNFCCC, and the projects themselves require several years to develop, this market is at this point mostly a forward market where purchases are made at a discount to their equivalent currency, the EUA, and are almost always subject to certification and delivery (although up-front payments are sometimes made). According to IETA, the market value of CDM/JI credits transacted in 2004 was €245 million; it is estimated that more than €620 million worth of credits was transacted in 2005.

Several non-Kyoto carbon markets are in existence or being planned, and these are likely to grow in importance and numbers in the coming years. These include the New South Wales Greenhouse Gas Abatement Scheme, the Regional Greenhouse Gas Initiative and Western Climate Initiative in the United States and Canada, the Chicago Climate Exchange and the State of California's recent initiative to reduce emissions.[412]

These initiatives taken together may create a series of partly linked markets, rather than a single carbon market. The common theme is the adoption of market-based mechanisms centered on carbon credits that represent a reduction of CO_2 emissions. The scheme would broaden the current carbon market far more than the current focus on the CDM/JI and EU ETS domains. An obvious precondition, however, is a realignment of penalties and fines to similar levels, since these create an effective ceiling for each market.[413]

---

411   A Survey of Organizations, Providers, and Research Involved in the Effort to Understand and Deal with Climate Change (last viewed June 28, 2013), www.kyotoprotocol.com.

412   Michael Grubb, *The Economics of the Kyoto Protocol* 4 WORLD ECONOMICS 143 (July-Sept. 2003), http://ynccf.net/pdf/CDM/The_economic_of_Kyoto_protocol.pdf.

413   *Id.*

2.1.4.ii. Post-Kyoto International reactions

Post-Kyoto negotiations refer to high-level talks attempting to address global warming by limiting GHG emissions, in particular concerning the period after the first "commitment period" of the Kyoto Protocol, which expired at the end of 2012. Negotiations have been mandated by the adoption of the Bali Road Map and Decision 1/CP.13 ("The Bali Action Plan"). UNFCCC negotiations are conducted within two subsidiary bodies, the Ad Hoc Working Group on Long-term Cooperative Action under the Convention (AWG-LCA) and the Ad Hoc Working Group on Further Commitments for Annex I Parties under the Kyoto Protocol (AWG-KP); negotiations are supported by a number of external processes, including the G8 process, a number of regional meetings and the Major Economies Forum on Energy and Climate that was launched by US President Barack Obama in March 2009. High-level talks were held at the meeting of the G8+5 Climate Change Dialogue in February 2007 and at some subsequent G8 meetings, leading to the adoption of the G8 leaders declaration "Responsible Leadership for a Sustainable Future" during the G8 summit in L'Aquila, Italy, in July 2009.[414]

2.2. REFERRING TO THE PACIFIC ISLANDS

2.2.1. Regional waves

"The Pacific island countries are subjected to the impacts of global warming caused by excessive fossil fuel burning, atmospheric pollution and deforestation of the land hemisphere."[415] "Despite a firm commitment at the United Nations Conference on Environment and Development in 1992 and at a subsequent meeting, there has been practically no progress towards reduction of green-

---

414 United Nations Climate-Change Conference Extended Extra Day. Fox News. 2007-08-03. Retrieved 2007-08-03.

415 Climate Change and the Pacific Islands, MINISTERIAL CONFERENCE ON ENVTL AND DEVELOPMENT IN ASIA AND THE PACIFIC 2000 (last updated May 8, 2000), http://www.unescap.org/mced2000/pacific/background/climate.htm [hereinafter Climate Change and the Pacific Islands]; Global Warming Fast Facts, National Geographic (June 14, 2007), http://news.nationalgeographic.com/news/2004/12/1206_041206_global_warming.html.

house gases. Japan is the only Annex 1 country in the Asia Pacific Region to obligate itself to reduce emissions."[416]

"It will require at least 50 years before any reduction begins to reverse predicted climate change and sea level rise."[417] "The longer the metropolitan countries delay, the worse the impacts will become; a situation that frustrates and angers Pacific island leaders."[418] "Pollution of the atmosphere by carbon dioxide and other GHGs is the most critical environmental problem faced by our world."[419] "It is also highly contentious and has sparked heated and prolonged debate, but very little action has occurred."[420]

"The Pacific Islands view climate change as a major disaster and have openly and continuously criticized the industrial nations for failure to take definitive steps towards abating pollution of the global atmosphere."[421] "There are three distinct impacts from this pollution; global warming, sea level rise and climate change."[422] "In fact, despite continuing improvement in measurements and predictive computer programs, nobody knows exactly what the outcome of atmospheric pollution will be, but if the current range of peculiar weather and catastrophic deaths of a wide range of important ecosystems are any indication, the small islands of the world have good cause to be worried."[423]

Global warming from increasing levels of greenhouse gases is expected to have serious effects on the Pacific Ocean. In the past two decades, for example, short-term extreme high temperatures contributed to a decline of coral reefs throughout the tropics. Corals, stressed by high temperatures, may eject their symbiotic algae. Coral bleaching, as this is called, renders the corals less able to cope with additional physiological stress and many of the colonies die. In a 1999 International Coral Reef Conference, some scientists expressed the opinion that

---

416 *Climate Change and the Pacific Islands, supra* note 530; A Survey of Organizations, Providers and Research Involved in the Effort to Understand and Deal with Climate Change (last viewed June 28, 2013), www.kyotoprotocol.com.

417 *Climate Change and the Pacific Islands, supra* note 530.

418 *Id.*

419 *Climate Change and the Pacific Islands, supra* note 530; Frank McDonald, *Climate Agreement Close After All-night Bargaining,* THE IRISH TIMES, Dec. 15, 2007.

420 *Climate Change and the Pacific Islands, supra* note 530.

421 *Id.*

422 *Id.*

423 *Id.*

it was now too late to save the coral reefs of the planet even if GHG emissions could begin to drop immediately.[424]

"This has significant impacts on organisms, such as fish, that depend on the living coral structures."[425] "In 1994, elevated sea temperatures killed over 90 percent of the living corals of American Samoa from the intertidal zone to a depth of 10 m and fishing catches declined drastically in the wake of the coral death."[426]

"Temperature also regulates the distribution of plants and animals."[427] Pelagic fish, the single most important fish in the Pacific,[428] Live near the surface and migrate along temperature boundaries.[429] In some cases, changes in temperature force these fish to change migration patterns, thereby moving away from traditional fishing areas.[430] "Samoa, for example, is on the edge of major tuna migrations, and fishing success can oscillate from extreme success to failure depending on ocean temperature regimes."[431]

In most Pacific Islands, the people, agricultural land, tourist resorts and infrastructure (including roads and airports) are concentrated in the coastal zones and are thus especially vulnerable to any rise in sea level. Determining how severe this problem is, or might be, is complicated by natural shifts in sea level associated with the recurring ice ages. For example, over the past 16,000 years, the sea level rose some 150 m in the South-West Pacific, reaching its present level about 6,000 years ago (Broecker, 1983).[432] This would indicate an aver-

---

424 *Climate Change and the Pacific Islands, supra* note 530; Finding Strength in Numbers: Pacific Stands Firm with AOSIS, PACIFIC ISLANDS FORUM SECRETARIAT, (last viewed June 30, 2013), http://www.forumsec.org.fj/pages.cfm/newsroom/press-statements/2011/pacific-in-busan-updates-from-cop17.html?printerfriendly=true.

425 *Climate Change and the Pacific Islands, supra* note 530.

426 *Climate Change and the Pacific Islands, supra* note 530; see Coral Reef Death in American Samoa, MINISTERIAL CONFERENCE ON ENVTL AND DEVELOPMENT IN ASIA AND THE PACIFIC 2000 (last updated May 18, 2000),

427 *Id.*

428 *Climate Change and the Pacific Islands, supra* note 530; *WPRFMC Reports: Important Pelagic Fishes of the Pacific* (last viewed June 30, 2013), http://www.wpcouncil.org/documents/pelagics.pdf (explaining that Oceanic and Pelagic fish are the most important fish in the Pacific. They are used for food and for sport).

429 *Id.*

430 *Climate Change and the Pacific Islands, supra* note 530.

431 *Id.*

432 Makereta Komai, *Pacific Countries Fight to Keep Kyoto Protocol to Safeguard the Adaptation Fund,* SOLOMON TIMES (June 3, 2010), http://www.solomontimes.com/news.aspx?nwID=5242

age rise of more than 15mm/year during the 10,000 years it took for sea level to reach its present level following the last glacial epoch. According to Australia's National Tidal Facility, the sea level rise in Australia has been stable over the past 21 years.[433]

Climate Change is causing sea level rise from thermal expansion as the sea warms up and from melting of the planet's ice caps. Some measurements of sea level rise, derived from TOPEX/POSWIDON satellite altimeter data, show a rise of 2.1 (plus or minus 1.3) mm/year on a global basis (Nerem et al., 1997). But this data is very preliminary, and the authors warn that the contribution of annual and decadal mean sea level variations cannot yet be isolated and that a longer time series of observations is needed before long-term climate change signals can be detected.[434]

Data compiled from 11 tide gauges by Australia's National Tidal Facility at Flinders University show considerable variability. For example, in September of 1997, the tide gauge in Samoa had been operating for 56 months and showed an average sea level rise of +19.2 mm per year. But the following year, when recalculated over 68 months of operation, the average sea level rise turned out to be falling at –19.5 mm per year. In Fiji, the calculated sea level rise over 61 months of operation was +21.5 mm a year in 1997, but after 73 months was recalculated as +5.2 mm a year. The conclusion is that changes in sea level are related to a multitude of variables, and no realistic trend can be detected from the data for many years to come.[435]

Climate change will shift rainfall patterns, causing prolonged droughts in some regions. Computer models predict that global warming will change rainfall patterns, resulting in extended drought conditions in some areas, and excessive rainfall in others. El Niño weather patterns have become more frequent since 1977, bringing an increase in rainfall in the North-East Pacific and a rainfall decrease in the South-West. These more frequent El Niño events are believed to be associated with global warming, although there is no clear evidence that they are not part of a long-term natural cycle. Each El Niño event has resulted in water shortages and drought in Papua New Guinea, Marshall Islands, Federated States of Micronesia, American Samoa, Samoa, Tonga, Kiribati and Fiji. More

---

433 *Climate Change and the Pacific Islands, supra* note 530.

434 *Id.*

435 *Id.*

frequent El Niño events also bring an increased risk of tropical cyclones, particularly for Tuvalu, Samoa, Tonga, Cook Islands and French Polynesia.[436]

The potential socio-economic impacts of climate change on the smaller Pacific island countries were estimated in a series of vulnerability studies. Depending on the worst-case scenario (one-meter sea level rise), the studies suggest that sea level rise will have adverse impacts on tourism, freshwater availability and quality, aquaculture, agriculture, human settlements, financial services and human health. Storm surges are likely to have a harmful impact on low-lying islands.[437]

Low-lying coastal areas of all islands were particularly vulnerable to a rising sea level, as well as to changes in rainfall, storm frequency and intensity. Inundation, flooding, erosion and intrusion of sea water are among the likely impacts. These catastrophes would result in economic and social costs beyond the capacity of most Pacific island countries and threaten the very existence of small atoll countries. Shifts in rainfall regimes and any increase in tropical cyclone intensity and frequency greatly amplify the impact of sea level rise. An increase of average sea level by one meter, when superimposed on storm surges, could easily submerge low-lying islands.[438]

The costs of responding to climate change depend on the options considered. They include (1) prevention: striving to prevent climate change; (2) adaptation: emphasizing strategies and measures for reducing expected damages; and (3) policies: indirectly inducing reduced emissions of GHGs. Although accurate estimates of costs of protection against climate change have not been finalized in Pacific Islands, IPCC estimates that adaptations to climate change could cost billions of dollars. Pacific Islanders are not impressed with these views, pointing out that for many islands, their entire culture, and perhaps their lives, are at risk.[439]

2.2.2. International responses and participation

The small island developing states of the world banded together into an Alliance of Small Island States[440] (AOSIS) during the 1990 Second World Climate

---

436   *Id.*

437   *Id.*

438   *Id.*

439   *Id.*

440   AOSIS http://aosis.org/

Conference in Geneva. This united front played a central role in shaping international policy on climate change and is a classic example of cooperation for environmental reform. With considerable justification, AOSIS claims that metropolitan countries will need to pay damages to their countries and must begin meaningful reductions of GHGs without further delay. Tuvalu points out that the damages might be very expensive as their islands may well become uninhabitable because of sea level rise.[441]

Since 1980, considerable effort has been made to: (i) raise awareness of climate change; (ii) monitor research developments; (iii) develop methodologies for vulnerability assessment; (iv) monitor sea level rise; and (iv) strengthen national capacity to understand the science, impacts and responses to climate change and sea level rise. These efforts have involved environment officials, planners, meteorologists and the general public. Most Pacific island countries have ratified the UNFCCC.[442]

The Pacific Islands Climate Change Assistance Programme (PICCAP) is a three-year South Pacific Regional Environmental Program (SPREP) activity funded by the Global Environment Facility (GEF). PICCAP began in 1997 to assist 10 Pacific Island countries that signed and ratified the UNFCCC with their reporting, training, and capacity building under the Convention. The Cook Islands, Federated States of Micronesia, Fiji, Kiribati, Republic of Marshall Islands, Nauru, Samoa, Solomon Islands, Tuvalu, and Vanuatu have appointed Climate Change Country Teams and a Climate Change Country Coordinator to: (i) conduct inventories of sources and sinks of GHGs; (ii) identify and evaluate mitigation options to reduce GHG emissions; (iii) assess vulnerability to climate change; (iv) develop adaptation options; (v) develop a national implementation strategy for mitigating and adapting to climate change over the long term.[443]

"A total of 23 participants from Cook Islands, FSM, Fiji, Kiribati, RMI, Nauru, Samoa, Solomon Islands, Tuvalu, Vanuatu and Niue attended an SPREP Regional Training Workshop on National Greenhouse Gas Inventory Methodology in 1998 for training in national inventories of GHG sources and sinks."[444]

Representatives from 12 countries (including Niue and PNG) participated in training on assessing climate change vulnerability and adaptation requirements

---

441 *Id.*

442 *Id.*

443 *Climate Change and the Pacific Islands, supra* note 530.

444 *Id.*

during a six-month training course on climate change vulnerability and adaptation assessment. This training took place at the International Global Change Institute (IGCI), University of Waikato, and New Zealand in 1998.[445]

The South Pacific Sea Level and Climate Monitoring Project, funded by AusAID and managed by the National Tidal Facility (NTF), based at the Flinders University of South Australia set up high-resolution monitoring stations in 11 island countries to measure the relative motions of land and sea at each station. These data will assist in long-term calibration of satellite altimetry and radio astronomy and provide a measure of regional vertical control, and exchange information and data with national, regional and international climate change centers. This will help the understanding of the complex problem of measuring changes in sea levels. The project also assists with information exchange and holds two-week training courses on the use of oceanographic, atmospheric and climate data in social and economic decision-making.[446]

"The Japanese government provided funds to develop an integrated coastal zone management Programme in Fiji, Marshall Islands, Samoa and Tuvalu to assess the impacts of sea-level rise and develop vulnerability assessment methodologies."[447]

Japan, Australia and the United States of America have conducted tests of the IPCC Common Methodology for sea-level rise impacts in Fiji, Kiribati, Marshall Islands, Palau, Samoa, Tonga and Tuvalu. In addition, the UNDP, Australia, and Japan contributed to an SPREP program to assist Fiji, Marshall Islands, Samoa and Tuvalu with planning for policy responses to climate change in the economic and environmental sectors, such as impacts on water supply, coastal protection, energy and coastal management planning.[448]

The IPCC Second Assessment Reports and many subsequent findings have vindicated the grave concern about potential impacts on fragile small island environments. It was, therefore, not surprising that SPREP's member countries, as part of the AOSIS made strong recommendations to the Kyoto discussions, calling for significant cuts in emissions of GHGs. The members of AOSIS played an extremely visible role at the Third Conference of the Parties to UNFCCC

---

445 *Id.*

446 *Id.*

447 *Id.*

448 *Id.*

meeting in Kyoto, Japan in 1997 and again at the Fourth Conference in Buenos Aires, Argentina, November 1998.[449]

Representatives of 38 small island developing countries gathered in Majuro, in the Marshall Islands, from July 12 to July 16 of 1999, to discuss the potential benefits and problems of the CDM of the Kyoto Protocol. The meeting was organized by the AOSIS and included representatives from 13 Pacific Island countries. The CDM would learn about developed countries investing in projects in developing countries, thus gaining credits for reductions in carbon dioxide that resulted from those projects. A share of the "proceeds" would be used to help countries most vulnerable to climate change to adapt to its adverse effects. Small island countries, which already established how vulnerable they are to climate change, hope to seek much-needed financial assistance from the CDM, to help with their adaptation measures, and to help them build up the new skills they need in future. Australia has organized a second CDM meeting in Nadi, Fiji, focusing more on investment aspects. This meeting will study what advantages there could be for businesses in using CDM to invest in various sectors in Pacific island countries.[450]

Climate Change and South Pacific Forum

In 1999, "the Forum recognized and endorsed members' deep concerns regarding the impact of GHG emissions on rising sea levels and changing weather patterns on all Forum members, especially low-lying island nations, as recorded in the "Forum Leaders' Statement on Climate Change" issued at the 28th South Pacific Forum and the "Statement on Climate Change and Sea Level rise" issued by the 7th Economic Summit of Smaller Island States Leaders."[451] It also "recognized the legally binding commitments agreed in the Kyoto protocol as a significant first step forward on the path to ensuring effective global action to combat climate change" and it "encouraged all countries to sign the Kyoto Protocol and to work toward its earliest possible ratification."[452]

"The Forum highlighted the importance of implementation of measures to ensure early progress toward meeting these commitments. They urged all

---

449 *Id.*

450 *Climate Change and the Pacific Islands, supra* note 530.

451 *Climate Change and the Pacific Islands, supra* note 530.

452 *Id.*

Annex 1 Parties, especially the United States, European Union, Russia, Japan, Canada and other major emitters to take urgent action in this regard."[453] "The Forum noted the recognition in the Kyoto Protocol of the importance of the adaptation needs of vulnerable Pacific island states."[454] " Leaders urged all parties to recognize the need for adaptation measures to be undertaken within Pacific island states."[455]

An important adaptation strategy that may be useful to deal with these impacts at the national level would be integrated coastal management (ICM). ICM is a continuous, iterative, adaptive and consensus-building process comprising a set of related tasks, all of which must be carried out to achieve a set of goals, including adapting to the effects of climate change, integration of policies and programs across and among sectors of the economy.[456]

Most Pacific island governments view climate change and sea-level rise and natural variability as priority issues, recognizing that they significantly impact the economic, environment, social, cultural and traditional sectors of PICs. However, governments wish to know what they have to do to address the problem. Traditional cultural practices were inextricably interwoven with conservation of the environment. Traditional knowledge has governed activities and survival of people in the region both in the past and present. From a socio-economic perspective, there has been a recent change from subsistence to a dual economy. Issues that need to be addressed include population concentration; the location of infrastructure; food security; culture and a wide range of other activities that are integral to sustainable livelihoods in Pacific island countries.[457]

Even if action is taken immediately by the industrial nations, the impacts of atmospheric pollution are going to get worse before they improve.[458]

"The options for the Pacific Islands, other than continuing to berate the industrial nations on their lack of concerted action, include migration, foreshore

---

453 *Id.*

454 *Id.*

455 *Id.*

456 *Id.*

457 *Climate Change and the Pacific Islands, supra* note 530; *see Climate Change Overview,* SPREP (last viewed July 1, 2013), http://www.sprep.org/Climate-Change/climate-change-overview.

458 *Climate Change and the Pacific Islands, supra* note 530; *see National Coral Reef Institute,* Nova Southeastern University (last viewed June 30, 2013), http://www.nova.edu/ocean/ncri.

stabilization, resettlement and decentralization to adapt to the impacts of climate and sea-level changes."[459]

All these options need planning as they have policy implications. Thus, future directions will have to be researched so that some response strategies can be planned and recommended for future adaptation. An integrated coastal management (ICM) approach may be useful in the development and implementation of adaptation strategies and could be valuable, with or without climate change, to permit effective planning to achieve sustainable development at the national level.[460]

2.2.3. South Pacific Regional Environmental Program

The South Pacific Regional Environment Programme (SPREP) was established in 1982 by the various governments of the Pacific region with the goal of protecting the environment.[461] There are 21 Pacific Island countries and territories, and 4 countries located outside of the Pacific Islands that have a direct interest in the Pacific Islands region, that encompass the SPREP.[462] This intergovernmental organization operates under its mission statement, which is "to promote co-operation in the South Pacific region and to provide assistance in order to protect and improve its environment and to ensure sustainable development for present and future generations."[463]

As part of its agenda, the SPREP Secretariat runs two distinct, but equally important, programs. The programs are:

- The Island Ecosystems program was created to work with the Pacific Island countries and territories to help them manage island

---

459 *Climate Change and the Pacific Islands, supra* note 530.

460 *Climate Change and the Pacific Islands, supra* note 530.

461 *South Pacific Regional Environment Programme,* U.S. Department of State (last viewed July 1, 2013), http://2001-2009.state.gov/g/oes/ocns/rsp/cta/12179.htm; *see About,* SPREP (last viewed July 1, 2013), http://www.sprep.org/About-Us.

462 *South Pacific Regional Environment Programme,* U.S. Department of State (last viewed July 1, 2013), http://2001-2009.state.gov/g/oes/ocns/rsp/cta/12179.htm (listing the members of the SPREP. The four developed countries with direct interests in the region are Australia, France, New Zealand and the United States of America).

463 *South Pacific Regional Environment Programme,* U.S. Department of State (last viewed July 1, 2013), http://2001-2009.state.gov/g/oes/ocns/rsp/cta/12179.htm; *see About,* SPREP (last viewed July 1, 2013), http://www.sprep.org/About-Us.

resources and marine ecosystems in a way that is sustainable so the islands can support life and livelihoods.

- The Pacific Futures program was designed to assist Pacific Island countries and territories in the planning and response of threats to the region and pressures on island and ocean systems because of climate change.[464]

SPREP is the secretariat for regional environmental conventions and their protocols, strengthening the regional legal frameworks for implementing global agreements. For example, the Waigani Convention provides for strict control over the transboundary movement of hazardous wastes and the sound management of these dangerous wastes. As such, the Waigani Convention has the potential to facilitate the implementation of the global chemicals conventions. Toward this end, the Pacific Joint Centre for Information and Technology Transfer for the implementation of the Basel and Waigani Conventions were established within SPREP in December 2003.[465]

With SPREP's assistance, some of the regional instruments are being amended to implement fully global MEAs. For example, the Convention for the Protection of the Natural Resources and Environment of the South Pacific Region (Noumea Convention) and its related Protocols provide a framework for cooperation in preventing pollution of the marine and coastal environment in the region.[466] For instance, the Apia Convention, which promotes the creation of protected areas, is being reviewed in the light of newer conventions such as CBD (Convention on Biological Diversity, adopted in 1992, and entered into force in 1993; CITES (Convention on International Trade in Endangered Species of Wild Fauna and Flora, adopted in 1973, and entered into force in 1975) and RAMSAR (Shorthand for the Ramsar Convention on Wetlands of International Importance, adopted in 1971, and entered into force in 1975) and may be amended to provide synergies.[467]

---

[464] *South Pacific Regional Environment Programme*, U.S. Department of State (last viewed July 1, 2013), http://2001-2009.state.gov/g/oes/ocns/rsp/cta/12179.htm

[465] MANUAL ON COMPLIANCE WITH AND ENFORCEMENT OF MULTILATERAL ENVIRONMENTAL AGREEMENTS 238 (2006)

[466] http://www.unep.org/climatechange/readywillingandable/home.aspx

[467] MANUAL ON COMPLIANCE WITH AND ENFORCEMENT OF MULTILATERAL ENVIRONMENTAL AGREEMENTS 238 (2006)

In order to so support SPREP Members, the Secretariat promotes coordination at the national level, provides technical and legal advice to states (for example in drafting national legislation), assists in preparing briefing papers for international negotiating conferences, coordinates pre-conference consultations to determine regional positions and strengthens regional legal frameworks. It also conducts research, offers training courses, and develops materials, promoting the placement of staff from other secretariats of Conventions and NGOs at its Headquarters.[468]

"Through the inter-linkages approach, SPREP facilitates the effective establishment of national coordination and consultation systems for the negotiation, ratification, and implementation of MEAs."[469]

2.2.4. Asia-Pacific Partnership for Clean Development and Climate

In 2006 The Asia-Pacific Partnership (APP) on Clean Development and Climate was launched at the Partnership's inaugural Ministerial meeting in Sydney. The APP was an international, voluntary, public-private partnership among Australia, Canada, India, Japan, The People's Republic of China, South Korea, and the United States. In 2011, the Partnership formally concluded, although some individual projects continue.

Foreign, Environment and Energy Ministers from partner countries agreed to cooperate in the development and transfer of technology, which enables reduction of GHG emissions that is consistent with and complementary to the UNFCCC and other relevant international instruments, and is intended to complement, but not replace, the Kyoto Protocol. Member countries account for over 50 percent of the world's GHG emissions, energy consumption, GDP, and population. Unlike the Kyoto Protocol, which imposes mandatory limits on GHG emissions, the Partnership engages member countries to accelerate the development and deployment of clean energy technologies, with no binding enforcement mechanism. This has led to criticism that the Partnership is worthless, by other governments, climate scientists, and environmental groups. Proponents, on the other hand, argue that unrestricted economic growth and emission reductions can only be brought about through active engagement by all major

---

468 *Id.*

469 MANUAL ON COMPLIANCE WITH AND ENFORCEMENT OF MULTILATERAL ENVIRONMENTAL AGREEMENTS 239 (2006).

polluters, which includes India and China, within the Kyoto Protocol framework because neither India nor China are yet required to reduce emissions.

The intent was to create a voluntary, non-legally binding framework for international cooperation in order to facilitate the development, diffusion, deployment, and transfer of existing, emerging and longer-term cost-effective as well as more efficient technologies and practices among the Partners. This would be done through concrete and substantial cooperation, so as to achieve practical results, promote and create enabling environments to assist in such efforts, facilitate attainment of the Partners' respective national pollution reduction, energy security and climate change objectives, and provide a forum for exploring the Partners' respective policy approaches.

The Partnership has been publicly supported as an alternative to the Kyoto Protocol by governments and business groups particularly in countries where the Kyoto Protocol has not been ratified. Many commentators have particularly welcomed the fact that the Partnership overcomes the impasse between developed and developing countries under the UNFCCC and the Kyoto Protocol and has led to India and China taking steps to address their GHG emissions. Mexico, Russia, and several ASEAN members have expressed interest in joining the Partnership in the future.

The Partnership has been criticized by environmentalists who have rebuked the proceedings as ineffectual without mandatory limits on greenhouse-gas emissions. A coalition of national environment groups and networks from all of the APP countries issued a challenge[470] to their governments to make the APP meaningful by agreeing to mandatory targets, creating financial mechanisms with incentives for the dissemination of clean energy technologies, and creating an action plan to overcome the key barriers to technology transfer. In the year since the Partnership went into effect, none of the parties have lowered emissions of GHGs.

Proponents of the Partnership have lauded the APP's achievements since its inception in 2006. In more than three years, the Partnership has established a record of achievement in promoting collaboration between our governments and the private sector in key energy-intensive sectors and activities. The Partnership has worked to develop and implement detailed action plans across key sectors of the energy economy, and to date has endorsed 175 collaborative projects

---

470 In April 2011, APP formally concluded. A number of projects continued and some other individual projects were cancelled.

including 22 flagship projects across all seven Partner countries. These projects have, *inter alia*, helped power plant managers improve the efficiency of their operations, trained cement plant operators how to save energy at their facilities, assisted in pushing solar photovoltaics toward commercialization, and improved design, equipment and operations of buildings and appliances. The Partnership has been widely noted for its innovative work in public-private sector cooperation and stands as an example of the benefits of international cooperative efforts in addressing climate change.[471]

2.2.5. Non-participants states: interests and arguments

In 2011, Canada, Japan, and Russia stated that they would not take on any further Kyoto targets.[472] On 12 December 2012, the Canadian government invoked Canada's legal right to withdraw formally from the Kyoto Protocol.[473] Although Canada was committed to cutting its greenhouse emissions to six percent below 1990 levels by 2012, in 2009 emissions were 17 percent higher than in 1990.

"On 12 November 1998, the United States signed the Protocol, in part because the Clinton Administration wanted to revitalize what was seen as some loss of momentum during COP-4."[474] "However, the treaty was not subsequently submitted to the Senate for approval in recognition of S.Res.98."[475] that indicated "disapproval of any treaty that did not include legally binding commitments for developing countries."[476] "In the United States, ratification of treaties can occur

---

[471] Shanghai Communiqué. Asia Pacific Partnership on Clean Development and Climate was an international public-private partnership among Australia, Canada, India, Japan, China, South Korea and the United States launched in January 2006 replaced by Global Superior Energy Performance Partnership (GSEP). http://ietd.iipnetwork.org/content/asia-pacific-partnership-clean-development-and-climate

[472] *Canada Pulls Out of, Denounces Kyoto Protocol*, CBS NEWS (Dec. 13, 2011), http://www.cbsnews.com/8301-202_162-57341907/canada-pulls-out-of-denounces-kyoto-protocol/.

[473] *Canada Pulls Out of Kyoto Protocol*, CBC NEWS (Dec. 12, 2011), http://www.cbc.ca/news/politics/story/2011/12/12/pol-kent-kyoto-pullout.html; United Nations Framework Convention on Climate Change, art. 2, June 12, 1992, 1771 U.N.T.S. 107,

    available at http://unfccc.int/resource/docs/convkp/conveng.pdf.

[474] Susan Fletcher, *98-2: Global Climate Change Treaty: The Kyoto Protocol*, Nat'l Council for Sci. and the Env't (March 6, 2000), http://cnie.org/NLE/CRSreports/Climate/clim-3.cfm [from now on Fletcher, 98-2: Global Climate Change].

[475] *Id.*

[476] HORACE M. KARLING, GLOBAL CLIMATE CHANGE REVISITED 105 (2007).

only after being submitted to and approved by the United States Senate."[477] "The United States would be obligated under the Protocol to a cumulative reduction in its GHG emissions of seven percent below 1990 levels for three major GHGs, including carbon dioxide, (and below 1995 levels for the three other, man-made gasses), averaged over the commitment period 2008 to 2012."[478]

"The United States had taken a firm position that 'meaningful participation' of developing countries in commitments made in the Protocol is critical both to achieving the goals of the Treaty and to its approval by the US Senate."[479] "This reflects the requirement articulated in S. Res. 98,[480] passed in 1997, that the United States should not become a party to the Kyoto Protocol until developing countries are subject to binding emissions targets."[481] "The US government also argued that success in dealing with the issue of climate change and global warming would require such participation."[482] "The developing country bloc argued that the Berlin Mandate clearly excluded them from new commitments in this Protocol, and they continued to oppose emissions limitation commitments by non-Annex I countries."[483]

"The November 2000 COP-6 meeting in The Hague was the last negotiation session on the Kyoto Protocol in which the United States participated."[484] After 2001, the US rejected the Kyoto Protocol and opted out of participation in Kyoto-related negotiations.[485] The Kyoto Protocol "was characterized as

---

477 *Id.*

478 Fletcher, *98-2: Global Climate Change, supra* note 598; see A Survey of Organizations, Providers, and Research Involved in the Effort to Understand and Deal with Climate Change (last viewed June 28, 2013), www.kyotoprotocol.com.

479 Fletcher, *98-2: Global Climate Change, supra* note 598.

480 *See* S. Res. 98, 105th Cong. (1997-1998).

481 Fletcher, *98-2: Global Climate Change, supra* note 598.

482 Fletcher, *98-2: Global Climate Change, supra* note 598.

483 Fletcher, *98-2: Global Climate Change, supra* note 598; United Nations Framework Convention on Climate Change, art. 2, June 12, 1992, 1771 U.N.T.S. 107, *available at* http://unfccc.int/resource/docs/convkp/conveng.pdf; *Kyoto Protocol Reference Manual on Accounting of Emissions and Assigned Amount,* Bonn, Germany: Climate Change Secretariat.

484 Horace M. Karling, Global Climate Change Revisited 109 (2007).

485 Susan Fletcher, *Global Climate Change: The Kyoto Protocol,* Nat'l Council for Sci. and the Env't (July 21, 2005), http://www.au.af.mil/au/awc/awcgate/crs/rl30692.pdf [hereinafter Fletcher, *Global Climate Change*].

"dead" regarding US policy."[486] "The cabinet-level review of US climate policy was ongoing, and the Bush Administration indicated that it would be interested in pursuing alternative approaches or cooperative efforts such as market-based incentives and voluntary measures, to address climate change concerns."[487]

Under the Kyoto treaty, all developed countries that ratify must decrease their GHG emissions to 1990 levels by 2012.[488] But many developing countries, including China, are not required to reduce emissions, but rather to simply monitor and report them to the UNFCCC.[489] China has criticized the US for not taking the lead in cutting emissions. Critics respond that China surpassed the US in 2006 in total GHG emissions to become the world's number one carbon polluter.[490] For any global reduction to be meaningful, the focus must be on reducing emissions in China. This has become a major point of contention for a new treaty that will replace the Protocol.

Such a treaty would have huge ramifications for China's economy.[491] In recent years, China has, on average, opened one new coal plant every week.[492] But since the burning of coal and other solid fuels (such as cow dung) releases "black carbon," the most damaging culprit of global warming,[493] China will be hard-pressed to meet the challenges that the rest of the world will undoubtedly seek to impose on it. The total impact of this problem on Chinese society and the economy seems immeasurable, and will not be known for many years to come.[494]

---

486 Fletcher, *Global Climate Change, supra* note 609, at 12.

487 *Id.*

488 *Kyoto Protocol*, UNITED NATIONS FRAMEWORK CONVENTION ON CLIMATE CHANGE (last viewed July 2, 2013),

489 Fletcher, *Global Climate Change, supra* note 609, at 2 (explaining that a total of 141 nations has no binding obligations under the treaty).

490 ZhongXiang Zhang, *Who Should Bear the Cost of China's Carbon Emissions Embodied in Goods for Export?* East-West Center 1, http://www.eastwestcenter.org/sites/default/files/private/econwp122. pdf (stating that China's CO2 emissions exceed US emissions by 8%).

491 *Id.*

492 Peter Galuszka, *China & India are Building 4 New Coal Power Plants – Every Week*, THE GLOBAL WARMING POLICY FOUNDATION (Nov. 14, 2012), http://www.thegwpf.org/china-india-building-4-coal-power-plants-week/.

493 About Black Carbon, EARTHJUSTICE (last viewed July 3, 2013), http://earthjustice.org/features/campaigns/about-black-carbon.

494 *Id.*

CHAPTER THREE

THE REFUGEE PERSPECTIVE

3.1. INTERNATIONAL REFUGEE LAW

3.1.1. Documents

3.1.1.i. 1951 Refugee Convention and the 1967 Protocol

The 1951 Convention relating to the Status of Refugees (Convention), with just one "amending" and updating Protocol adopted in 1967 (1967 Protocol), is the central feature of today's international regime of refugee protection,[495] and some 144 States (out of a total United Nations membership of 192) have now ratified either one or both of these instruments (as of August 2008).[496] The Convention, which entered into force in 1954, is by far the most widely ratified refugee treaty and remains central also to the protection activities of the United Nations High Commissioner for Refugees (UNHCR).[497]

---

[495] Kate Jastram & Marilyn Achiron, *Refugee Protection: A Guide to International Refugee Law*, INTER-PARLIAMENTARY UNION 8 (2001), http://www.ipu.org/pdf/publications/refugee_en.pdf.

[496] *The 1951 Convention Relating to the Status of Refugees and its 1967 Protocol*, UNHCR (Sept. 2011), *available at* http://www.unhcr.org/4ec262df9.html.

[497] Guy Goodwin-Gill, *Convention Relating to the Status of Refugees Protocol Relating to the Status of Refugees*, U.N. AUDIOVISUAL LIBRARY OF INT'L LAW 1 (2008), http://untreaty.un.org/cod/avl/pdf/ha/prsr/prsr_e.pdf; *See The 1951 Refugee Convention*, UNHCR, http://www.unhcr.org/pages/49da0e466.html.

In the aftermath of the Second World War, refugees, and displaced persons were high on the international agenda. At its first session in 1946, the United Nations General Assembly recognized not only the urgency of the problem but also the cardinal principle that "no refugees or displaced persons who have finally and definitely ... expressed valid objections to returning to their countries of origin ... shall be compelled to return ..."[498]. The United Nations' first post-war response was a specialized agency, the International Refugee Organization (IRO, 1946-1952),[499] but notwithstanding its success in providing protection and assistance and facilitating solutions, it was expensive and also caught up in the politics of the Cold War. As a result, it was soon replaced with a temporary organization with updated treaty provisions on the status of refugees.[500]

The historical context also helps to explain both the nature of the Convention and some of its apparent limitations. Just six years before its conclusion, the Charter of the United Nations had identified the principles of sovereignty, independence and non-interference within the reserved domain of domestic jurisdiction as fundamental to the success of the Organization (Article 2 of the Charter of the United Nations). In December 1948, the General Assembly adopted the Universal Declaration of Human Rights, article 14, paragraph 1, of which recognizes that, "Everyone has the right to seek and to enjoy in other countries asylum from persecution,"[501] but the individual was only then beginning to be seen as the beneficiary of human rights in international law.

The General Assembly replaced the IRO with the Office of the United Nations High Commissioner for Refugees on January 1, 1951. Initially set up for three years, the High Commissioner's mandate was regularly renewed thereafter for five-year periods until 2003, when the General Assembly decided "to continue the Office until the refugee problem is solved."[502]

---

498 "Question of Refugees," UNHCR http://www.unhcr.org/print/3ae69ee78.html

499 *International Refugee Organization definition*, ENCYCLOPEDIA BRITANNICA (last visited July 4, 2013), http://www.britannica.com/EBchecked/topic/291218/International-Refugee-Organization.

500 Goodwin-Gill, *supra* note 619, at 1; *International Refugee Organization definition*, ENCYCLOPEDIA BRITANNICA (last visited July 4, 2013), http://www.britannica.com/EBchecked/topic/291218/International-Refugee-Organization (explaining that the IRO was succeeded by the Office of the United Nations High Commissioner for Refugees).

501 *The Universal Declaration of Human Rights.* http://www.un.org/en/documents/udhr/

502 Goodwin-Gill, *supra* note 619, at 1-2; G.A. Res. 58/153, ¶ 9, U.N. Doc. A/RES/58/153 (Dec. 22, 2003), *available at*
http://www.un.org/ga/search/view_doc.asp?symbol=A/RES/58/153&Lang=E.

The High Commissioner's primary responsibility, set out in paragraph 1 of the Statute annexed to resolution 428 (V), is to provide "international protection" to refugees and, by assisting governments, to seek "permanent solutions for the problem of refugees." Its protection functions specifically include "promoting the conclusion and ratification of international conventions for the protection of refugees, supervising their application and proposing amendments thereto" (paragraph 8 (a) of the Statute).[503]

A year earlier, in 1949, the United Nations Economic and Social Council appointed an Ad Hoc Committee to "consider the desirability of preparing a revised and consolidated Convention relating to the international status of refugees and stateless persons and, if they consider such a course desirable, draft the text of such a convention."[504]

The Ad Hoc Committee decided to focus on refugees and produced a draft convention. Its provisional draft identified several categories of refugees, such as the victims of different political regimes and those recognized under previous international agreements. Additionally, it also adopted the general criteria of the well-founded fear of persecution and lack of protection (See United Nations doc. E/AC.32/L.6, 23 January 1950).[505]

The Conference met in Geneva from 2 to 25 July 1951 and took as its basis for discussion the draft which had been prepared by the Ad Hoc Committee on Refugees and Stateless Persons, save that the Preamble was that adopted by the Economic and Social Council, while Article 1 (definition) was as recommended by the General Assembly and annexed to resolution 429 (V). On adopting the final text, the Conference also unanimously adopted a Final Act, including five recommendations covering travel documents, family unity, NGOs, asylum and application of the Convention beyond its contractual scope.[506]

A stark difference existed between the responsibilities of the UNHCR, and the scope of the new Convention—the mandate of the UNHCR was universal and unconstrained by geographical or temporal limitations while the General

---

503 Goodwin-Gill, *supra* note 619, at 2; *see Refugees*, UNITED NATIONS (last viewed July 4, 2013), http://www.un.org/en/globalissues/briefingpapers/refugees/nextsteps.html.

504 Goodwin-Gill, *supra* note 619, at 2.

505 Goodwin-Gill, *supra* note 619, at 2.

506 Goodwin-Gill, *supra* note 619, at 2.

Assembly's definition applied only to those who became refugees by as a result of an event that occurred prior to 1 January 1951.[507]

Article 1A, paragraph 1, of the 1951 Convention applies the term "refugee," first, to any person considered a refugee under earlier international arrangements. Article 1A, paragraph 2, together with the 1967 Protocol offers a general definition of the refugee as including any person who is outside their country of origin and unable or unwilling to return there or to avail themselves of its protection, on account of a well-founded fear of persecution for reasons of race, religion, nationality, membership of a particular group or political opinion. Stateless persons may also be refugees because the country of origin (citizenship) is understood as "country of former habitual residence." Those who possess more than one nationality will only be considered refugees within the Convention if such other nationality or nationalities are ineffective (that is, do not provide protection).[508]

The refugee must be "outside" his or her country of origin, and must have fled his or her country and crossed an international border. However, it is not necessary to have fled by reason of fear of persecution, or even actually to have been persecuted.[509]Although the risk of persecution is key to the refugee definition, the term "persecution" is not defined in the 1951 Convention. Articles 31 and 33 refer to those whose life or freedom "was" or "would be" threatened, so clearly it includes the threat of death, or the threat of torture, or cruel, inhuman or degrading treatment or punishment. A comprehensive analysis today will require the general notion to be related to developments in the broad field of human rights (cf. 1984 Convention against Torture, Article 7; 1966 International Covenant on Civil and Political Rights, Article 3; 1950 European Convention on Human Rights, Article 6; 1969 American Convention on Human Rights, Article 5; 1981 African Charter on Human and Peoples' Rights).[510]

At the same time, fear of persecution and lack of protection are themselves interrelated elements. The persecuted do not have the protection of their country of origin while evidence of the lack of protection on either the internal or external level may create a presumption as to the likelihood of persecution and

---

507 Goodwin-Gill, *supra* note 619, at 2.

508 Goodwin-Gill, *supra* note 619, at 3; *The 1951 Convention Relating to the Status of Refugees and its 1967 Protocol*, UNHCR (Sept. 2011), *available at* http://www.unhcr.org/4ec262df9.html.

509 Goodwin-Gill, *supra* note 619, at 3.

510 Goodwin-Gill, *supra* note 619, at 3.

fear. However, there is no necessary linkage between persecution and government authority. A Convention refugee, by definition, must be *unable* or *unwilling* to avail him or herself to the protection of the state or government, and the notion of inability to secure the protection of the state is broad enough to include a situation where the authorities cannot or will not provide protection, for example, against the persecution of non-state actors.[511]

The Convention requires that the persecution feared to be for reasons of "race, religion, nationality, membership of a particular social group (added at the 1951 Conference), or political opinion.[512] This language, which recalls the language of non-discrimination in the Universal Declaration of Human Rights and subsequent human rights instruments, gives an insight into the characteristics of individuals and groups that are considered relevant to refugee protection. Persecution for the stated reasons implies a violation of human rights of particular gravity; it may be the result of cumulative events or systemic mistreatment, but equally it could comprise a single act of torture.[513]

Persecution under the Convention is thus a complex of reasons, interests and measures. The measures are taken against groups or individuals for reasons of race, religion, nationality, membership of a particular social group or political opinion. These reasons show that the groups or individuals are identified via a classification that ought to be irrelevant to the enjoyment of fundamental human rights.[514]

The Convention does not just say who is a refugee, however. It goes further and sets out when refugee status comes to an end (Article 1C; for example, in the case of a voluntary return, acquisition of a new, effective nationality or change of circumstances in the country of origin). For particular, political reasons, the Convention also puts Palestinian refugees outside its scope, at least while they continue to receive protection or assistance from other United Nations agencies (Article 1D), and excludes persons who are treated as nationals in their state of refuge (Article 1E). Finally, the Convention definition categorically excludes from the benefits of refugee status anyone who is suspected to have committed

---

511 Goodwin-Gill, *supra* note 619, at 3.

512 *The 1951 Convention relating to the Status of Refugees and its 1967 Protocol*, UNHCR http://www. refugeelegalaidinformation.org/sites/default/files/uploads/1951%20convention%20and%201967%20 protocol.pdf

513 Goodwin-Gill, *supra* note 619, at 3-4.

514 Goodwin-Gill, *supra* note 619, at 4. International Covenant on Civil and Political Rights, New York, 16 December 1966, United Nations, *Treaty Series*, vol. 999, p. 171.

a war crime, a serious non-political offense prior to admission, or acts contrary to the purposes and principles of the United Nations (Article 1F).[515] From the very beginning, therefore, the 1951 Convention has contained clauses sufficient to ensure that the serious criminal and the terrorist do not benefit from international protection.[516]

"Besides identifying the essential characteristics of the refugee, states party to the Convention also accept a number of specific obligations that are crucial to achieving the goal of protection, and are thereafter an appropriate solution."[517]

The origins of the 1967 Protocol relating to the Status of Refugees, which reflected recognition by UNHCR and the states members of its Executive Committee that there was a disjuncture between the universal, unlimited UNHCR Statute and the scope of the 1951 Convention, were quite different from those of the latter. Instead of an international conference under the auspices of the United Nations, the issues were addressed at a colloquium of some 13 legal experts, which met in Bellagio, Italy, from 21 to 28 April 1965. The Colloquium did not favor a complete revision of the 1951 Convention but opted instead for a Protocol by way of which parties would agree to apply the relevant provisions of the Convention, but without necessarily becoming a party to that treaty. The approach was approved by the UNHCR Executive Committee, and the draft Protocol was referred to the Economic and Social Council for transmission to the General Assembly. The General Assembly took note of the Protocol (the General Assembly commonly "takes note" of, rather than adopts or approves, instruments drafted outside the United Nations system), and requested the Secretary-General to transmit the text to states with a view to enabling them to accede (resolution 2198 [XXI] of 16 December 1966). The Protocol required just six ratifications, and it duly entered into force on 4 October 1967.[518]

The Protocol is often referred to as "amending" the 1951 Convention, but in fact, and as noted above, it does not. The Protocol is an independent instrument, not a revision within the meaning of Article 45 of the Convention. States parties to the Protocol, which can be ratified or acceded to by a state without becoming a party to the Convention merely agrees to apply Articles 2 to 34 of the Convention to refugees defined in Article 1 thereof as if the dateline

---

515 http://www2.ohchr.org/english/law/pdf/protocolrefugees.pdf

516 Goodwin-Gill, *supra* note 619, at 4.

517 Goodwin-Gill, *supra* note 619, at 4.

518 Goodwin-Gill, *supra* note 619, at 7.

was, omitted (Article I of the Protocol). As of 2008, Cape Verde, Swaziland, the United States of America and Venezuela have acceded only to the Protocol, while Madagascar, Monaco, Namibia and St. Vincent and the Grenadines are party only to the Convention (and the Congo, Madagascar, Monaco, and Turkey have retained the geographical limitation).[519]

"Article II on the cooperation of national authorities with the United Nations is equivalent to Article 35 of the Convention while the few remaining articles (just 11 in all) add no substantive obligations to the Convention regime."[520]

The Convention is sometimes portrayed today as a relic of the cold war and as inadequate in the face of "new" refugees from ethnic violence and gender-based persecution. It is also said to be insensitive to security concerns, particularly terrorism and organized crime, and even redundant, given the protection now due in principle to everyone under international human rights law.[521]

The Convention does not deal with the question of admission, and neither does it oblige a state of refuge to accord asylum as such, or provide for the sharing of responsibilities (for example, by prescribing which state should deal with a claim to refugee status). The Convention also does not address the question of "causes" of flight, or make provision for prevention; its scope does not include internally displaced persons, and it is not concerned with the better management of international migration. At the regional level, and notwithstanding the 1967 Protocol, refugee movements have necessitated more focused responses, such as the 1969 OAU/AU Convention on the Specific Aspects of Refugee Problems in Africa and the 1984 Cartagena Declaration; while in Europe, the development of protection doctrine under the 1950 European Convention on Human Rights has led to the adoption of provisions on "subsidiary" or "complementary" protection within the legal system of the European Union.[522]

Nevertheless, within the context of the international refugee regime, which brings together states, UNHCR and other international organizations, the UNHCR Executive Committee, and NGOs, among others, the Convention continues to play a significant role in the protection of refugees, in the promotion

---

519 Goodwin-Gill, *supra* note 619, at 7. Handbook on Procedures and Criteria for Determining Refugee Status under the 1951 Convention and the 1967 Protocol relating to the Status of Refugees HCR/IP/4/Eng/REV.1Reedited, Geneva, January 1992, UNHCR 1979.

520 Goodwin-Gill, *supra* note 619, at 7.

521 Goodwin-Gill, *supra* note 619, at 7.

522 Goodwin-Gill, *supra* note 619, at 8.

and provision of solutions for refugees, in ensuring the security of states, sharing responsibility and generally promoting human rights. A Ministerial Meeting of States Parties, convened in Geneva in December 2001 by the government of Switzerland to mark the 50th anniversary of the Convention, expressly acknowledged, "the continuing relevance and resilience of this international regime of rights and principles."[523]

3.1.1.ii. The 1984 Cartagena Declaration

Cartagena Declaration on Refugees (CD)[524] is a declaration written in November 1984 by various experts from the Americas. This Declaration broadens the refugee definition and includes "...persons who have fled their country because their lives, safety or freedom have been threatened by generalized violence, foreign aggression, internal conflicts, massive violation of *human rights* or other circumstances that have seriously disturbed public order."[525]The Cartagena Declaration's provisions are implemented throughout Central America and even written in certain *national laws.*

The CD was drafted to complement and build upon the protection already afforded to some by the 1951 Convention. It was heavily influenced by the Organization of African Unity's (OAU) 1969 Convention on the Specific Aspects of Refugee Problems in Africa, improving upon some of its provisions, and retracing steps in others. With the advent of the CD, the terminology of International Refugee Law was significantly changed. The definition was broadened while simultaneously expanding states' obligations towards a wider variety of individuals and groups. Conclusion No.3 of the CD reads as follows: the definition or concept of a refugee to be recommended for use in the region is one in which, in addition to containing the elements of the 1951 Convention and the 1967 Protocol, includes among refugees persons who have fled their country because their lives, safety or freedom have been threatened by generalized

---

523 Goodwin-Gill, *supra* note 619, at 8; G.A. Res. 428 (V) (Dec. 1950).

524 Cartagena Declaration on Refugees, Nov. 22, 1984, Annual Report of the Inter-American Commission on Human Rights, OAS Doc. OEA/Ser.L/V/II.66/doc.10, rev. 1, at 190-93 (1984-85).

525 Cartagena Declaration on Refugees, *supra* note 648 at p.3.

violence, foreign aggression, internal conflicts, massive violations of human rights or other circumstances which have seriously disturbed public order.[526]

The 1951 Refugee Convention requires that an individual asylum seeker demonstrates a 'well-founded fear of persecution' based upon one of the five Convention grounds. The onus is on the individual asylum seeker to convincingly prove the nexus between subjective fear and objective reasons for such fear. This linkage between subjective fear and objective conditions was completely eradicated in the OAU Convention refugee definition, which leaves open the possibility that the basis or rationale for the harm may be indeterminate.[527]

The CD refugee definition represents something of a compromise between the all-inclusive OAU Convention definition, which defers to an individual's perception of peril and the Convention standard. It accepts claims in which the rationale for harm is indeterminate; however, this acceptance is qualified. In Conclusion No.3, it is stipulated that an individual must demonstrate that they have "fled their country because their lives, safety or freedom have been threatened." In other words, an individual must be personally at risk. Under the CD, it is implied that an individual or group of applicants must demonstrate that there is a "prospective" threat to their lives, security or liberty. However, the "threat" provided for in the CD refugee definition establishes a threshold that is significantly lower than the "well-founded fear" element of the 1951 Convention.[528]

The CD marks a step forward in the development of international refugee law by formalizing the natural consequences of armed conflict as a basis for refugee status. This is not to say that previous to the establishment of the CD, individuals fleeing risks emanating from such situations were not afforded protection. State practice has repeatedly accommodated these victims. Nevertheless, the inclusion of such people and groups under the RC required a liberal interpretation of the text of the treaty. The broadened definition of the CD provides textual clarity, thereby pre-empting efforts by states to prevent individuals who are fleeing their countries because of civil war, internal violence or general disregard for human rights from acquiring protection under the 1951 Convention.[529]

---

526 Claire Reid, *International Law, and Legal Instruments,* FORCED MIGRATION ONLINE (June 2005), http://www.forcedmigration.org/research-resources/expert-guides/international-law-and-legal-instruments/alldocuments

527 Reid, *supra* note 650.

528 Reid, *supra* note 650.

529 Reid, *supra* note 650.

The grounds for granting asylum stipulated in the CD referring to massive violations of human rights is in some ways analogous to the general term persecution used in the RC, neither of which provide a definition of the term. Given the general qualification in the CD that any violation must threaten life, liberty or security, it can be assumed that the drafters assumed that massive violations of human rights or persecution fundamentally includes the threat of deprivation of life or physical freedom. Yet, the International Conference on Central American Refugees (CIREFCA), in its Principios y Criterios, stipulates that massive violations of human rights can and do include other rights, including economic, social and cultural rights, provided that a link is made to the subjective element of "threat to life, liberty, or security." Therefore, measures such as the imposition of serious economic disadvantage, denial of employment opportunities, the denial of access to education, professions and so forth ought to be included as measures that could potentially lead to the granting of refugee status.[530]

Some have argued that the CD is too expansive because, inter alia, it contains no cessation or exclusion clauses. While it is true that no specific provisions are included, this does not imply that cessation and exclusion do not apply to refugees under the CD. According to the Executive Committee of UNHCR (ExComm), the underlying rationale for cessation clauses is that: refugee status should not be granted for a day longer than was absolutely necessary, and should come to an end if, in accordance with the terms of the Convention or the Statute, a person had the status of *de facto* citizenship, that is to say, if he really had the rights and obligations of a citizen of a given country. That an individual may cease to be protected under the CD is implied by the Declaration's affirmation of voluntary repatriation of refugees, in Conclusion, No.12. In addition, Conclusion No.3 indicates that the CD simply adds to the elements of the RC. Cessation clauses are provided for in Article 1C of the RC and exclusion clauses in Article 1F. The text of the CD indicates that these same provisions apply to individuals applying under the CD. Indeed, all that the CD really does is broaden the inclusion clauses, by expanding the definition.[531]

The CD was inspired by the OAU 1969 Convention on the Specific Aspect of Refugee Problems in Africa, which contains cessation and exclusion clauses in Article 1(4) and 1(5), respectively. That the OAU Convention is expressly

---

530 Reid, *supra* note 650. http://web.presidencia.gov.co/english/2008/declara_ing.pdf

531 Reid, *supra* note 650. http://www.basel.int/COP10/CartagenaDeclaration/tabid/2433/Default.aspx

mentioned as a "precedent" for the CD indicates that the CD would include those cessation and exclusion provisions provided for in that instrument to the extent that they were regionally appropriate, i.e., excluding Articles 1(4)(f)(g) and (5)(c), which are purely regional in character.[532]

Finally, the inclusion clauses of the Declaration can be applied *"a contrario sensu."* In other words, when the conditions that gave rise to flight disappear, refugee status ceases, unless the individual has particular reasons to maintain his or her status. To determine the validity of such reasons, recourse must be had to the RC. Cessation clauses are implied in the CD: if the conditions that caused flight have fundamentally changed, the refugee is no longer a refugee, and all things being equal, he or she can be required to return home like any other foreign national. If the conditions have fundamentally changed, yet the individual applicant wishes to maintain their refugee status, they must demonstrate that a nexus exists between the facts and the particular individual applicant such that a "well-founded fear of persecution" exists. To establish this, decision makers in respective countries must consider Article 1 of the 1951 Convention and all of its implications.[533]

3.1.2. United Nations High Commissioner for Refugees

Following the demise of the League of Nations and the formation of the United Nations, the international community was acutely aware of the refugee crisis following the end of World War II. In 1947, the International Refugee Organization (IRO) was founded by the United Nations. The IRO was the first international agency to deal comprehensively with all aspects pertaining to the lives of refugees.[534]

In the late 1940s, the IRO fell out of favor, but the United Nations agreed that a body was required to oversee global refugee issues. Despite many heated debates in the General Assembly, the UNHCR was founded as a subsidiary organ of the General Assembly by Resolution 319 (IV) of the United Nations General Assembly of December 1949. However, the organization was only intended to

---

532 Reid, *supra* note 650.

533 Reid, *supra* note 650.

534 GIL LOESCHER, THE UNHCR, AND WORLD POLITICS: A PERILOUS PATH (2001).

operate for three years, from January 1951, due to the disagreement of many United Nations member states over the implications of a permanent body.[535]

UNHCR's mandate was originally set out in its Statute, annexed to Resolution 428 (V) of the United Nations General Assembly of 1950. This mandate has been subsequently broadened by numerous resolutions of the General Assembly and its Economic and Social Council (ECOSOC). According to UNHCR, its mandate is to provide, on a non-political and humanitarian basis, international protection to refugees and to seek permanent solutions for them.

Soon after the signing of the 1951 Convention relating to the Status of Refugees, it became clear that refugees were not solely restricted to Europe. In 1956, UNHCR was involved in coordinating the response to the uprising in Hungary. Just a year later, UNHCR was dealing with Chinese refugees in Hong Kong, while also responding to Algerian refugees who had fled to Morocco and Tunisia in the wake of Algeria's war for independence. The responses marked the beginning of a wider, global mandate in refugee protection and humanitarian assistance.[536] Decolonization in the 1960s triggered large refugee movements in Africa, creating a massive challenge that would transform UNHCR; unlike the refugee crises in Europe, there were no durable solutions in Africa and many refugees fled one country only to find instability in their new country of asylum.

By the end of the decade, two-thirds of UNCHR's budget was focused on operations in Africa and in just one decade, the organization's focus had shifted from an almost exclusive focus on Europe to other countries. In the 1970s, UNHCR refugee operations continued to spread around the globe, with the mass exodus of East Pakistanis to India shortly before the birth of Bangladesh. Adding to the woes in Asia was the Vietnam War, with millions fleeing the war-torn country. In the 1980s, UNHCR was faced with new challenges as many member states were unwilling to resettle refugees due to the sharp rise in refugee numbers over the past decade. Often, these refugees were not fleeing wars between states, but an inter-ethnic conflict in newly independent states. The targeting of civilians as military strategy added to the displacement in many nations, so even "minor" conflicts resulted in a large number of displaced persons. Whether, in Asia, Central America, or Africa, these conflicts were not easy to find durable solutions for and they continued to be a massive challenge for the UNHCR. As

---

535 History of UNHCR, UNHCR (last viewed Nov. 1, 2009), http://www.unhcr.org/pages/49c3646cbc.html

536 *See* Basic facts, UNHCR (2010), http://www.unhcr.org/4dfdbf340.pdf.

a result, the UNHCR became more heavily involved with assistance programs within refugee camps, often located in hostile environments. The end of the cold war marked continued inter-ethnic conflict and contributed heavily to refugee flight. In addition, humanitarian intervention by multinational forces became more frequent, and the media began to play a big role. The genocide in Rwanda (1994) or the NATO mission in ex-Yugoslavia (1999) caused massive refugee crisis, again highlighting the difficulties for UNHCR to uphold its mandate, and the UNHCR continued to battle against restrictive asylum policies in so-called "rich" nations.

UNHCR's mandate has expanded since 1920 over the years, becoming a world oriented organization rather it's initial European limited mandate and now also focuses on protecting and providing humanitarian assistance to those who are "of concern," meaning people who have been internally displaced (IDPs). Such IDPs fit under the definition of the 1951 Convention, the 1967 Protocol, the 1969 Organization for African Unity Convention, and other treaties as long as they left their communities, but currently remain in their country of origin.

3.2. PROTECTION OF THE REFUGEES

3.2.1. Refugee Protection under international and human rights law

"Predictions for mass migrations owing to the effects of climate change are shocking—200 million people by 2050—and have led to the adoption of a new category of displaced persons known as climate refugees."[537]

"Nineteen years ago, when IPCC released its First Assessment Report, the report's authors suggested that large-scale, global migrations might represent the "greatest single impact" on world security resulting from climate change."[538]

There is now increasing scientific evidence to suggest that these concerns were well founded. In 2010, during a climate science summit in Copenhagen, experts rose earlier predictions of the sea-level rise in this century to three times

---

537 Benjamin Glahn, 'Climate Refugees'? Addressing the International Legal Gaps, Int'l Bar Assoc. (last viewed July 5, 2013),

http://www.ibanet.org/Article/Detail.aspx?ArticleUid=B51C02C1-3C27-4AE3-B4C4-7E350EB0F442.

538 Glahn, *supra* note 666.

those given by the IPCC just two years ago. And in February, the noted British economist, and author of the Stern Review on the Economics of Climate Change, Nick Stern, warned of climate-induced migration on a massive scale. Stern said that hundreds of millions and even billions of people would have to move with even a 4, 5, or 6-degree increase.[539]

"These kinds of predictions—and the increasing humanitarian concerns that accompany them—have now also given rise to a new nomenclature in the ever-expanding lexicon of climate change concerns: the 'climate refugee.'"[540]

Within the international humanitarian community, however, the notion of the "climate refugee" is problematic and controversial—problematic because it has no legal standing under existing international refugee and asylum law, and controversial because there is little agreement as to what to do about the problems it presents.[541] Over the past several years, numerous policy researchers and humanitarian agencies have tried to address some of these problems by pointing to the fact that "climate refugees" represent an unrecognized category of migrants that risks falling through the cracks of international refugee and immigration policy.

Currently, a central problem with the term "climate refugee" is that it is not an officially recognized category under existing international law. There are no frameworks, no conventions, no protocols and no specific guidelines that can provide protection and assistance for people crossing international borders because of climate change. Although existing international humanitarian law may apply in some cases of environmental displacement, the existing rights guaranteed to refugees—specifically those of international humanitarian assistance and the right of return—do not apply.

The current body of international law, and specifically the 1951 Convention relating to the Status of Refugees and its 1967 Protocol, was drafted at a time when the dangers of climate change were unknown. The 1951 Convention protects distinctively against persecution, and official recognition of "refugees" is therefore limited to a very explicit legal category—namely, only a person who "owing to well-founded fear of being persecuted for reasons of race, religion, nationality, membership of a particular social group or political opinion, is

539 Glahn, *supra* note 666.

540 Glahn, *supra* note 666; Warren, *supra* note 181.

541 Nicholls, *supra* note 182, at 9.

outside the country of his nationality and is unable, or owing to such fear, is unwilling to avail himself of the protection of that country.[542]

Thus, it is worth making clear that neither climate change nor environmental degradation is mentioned in any of the key legal conventions or norms that currently provide protections for refugees and asylum seekers. Use of the term "climate refugee" is, in other words, nothing more than a quasi-definitional description, not legally enforceable under any current international treaty, convention or instrument. More importantly, there is no structural process yet available within the international arena that can provide services for, and uphold the rights of, this new, unrecognized "category" of migrant.[543]

Without an official definition of what constitutes a "climate refugee," and lacking some form of official recognition under the international law, persons forced to migrate across international borders as a result of climate change may continue to be, as the International Organization for Migration has said, "almost invisible in the international system... unable to prove political persecution in their country of origin they fall through the cracks of asylum law."[544]

At present, however, there appear to be at least three possibilities that could advance the international debate about "climate refugee" protections and fill existing gaps in international law. The first option is to revise the 1951 Convention on the Status of Refugees to include climate (or environmental) refugees and to offer legal protections similar to those for refugees fleeing political persecution. The UNHCR is opposed to this option. While it recognizes that environmental degradation and climate change can contribute to forced, cross-border migrations, it does not perceive them to be grounds for granting refugee status under international law.[545]

A second, more ambitious option is to negotiate a completely new convention, one that would try to guarantee specific rights and protections to climate or environmental "refugees." There are several serious problems with this approach.

542 Glahn, *supra* note 666.

543 Glahn, *supra* note 666; Munich Re Group, *Megacities—Megarisks: Trends and Challenges for Insurance and Risk Management,* Munich Reinsurance Company (2004), http://www.preventionweb. net/files/646_10363.pdf.

544 Glahn, *supra* note 666; M. C. Zinyowera, and R.H. Moss, eds., *Climate Change 1995—Impacts, Adaptations and Mitigation of Climate Change: Scientific-Technical Analyzes* (Cambridge, UK: Cambridge University Press, 1996).

545 Glahn, *supra* note 666. G. J. Nagy et al., *Understanding the Potential Impact of Climate Change and Variability in Latin America and the Caribbean,* report prepared for N. H. Stern et al., *The Stern Review on the Economics of Climate Change* (2006).

First, there is a difference between people who were forced to relocate and those who have done so on their own accord. In cases of slow-onset disasters—such as drought and agricultural degradation—this difference that becomes difficult to determine. Additionally, it remains challenging to separate "climate disasters" and "natural disasters." How can one know whether a particular disaster happened with or without climate change?[546] Finally, there seems to be little agreement within the international humanitarian community as to whether a new convention is either possible or advisable.[547]

A third and perhaps final option is to follow the example of the 1998 Guiding Principles on Internal Displacement and develop a synthesis of existing international legal mechanisms. This option would seek to create a non-binding, but universally agreed on a set of principles that could protect "environmentally displaced persons."

Despite these options, however, significant questions still exist. Predictions for the number of possible "climate refugees" —200 million by 2050—represent nearly a four-fold increase in the number of displaced persons and refugees currently eligible for protection under the UNHCR mandate. And in 2007, the IPCC suggested that more than 600 million people currently living in low-lying coastal zones—438 million in Asia and 246 million in the least developed countries—will be directly at risk to potential threats of climate change in this century. The so-called "climate hotspots"—low-lying islands, coastal regions, large river deltas and underdeveloped regions—remain in danger of catastrophic environmental change. Under current international law, any climate-induced, cross-border migrations from these areas would trigger little if any protections or assistance mechanisms that could help provide aid to them.[548]

Thus, questions about where climate-displaced persons are likely to come from, where they might go and how international and domestic systems of legal rights, obligations and instruments can best be mobilized to protect them are currently of critical importance.[549]

---

546 Robert Nicholls, *Case Study on Sea-level Rise Impacts*, ORGANIZATION FOR ECONOMIC CO-OPERATION AND DEVELOPMENT (2003)?

547 Glahn, *supra* note 666.

548 Glahn, *supra* note 666; Nicholls, *supra* note 677.

549 Glahn, *supra* note 666.

3.2.2. The Principle of *Nonrefoulement*

A principle of paramount importance, the principle of nonrefoulement (prohibition to return) applies to any refugee, asylum-seeker or an alien who needs some form of shelter from the state whose control he/she is under. The *nonrefoulement* principle means that states cannot return aliens to territories where they might be subjected to torture, inhumane or degrading treatment, or where their lives and freedoms might be at risk. Given the absolute prohibition under international law of *refoulement*, the international community must address whether asylum-seekers are entitled to enter the territory of the state where they seek asylum and whether states are under an obligation to provide asylum seekers access to their territory.[550]

States are entitled to control immigration; a practice recognized to be within the reserved domain of their sovereignty. Immigration control presupposes two prerogatives—denying or blocking access to state territory, and ensuring the return of those aliens who have succeeded in entering. At the same time, immigration control as an expression of state sovereignty is subject to the principles and norms of international human rights law.[551] However, immigration control and human rights protection come into conflict when asylum seekers flee their countries and try to find safe shelter. In fact, potential countries of asylum seek to prevent asylum seekers from reaching their territory as well as return those who have managed to enter.[552] When states implement such security mechanisms, no distinction between refugees and other immigrants is made. The procedure for determining immigrants' status and for identifying the real refugees is expensive and time-consuming. Consequently, states prefer not to take the responsibility of offering protection.[553]

Article 14 of the Universal Declaration of Human Rights recognizes the right "to seek and to enjoy in other countries asylum from persecution." "Asylum" is protection offered by states to people who flee persecution and human rights

---

[550] Vladislava Stoyanova, *The Principle of Non-Refoulement and the Right of Asylum-Seekers to Enter State Territory, 3:1* CASIN 2 (2008-2009),

http://works.bepress.com/cgi/viewcontent.cgi?filename=0&article=1001&context=vladislava stoyanova&type=additional; http://www.unhcr.org/cgi-bin/texis/vtx/refworld/rwmain?docid=438c6d972

[551] Ian Brownlie, Principles Of Public International Law, 6th ed., 293 (Oxford University Press, 2003).

[552] Matthew J. Gibney and Randall Hansen, *Deportation and the Liberal State: the Forcible Return of Asylum Seekers and Unlawful Migrants in Canada, Germany, and the United Kingdom.*

[553] Stoyanova, *supra* note 682, at 2-3.

violations. When they do not receive asylum or refugee status and when they have no other legal ground to stay in the country, they must leave. Asylum seekers are potential refugees, and they receive the status of "refugee" if they can prove that they have a well-founded fear "of being persecuted for reasons of race, religion, nationality, membership of a particular social group or political opinion."[554]

The most important international human rights instruments, which prohibit exposure to *refoulement*, are the Geneva Convention relating to the Status of Refugees, the United Nations Convention against Torture and Other Cruel, Inhuman or Degrading Treatment or Punishment and the European Convention on Human Rights. Each imposes a prohibition on *refoulement*.

The principle of *nonrefoulement* applies to asylum seekers who are still under the refugee status determination procedure; to individuals who cannot be returned since there is a risk that they will be subjected to torture or inhumane or degrading treatment or punishment; and to individuals who have been recognized as refugees within the meaning of Article 1 of the Refugee Convention.[555] Any act of removal is prohibited, which means that the formal description of the act—deportation, expulsion, extradition, return—is not material.[556]

Article 13 of the Universal Declaration of Human Rights stipulates that "Everyone has the right to freedom of movement and residence *within the borders* of each state" and "Everyone has the right to leave *any* country, including his own, and to return to *his* country." Accordingly, asylum seekers have the right to leave their countries, but they are not entitled to enter other countries. While freedom of movement within the borders of each state is recognized, freedom of movement across international borders is a controversial issue.[557]

There is no explicit international norm that obliges states to grant asylum and consequently to accept refugees into their territories. Some scholars[558] find that state practice permits only one conclusion: the individual has no right to be granted asylum and further explains that there is no necessary connec-

---

554 Stoyanova, *supra* note 682, at 3; James Hathaway, The Law of Refugee Status 20 (Butterworth's, 1991).

555 Convention against Torture and Other Cruel, Inhuman or Degrading, Treatment or Punishment, GA Res. 39/46, United Nations GAOR, 1984, Supp. No. 51, United Nations Doc. A/39/51 (1984).

556 Stoyanova, *supra* note 682, at 3-4.

557 Stoyanova, *supra* note 682, at 4.

558 Goodwin-Gill, The Refugee In International Law 202 (Clarendon, 1996).

tion between nonrefoulement and admission or asylum; the discretion to grant asylum and the obligation to abide by *nonrefoulement* remain divided. Others[559] affirm that there is no international recognition of the right to be granted asylum of universal scope. Similarly, the *nonrefoulement* principle provided for in Article 33(1) of the Refugee Convention does not give individuals the right to receive asylum in a particular state. The prohibition for *refoulement*, therefore, does not negate the sovereign right of states to regulate the entrance of aliens in their territory. *Nonrefoulement* is not so much about admission to a state as it is about not returning refugees to where their lives or freedom may be endangered.[560]

At the same time, it has been recognized that *nonrefoulement* to a certain degree limits state sovereignty, because the prohibition in Article 33(1) could in certain situations amount to a *de facto* obligation to accept asylum seekers in a state's territory if the denial of acceptance "in any manner whatsoever" results in exposure to risk. However, the acceptance in a state's territory could be the only way the consequences from risk exposure can be avoided.[561]

Corroborated, "Articles 1 and 33 of the Refugee Convention place a duty on States parties to grant, at a minimum, access to asylum procedures for the purpose of refugee status determination."[562] Further, the "access to asylum procedures is an implied right under the 1951 Convention, without which obligations of *nonrefoulement*, including rejection at the frontier, could be infringed."[563]

Nonrefoulement cannot be guaranteed without granting asylum-seekers access to state territory. Denial of access to state territory equates to a denial of fair refugee status determination procedure. If a refugee status determination procedure is not conducted, it becomes impossible to identify those asylum seekers who face the risk of persecution if denied protection. Since *nonrefoulement* prevents violations of human rights, which are recognized to hold such significant value (like the prohibition of torture) that states should invest

---

559 María- Teresa Gil Bazo, New issues in Refugee Research, UNHCR Research Paper No.136, *Refugee Status, Subsidiary Protection, and the Right to be Granted Asylum under EU Law.*

560 Stoyanova, *supra* note 682, at 4; Goodwin-Gill, The Refugee in International Law 202 (Clarendon, 1996).

561 Stoyanova, *supra* note 682, at 5; James Hathaway, The Rights of Refugees under International Law 301 (Cambridge University Press, 2005).

562 Stoyanova, *supra* note 682, at 5; Alice Edwards, *Human Rights, Refugees, and the Right To Enjoy Asylum*, 17 Int'l J. Refugee L. 302 (2005).

563 Stoyanova, *supra* note 682, at 5.

extraordinary efforts to achieve some degree of certainty that these rights are not breached.[564]

Another pertinent issue, except the right to appeal, would be whether asylum seekers have access to legal assistance. Without legal help, asylum seekers are at the mercy of state immigration officials, which is a premise for arbitrariness. Further, although the duty to ascertain and evaluate all relevant facts is shared between the applicant and the examiner, generally, the burden of proof lies with the individual submitting a claim. Demonstrating that the particular situation of an asylum seeker falls within the conditions of Article 1A of the Refugee Convention is an arduous endeavor even for a person with a legal background. It follows that access to state territory also means access to legal aid and real chances for asylum seekers to prove their asylum claims.[565]

Equally important is the availability of an interpreter. Preliminary interviews at state borders and in international zones might not include an interpreter, which makes it impossible for asylum seekers to communicate their stories. Consequently, there is a clear connection between the prohibition on *refoulement* and access to state territory. Access to state territory means access to the fair and efficient procedure for determining if an asylum seeker needs protection.[566]

Therefore, the practices applied by states to block potential access to their territory are in violation of the prohibition of *refoulement*. Interception of asylum seekers on the high seas is an example of such a practice. Similarly, asylum-seekers rescued at sea and stowaway asylum-seekers are vulnerable groups, since states do not allow them to enter their territory and to submit applications for asylum.[567]

The United States' practice of returning asylum seekers from Haiti is a notorious example of denying access to state territory. It is also an example of how states can exercise extraterritorial jurisdiction and, after that, claim that they are not responsible for the actions of their officials committed outside national borders. In the *Sale v. Haitian Centers Council* decision, the majority of the

---

564 Sir Elihu Lauterpacht and Daniel Bethlehem, T*he scope, and content of the principle of nonrefoulement: Opinion*, at 112, *available at* http://www.unhcr.org/publ/.

565 Stoyanova, *supra* note 682, at 5-6.

566 Stoyanova, *supra* note 682, at 6; Paul Weis, The Refugee Convention, 1951: The Travaux Preparatoires Analyzed with a Commentary by Dr. Paul Weis 342 (Cambridge University Press, 1995).

567 Stoyanova, *supra* note 682, at 6.

USA Supreme Court held that United Nations Protocol Relating to the Status of Refugees does not apply to actions taken by the Coast Guard on the high seas. Accordingly, in the opinion of the majority, the *nonrefoulement* principle embodied in Article 33(1) from the Refugee Convention is inapplicable outside USA borders.[568]

The idea that states are not responsible for human rights violations committed by their agents in so-called international zones is unacceptable. Article 2(1) of the International Covenant on Civil and Political Rights stipulates, "Each State Party to the present Covenant undertakes to respect and to ensure to all individuals *within its territory and subject to its jurisdictio*n the rights recognized in the present Covenant..." The United Nations Human Rights Committee has stated that the phrase "within its territory and subject to its jurisdiction" refer not to the place, but to the connection between the individual and the state. States should respect the rights of all individuals under their effective control, even if they are not in the states' territory. A narrow interpretation of Article 33(1) of the Refugee Convention allows the return of asylum seekers to persecution with the justification that they have not set foot on state territory and accordingly states do not have any obligations regarding them. However, such interpretation is unacceptable since it is inconsistent with the objectives of the Refugee Convention.[569]

Intercepted asylum seekers could turn into people in distress at sea. In this case, the issue that arises is which states are responsible for the rescued asylum seekers. International refugee law and international maritime law are both relevant when examining the problem. Many questions need to be answered, like those that deal with the obligations of the coastal state and with the ship that rescued the asylum seekers. The duty to render assistance to persons in distress at sea is established in both international treaties and customary law. However, the case of rescued asylum seekers constitutes a problem for the following reasons—the asylum seekers do not want to go back to their countries of origin and at the same time no other state is obliged to accept them in its territory. Asylum seekers in distress on the high seas have to be rescued; however, it is not clear who should take responsibility for them after their rescue. No state is required to accept them. It is also not clear which state is responsible for reviewing their

---

568 Stoyanova, *supra* note 682, at 6; Alice Edwards, *Human Rights, Refugees, and the Right to Enjoy Asylum*, 17 Int'l J. Refugee L. 302 (2005).

569 Stoyanova, *supra* note 682, at 6-7.

applications for asylum: without procedure aimed at identifying the refugees, the observance of *nonrefoulement* cannot be ensured.[570]

The incident of the Norwegian ship *Tampa* and Australia's unwillingness to accept asylum seekers on its territory illustrates how asylum seekers rescued at sea fall into a legal limbo. After rescuing asylum seekers in distress at sea, *Tampa* was not allowed to enter Australian territorial waters and port. The position of Australia was that Tampa carried individuals, who intended to enter Australia illegally, which is a breach of the conditions for admission.[571] Consequently, closure of the Australian harbor was necessary for the prevention of the entrance of illegal immigrants.[572]

"Further, the international maritime law entitles coastal states to demand that a ship, which carries illegal immigrants, should leave their territorial waters. It could be concluded that current maritime law does not take into consideration the problem of asylum seekers."[573]

However, an issue that should be raised is whether the individuals saved by *Tampa* could be labeled as illegal immigrants. Australia cannot define them as illegal immigrants since it has not conducted refugee status determination procedures. From the perspective of international refugee law, it has to be mentioned that no provision explicitly indicates where the obligation for reviewing the asylum application arises.[574] In respect to the *Tampa* case, it should be emphasized that the ship entered Australian territorial waters, in which Australia has full sovereign rights. The asylum-seekers expressed their desire to submit applications for asylum and to seek protection in Australia. Accordingly, by denying review of their asylum applications, Australia exposed them to potential *refoulement*.[575]

International human rights law does not contain specific binding rules concerning stowaway asylum-seekers. An international convention—the Brussels

---

570 Stoyanova, *supra* note 682, at 7-8; Joan Fitzpatrick, *Revitalizing the 1951 Refugee Convention*, 9 Harv. Hum. Rts. J.229, 232 (1996). 2008-2009] The Principle of Non-Refoulement.

571 The Office of the United Nations High Commissioner for Refugees, *The State of World's Refugees Human Displacement in the New Millennium* (2006), at 41.

572 Stoyanova, *supra* note 682, at 8.

573 Stoyanova, *supra* note 682, at 8.

574 Richard Plender and Nuala Mole, *Beyond the Geneva Convention: Construction a de facto Right to Asylum from International Human Rights Instruments*, in Refugee Rights And Realities 86 (Cambridge University Press, 1999).

575 Stoyanova, *supra* note 682, at 8-9.

Convention—relating to stowaways was adopted in 1957, but it has not yet entered into force due to the absence of a sufficient number of ratifications by states. Article 1 of the Brussels Convention defines a stowaway "as a person who, at any port or place in the vicinity thereof, secretes himself in a ship without the consent of the ship owner or the Master or any other person in charge of the ship and who is on board after the vessel has left that port or place." If a stowaway is found on board, the Master may deliver him to the appropriate authority at the first port in a state party to the convention at which the ship calls after the stowaway is found. The state of the first port of disembarkation only temporarily accepts the stowaway. That state may return the stowaway to his or her country of nationality, to the state where his or her port of embarkation is considered to be situated, or to the state in which the last port at which the ship called prior to his or her being found is situated.[576]

The Brussels Convention does not provide an adequate solution to the problem of stowaway asylum-seekers. The possibility for chain transferring equates to a lack of any responsibility on the part of a state for conducting a refugee status determination procedure. The process of the transfer itself could even amount to inhumane and degrading treatment. If the problem is approached from the international maritime law perspective, it should be pointed out that once a ship enters the port of a coastal state, that state is then entitled to exercise full immigration control.[577] Further, Article 24 of the Convention on the Territorial Sea and the Contiguous Zone stipulates that "in a zone of the high seas contiguous to its territorial sea, the coastal state may exercise the control necessary to prevent infringement of its customs, fiscal, *immigration*, or sanitary regulations within its territory or territorial sea." Hence, not only in the port and in the territorial sea but also in the zone contiguous to the territorial sea, coastal states have jurisdiction. Accordingly, from the international refugee law perspective, once a stowaway is found on board, and once the ship enters the contiguous zone of a coastal state, the stowaway asylum-seeker is within the jurisdiction of that coastal state.[578]

---

576 Stoyanova, *supra* note 682, at 9; Joan Fitzpatrick, *Revitalizing the 1951 Refugee Convention*, 9 Harv. Hum. Rts. J. 229, 232 (1996).

577 International Organization for Migration, Carrier Responsibilities, *available at* http://www.iom.int/jahia/Jahia/pid/604.

578 Stoyanova, *supra* note 682, at 9-10; Seminar *Non-Refoulement Under Threat*, THE REDRESS TRUST&THE IMMIGR. LAW PRACTITIONERS' ASS'N (May 16, 2006), http://www.redress.org/downloads/publications/Non-refoulementUnderThreat.pdf

Immigration laws of coastal states require that shipmasters notify the authorities of the presence of stowaways upon arrival at the port of entry and that stowaways are held on board until they can be presented to the authorities for examination. When coastal states face a situation with stowaway asylum-seekers, they might demand from the shipmaster to hold the stowaways on board. The coastal state could require that the flag state takes responsibility for the stowaways if the next port of disembarkation is not an acceptable option. Allowing disembarkation under the condition of subsequent resettlement is another possible alternative.[579] The immigration authorities of the coastal state could intercept the ship, and officials could embark to determine if the stowaways are "genuine" asylum seekers. Subsequently, some form of a refugee status determination procedure could be initiated. However, such a practice is very challenging.[580]

It is difficult to imagine how an asylum seeker, who is scared and exhausted by the long journey, with barely any knowledge of the foreign language, could reveal his/her reasons for fleeing his/her country of origin. The absence of an interpreter constitutes another problem. The interviews at ships are not real refugee status determination interviews; they are a preliminary procedure, on whose basis immigration officials make an assessment whether to allow asylum seekers to disembark the ship in order to submit applications for asylum. Initial interviews at ships are of paramount significance since asylum seekers will not have the chance to submit an application for asylum if they are not allowed to disembark.[581] A possible solution to the problem of stowaway asylum-seekers, which would guarantee them access to international protection, could be the following: the state, at whose port the ship first calls (after stowaways are found on board by the shipmaster) should accept them on its territory and that state is then responsible for the conduction of a refugee status determination procedure. If it transpires that the state at whose port the ship first calls after stowaways are found is not an acceptable destination, then the state whose flag the ship flies should take appropriate measures to ensure that the stowaway asylum-seekers

---

579 Stoyanova, *supra* note 682, at 10.

580 Stoyanova, *supra* note 682, at 10.

581 Francesco Messineo, "Non-Refoulement Obligations in Public International Law: Towards a New Protection Status?" *Social Science Research Network. April 4, 2011.* http://papers.ssrn.com/sol3/papers.cfm?abstract_id=1802800

are not exposed to *refoulement* and their applications for asylum be reviewed.[582] The overall consideration should be that the asylum applications be reviewed as soon as possible.[583]

3.3. JURISDICTION AND REFUGEES' RIGHTS IN THE PACIFIC

3.3.1. Refugee Tide

Population resettlement is not a new phenomenon in the Pacific Islands region, yet it remains under-studied. There are many reasons for examining cases of population resettlement in the Pacific. There have been relocations on or from numerous islands since the middle of the 19th century, affecting many parts of the region (Lieber, 1977). Population resettlement necessitated by rising sea levels, coastal erosion, economic pressures, resource exploitation or dwindling populations make the study of past cases relevant, if not a necessity, to ensure successful resettlements in future. [584]

Much of the work on resettlement and forced migration in the Pacific has had an anthropological or geographical focus, and more recent study has tended to be almost entirely promulgated by groups or persons associated with the affected population (Sigrah and King, 2001; Niedenthal, 2001). Forced Migration is the term used to describe the event of being pushed or required to relocate from one's current place of residence. Forced migration is best defined as "the process of collective dislocation and/or settlement of people away from their usual habitat by a superior force" (Shami, 2003: 4-5). This superior force can vary from an environmental change to warfare or even development projects (Bates, 2002).[585]

There have been a number of cases of forced migration in the Pacific, most notably since the Second World War (WWII). The two best known are the cases

---

582 Guy Goodwin-Gill, The Refugee In International Law 132.

583 Stoyanova, *supra* note 682, at 10-11.

584 Dominic Collins, *Forced Migration and Resettlement in the Pacific: Development of a Model Addressing the Resettlement of Forced Migrants in the Pacific Islands Region from Analysis of the Banaban and Bikinian Cases*, Univ. of Canterbury 4 (2009), http://ir.canterbury.ac.nz/bitstream/10092/3234/1/thesis_fulltext.pdf [hereinafter Collins, *Forced Migration*].

585 Collins, *Forced Migration*, *supra* note 722, at 4-5.

of the Banabans being moved to Rabi (pronounced "Ram-bee"), and the Bikinians being moved to Kili Island. These cases both involved the forced removal of an entire ethnic group from their homeland and a resettlement elsewhere in order for their islands to be used for other purposes by their respective "colonial" governments. Due to the connection between climate change, sea level rise and future potential for forced migration, it is important to examine past such cases.[586]

Reasons for studying population resettlement in the Pacific Islands are not hard to find. The fact that many ignored this region is justification enough. Low populations, isolation and lack of publicity have resulted in many cases of Pacific island resettlement going practically unreported and. Therefore, those cases have remained largely unexamined by theorists and academics. With the current attention being paid to the threats of water shortages, climate change, and global warming, it is important to assess what can be done to ameliorate the potential dangers to Pacific Island populations. It is also important to assess what can be done if efforts to avoid the catastrophic predictions of low-lying Pacific Islands and atolls become a reality. Assessing past cases gives some guidance as to how to avoid the catastrophic predictions of low-lying Pacific Islands.[587]

In order to assess the phenomena of forced displacement and resettlement in a meaningful and instructive way, this study assesses past cases from the Pacific Islands region to inform future relocations. Using a model based on current theory, the Banaban and Bikinian cases of relocation are studied, focusing on the overall resettlement process, relevant variables, culture and the avoidance of marginalization.

Of all Pacific island states, Tuvalu is the one that currently appears to be the most at risk of needing to resettle its entire population. The coral atolls that make up the tiny nation are being eroded and flooded by encroaching seas. In many areas, sea walls that were erected to protect the islands are regularly breached and act as retaining walls for the salt water. Predictions of increased storm activity and rising sea levels do not look promising for the people of Tuvalu and as a result, many have already resettled on the Fijian Island of Kioa, and many others have plans to relocate. It is as yet uncertain what the official

---

586 Collins, *Forced Migration, supra* note 722, at 5.

587 Collins, *Forced Migration, supra* note 722, at 6; Maxine Burkett, *The Nation Ex-Situ: On Climate Change, Deterritorialized Nationhood and the Post-Climate Era*, 2 Climate Law 345 (2011), *available at* http://iis-db.stanford.edu/evnts/6809/The_Nation_Ex-Situ_Maxine_Burkett.pdf.

stance of the Tokelau administration and New Zealand government will be, but mass emigration to Kioa or New Zealand is likely.[588]

> *"International legal experts are discovering climate change law, and the Pacific island nation of Tuvalu is a case in point: The Polynesian archipelago is condemned to disappear beneath the ocean."*[589]

> *"The photographs of the Tuvaluans are meant to give climate change a human face."*[590]

"The group of islands lies just 10 centimeters (roughly four inches) above sea level; if the average sea level continues to rise, in just 50 years there will be nothing here but waves."[591]

Some of the islands are already uninhabitable; the ocean nibbles at the narrow landmass from all sides. Nine islands totaling just 26 square kilometers (10 square miles) in the area make up the fourth-smallest country in the world. There's hardly any industry, no military, few cars and just eight kilometers of paved roads.[592]

"The majority of the people make their living from fishing and agriculture."[593] "The country is so small that there is only a rough division of labor, with people acting as cooks and captains, ice cream salesmen and politicians."[594]

"Over 3,000 Tuvaluans have already left their homeland."[595] "In the meantime, however, refugees are increasingly knocking on locked doors, particularly in nearby Australia, where immigration has long been an election issue."[596]

---

588 Collins, *Forced Migration, supra* note 722, at 15; Peter King, *Integration of Climate Change into National Planning in Asia-Pacific,* INT'L INST. FOR SUSTAINABLE DEV., 42 (Sept. 1, 2009), *available at* http://www.sdplannet-ap.org/Documents/CC_SDplanNet-Peter.pdf

589 Anwen Roberts, *Islanders Without an Island: What Will Become of Tuvalu's Climate Refugees?,* Spiegel Online (2007), http://www.spiegel.de/international/world/islanders-without-an-island-what-will-become-of-tuvalu-s-climate-refugees-a-505819.html.

590 Roberts, *supra* note 733.

591 Roberts, *supra* note 733.

592 Roberts, *supra* note 733.

593 Roberts, *supra* note 733.

594 Roberts, *supra* note 733.

595 Roberts, *supra* note 733.

596 Roberts, *supra* note 733.

The Tuvalu government has opted, therefore, for political pressure. Since it joined the United Nations in 2000, the island nation has managed to place its concerns high on the organization's agenda. Its efforts seem to have borne fruit: Tuvalu is now regarded as a prime example of just how much damage climate change can do to a country.[597]

"Some experts now believe changes will have to be made to the international law to deal with the impact of climate change."[598] "Tuvalu is not alone—other small island nations like Kiribati, the Marshall Islands, and the Maldives are also concerned about their future."[599]

"Regardless of what happens, the island nation of Tuvalu will, at least, survive its physical demise in the virtual world."[600] "Even today the country's primary source of income is from selling the rights to its national '.tv.' internet domain."[601]

So, where can climate refugees from submerged states go to seek justice? The Pacific Islands have been brought together under the AOSIS, an umbrella group seeking to link the effects of global warming and human rights. Led by the Maldives, the cause has been brought to the United Nations Human Rights Council. It has been challenging to persuade delegations to ask the High Commissioner for Human Rights to commission an impact study. Many countries resisted, including the US and Australia. Other countries like New Zealand only wished to accept 75 Tuvalu migrants a year.[602]

Specialists have predicted that in the next 40 years, climate change could produce eight million refugees in the Pacific Islands, with 75 million in the Asia-Pacific region alone.[603]

"The Oxfam report points out that 'For countries like Kiribati, Tuvalu, Tokelau, the Marshall Islands, Fiji, Vanuatu, Papua New Guinea and the Federated States of Micronesia climate change is not something that could happen in the future

---

597 Roberts, *supra* note 733;

598 Roberts, *supra* note 733.

599 Roberts, *supra* note 733.

600 Roberts, *supra* note 733.

601 Roberts, *supra* note 733.

602 Armanios, *supra* note 748.

603 *Climate Change: 75 Million Environmental Refugees to Plague Asia-Pacific* (Aug. 2005), *available at:* http://prodip.wordpress.com/tag/climate-change/.

but something they are experiencing now.'"[604] "The report documents how people are coping with more frequent flooding and storm surges, losing land and being forced from their homes, facing increased food and water shortages, and dealing with rising incidence of malaria and dengue."[605]

The Oxfam report argues that unless developed countries take urgent action to curb emissions, some Pacific island nations face the very real threat of becoming uninhabitable. The report calls on Australia—one of the biggest polluters in the world—and New Zealand to reduce carbon emissions by 40 percent by 2020 and by 95 percent by 2050.[606] It also urged the two governments to contribute more money toward helping these island nations adapt to climate change.[607]

3.3.2. Pacific Refugees' categorical definitions

3.3.2.i. Climate Change Refugees: the time for recognition

In 2007, the International Organisation for Migration (IOM) proposed the following definition for environmental migrants:[608]

> *"Environmental migrants are persons or groups of persons who, for compelling reasons of sudden or progressive changes in the environment that adversely affect their lives or living conditions, are obliged to leave their habitual homes, or choose to do so, either temporarily or permanently, and who move either within their country or abroad."*

While IOM proposed the definition above, there is no universally accepted definition of "environmental migration" yet. IOM attempted to encompass the

---

604 Neena Bhandari, *Climate Change: 75 Million Environmental Refugees to Plague Asia-Pacific* (Aug. 3, 2009), http://www.ipsnews.net/2009/08/climate-change-75-million-environmental-refugees-to-plague-asia-pacific/; http://www.oxfam.org/en/about/annual-reports

605 Bhandari, *supra* note754.

606 http://policy-practice.oxfam.org.uk/publications/growing-a-better-future-food-justice-in-a-resource-constrained-world-132373

607 Bhandari, *supra* note754.

608 Migrations, Environment and Climate Change: Assessing the Evidence IOM Report 2009
http://publications.iom.int/system/files/pdf/migration_and_environment.pdf

complexity of the topic, suggesting that there are three types of environmental migrants:

- Environmental emergency migrants: people who flee temporarily due to an environmental disaster or sudden environmental event (e.g. someone forced to leave due to a hurricane, a tsunami, or an earthquake)

- Environmental forced migrants: people who have to leave due to deteriorating environmental conditions (e.g. someone forced to leave due to deterioration of their environment, such as deforestation, coastal degradation, etc.)

- Environmental motivated migrants also known as environmentally induced economic migrants: people who choose to leave to avoid possible future problems (e.g. someone who leaves due to declining crop productivity caused by desertification)

Much of the literature produced in the context of "environmental migration" assumes the nexus to be self-evident. However, there is no evidence that the concept can be used to achieve generalizable truths. In brief, this is because the degree to which any given environmental factor is meaningful at the societal level—let alone to any specific aspect of human activity, such as migration—is entirely conditional on socio-economic and political contingencies."[609]

There has been little work that has bolstered the conceptual integrity of the concept. The concept lacks an agreed definition, and as a consequence also lacks clear-cut evidence. Predictive models have therefore proved elusive, despite high-profile "scoping studies," leading to a wide range of estimates, such as that conducted by the European Commission-funded EACH-FOR project. Research[610] Conducted in areas of "environmental degradation," which attempted to demonstrate a statistically significant correlation between migration and environmental degradation (including climate change) have so far lacked falsifiability and

---

609 Afifi, T., Warner, K. 2007 *The Impact of Environmental Degradation on Migration Flows across Countries* UNU-EHS working paper no. 3. Bonn.

610 Karen McNamarma, *Conceptualizing Discourses on Environmental Refugees at the United Nations*, 29 POPULATION AND ENVIRONMENT 14 (2007).

have been marked by an absence of false evidence that has made it impossible to draw any generalizable conclusions from the findings.

In 2010 and 2011, according to the Internal Displacement Monitoring Centre, more than 42 million people were displaced in Asia and the Pacific. That number makes up more than twice the population of Sri Lanka. This figure includes those displaced by storms, floods, and heat and cold waves. Still others were displaced drought and sea-level rise. Most of those compelled to leave their homes eventually returned when conditions improved, but an undetermined number became migrants, usually within their country, but also across national borders.[611]

Climate-induced migration is a highly complex issue that needs to be understood as part of global migration dynamics. Migration typically has multiple causes, and environmental factors are intertwined with other social and economic factors, which themselves can be influenced by environmental changes. Environmental mobility should not be treated solely as a discrete category, set apart from other migration flows. A 2012 Asian Development Bank study argues that climate-induced migration should be addressed as part of a country's development agenda, given the significant implications of migration on economic and social development. The report recommends interventions both to address the situation of those who have migrated, as well as those who remain in areas subject to environmental risk. It says: "To reduce migration compelled by worsening environmental conditions, and to strengthen resilience of at-risk communities, governments should adopt policies and commit financing to social protection, livelihoods development, basic urban infrastructure development, and disaster risk management."[612]

Additionally, it is maintained that the poor populate areas that are most at risk for environmental destruction and climate change, including coastlines, flood lines and steep slopes. As a result, climate change threatens areas already suffering from extreme poverty. "The issue of equity is crucial. Climate affects us all, but does not affect us all equally," United Nations Secretary-General Ban Ki-moon told delegates at a climate conference in Indonesia. Africa is also one

---

611 Afifi, T., Warner, K. 2007 *The Impact of Environmental Degradation on Migration Flows across Countries* UNU-EHS working paper no. 3. Bonn.

612 Addressing Climate Change Migration in Asia and the Pacific, ASIAN DEVELOPMENT BANK viii (2012), http://reliefweb.int/sites/reliefweb.int/files/resources/addressing-climate-change-migration_0.pdf.

of the world regions where environmental displacement is critical largely due to due to droughts and other climate-related eventualities.[613]

The International Organization for Migration (IOM) expects the scale of global migration to rise as a result of accelerated climate change.[614] IOM recommends policymakers to take a proactive stance on the matter.[615] The IOM is composed of 146 member states and 13 observer states and "works closely with governments in promoting migration management that ensures humane and orderly migration that is beneficial to migrants and societies."[616] Additionally, when interviewing Oliver-Smith, an anthropologist and member of the United Nations group, National Geographic Magazine noted that "there are at least 20 million environmental refugees worldwide, the [United Nations] group says more than those displaced by war and political repression combined." Therefore, it is imperative that we begin to recognize this recent division of refugees.[617]

The Environmental Justice Foundation (EJF) has argued that the people who will be forced to move due to climate change currently have no adequate recognition in international law.[618] The EJF contends that a new multilateral legal instrument is required to specifically address the needs of "climate refugees" to confer protection to those fleeing environmental degradation and climate change.[619] They have also asserted that additional funding is needed to enable developing countries to adapt to climate change. Sujatha Byravan and Sudhir Chella Rajan have argued for the use of the term "climate exiles" and for international agreements to provide them political and legal rights, including citizen-

613 Susana Adamo & Alexander de Sherbinin, *The Impact of Climate Change on the Spatial Distribution of Populations and Migration, in* POPULATION DISTRIBUTION, URBANIZATION, INTERNAL MIGRATION AND DEVELOPMENT: AN INTERNATIONAL PERSPECTIVE (2011),

http://www.un.org/esa/population/publications/PopDistribUrbanization/PopulationDistributionUrbanization.pdf.

614 International Organization for Migration's Perspective on Migration and Climate Change.

615 International Organization for Migration: Key Principles for Policy Making on Migration, Climate Change & the Environmental Degradation.

616 International Organization for Migration: Key Principles for Policy Making on Migration, Climate Change & the Environmental Degradation.

617 Stefan Lovgren, *Climate Change Creating Millions of "Eco Refugees, United Nations Warns*, NATIONAL GEOGRAPHIC NEWS (Oct. 18 2005), http://news.nationalgeographic.com/

618 No place like home— Where next for climate refugees?, The Environmental Justice Foundation, 2009 http://ejfoundation.org/sites/default/files/public/no%20place%20like%20home.pdf

619 "Global warming could create 150 million climate refugees by 2050" John Vidal, The Guardian, 3rd November 2009.

ship in other countries, bearing in mind those countries' responsibilities and capabilities.[620]

In some cases, climate change may lead to conflict arising between countries that as a result of flooding or other conditions produce a large number of refugees and bordering countries that build fences to keep out these refugees. The Bangladesh-India border is widely separated via a fence, and case studies suggest the possibility of violent conflict arising due to people fleeing from areas suffering from the destruction of arable land. Current migration has already resulted in low-scale conflicts.[621]

Despite concerns regarding its capacity to say anything meaningful about the complex relationship between environmental drivers and human migration, the notion of "environmental migrant," and particularly "climate refugee," has gained traction in popular culture. A documentary entitled *Climate Refugees* has been released in 2010, which engages uncritically with the neo-Malthusian understandings of the climate change migration nexus.[622] More recently, Short Documentary Academy Award Nominee, Sun Come Up (2011), tells the story of Carteret islanders who are forced to leave their ancestral land in response to climate change and migrate to war-torn Bougainville.[623] Since 2007, German artist Hermann Josef Hack has shown his World Climate Refugee Camp in the centers of various European cities. The model camp, made of roughly 1,000 miniature tents, is a public art intervention that depicts the social impacts of climate change.

---

620 "Before the Flood" Sujatha Byravan and Sudhir Chella Rajan, The New York Times, May 9, 2005.

621 Litchfield, William Alex. "Climate Change Induced Extreme Weather Events & Sea Level Rise in Bangladesh leading to Migration and Conflict". *American University*. ICE Case Studies. Retrieved 19 June 2011.

622 Sun Come Up: Home." Sun Come Up. N.p., n.d. Web. 13 Mar. 2012. <http://www.suncomeup.com/film/Home

623 Climate Refugees at Sundance Film Festival 2010.

3.3.2.ii. Economic Refugees

An *economic refugee* is someone person whose economic prospects have been ruined and who strives to escape oppressive poverty in his or her country of origin. Many such economic refugees are coming from third world countries.[624]

The first economic refugees were in the Carteret Islands. "The Carteret Islands (also known as Carteret Atoll, Tulun or Kilinailau Islands/Atoll) are Papua New Guinea islands located 86 km (53 mi) north-east of Bougainville in the South Pacific."[625] These islands were named after the British navigator Philip Carteret, who was the first European to discover them, arriving in the sloop *Swallow in 1767. As of 2012, about 2600 people live on the islands.*[626]

Since about 1000 years before European contact in 1880, locals have been engaged in cultivating taro and coconut and have been fishing. The population grew rapidly in the early 1900s, which caused overcrowding in the 1930s and hence, a population decline.[627] Since the 1960's, food shortages caused by international commercial fishers contributed to the resettlement of some islanders to the Kuveria area of Bougainville from 1984 through the late 1980s.[628] In the 1990s, the people living on the islands were classified as economic refugees.[629]

3.3.3. International migration impact

"Policies of migrant-receiving countries vary significantly, with the triangle of policies framed by Singapore's skilled vs. low-skilled employees rotation scheme, Japan's mostly closed doors to low-skilled foreign workers, and the

---

624 What Are Economic Refugees?, FLICKR (July 6, 2012),

http://www.flickr.com/groups/global_photojournalism_news_protest_and_culture/discuss/72157630448657748/

625 Background Information on the Carteret Islands,

626 "I need a new home, my island has sunk," UNESCO, accessed August 15, 2014, http://www.unesco.org/new/en/rio-20/single-view/news/i_need_a_new_home_my_island_has_sunk/#.Vd10RSlR-gE

627 Morrell, Benjamin (1832). *A Narrative of Four Voyages to the South Sea, North and South Pacific Ocean.* New York: J & J Harper. Retrieved 2008-01-04.

628 Bougainville Province Agricultural System: 02, Subsystem: 01 Page 2" (PDF). MASP Working Papers. Australian National University. Archived from the original on 2007-09-02. Retrieved 2008-01-04.

629 Royle, Stephen A. (2001). A Geography of Islands. Routledge. p. 39.

dependence of Gulf oil exporters on migrants to fill 90 percent of private-sector jobs."[630]

"This economic success may encourage some Asian leaders to believe that they can achieve another success in managing internal and international labor migration to achieve goals that include protecting migrants and local workers, enhancing cooperation between governments in labor-sending and receiving areas to better manage migration, and ensuring that migration promotes development in labor-sending areas."[631] "Second, there is more diversity in national labor migration policies than in national economic policies."[632] "The policy extremes can be approximated by a triangle."[633]

The history of the Pacific is a history of migration. Yet current barriers to migration impede development in the Pacific island countries facing degraded resources, high rates of natural population increase, low-lying geographies and limited opportunities for international movement through citizenship or preferred visa status. This chapter examines international migration in the Pacific, and argues that there should be greater opportunities for the people of Pacific countries to migrate between their home states and the developed states of the Pacific Rim. Creating more permeable borders is an important means of redressing past and current injustices, expanding opportunities for human development and fostering stronger regional relations. Both the United States and New Zealand have been reasonably generous in facilitating migration from Micronesia and Polynesia.[634] Australia stands out as the Pacific neighbor with the greatest possibility to develop new migration streams.[635]

Added to the problems of a poor endowment of resources, the populations of many Pacific countries are growing rapidly, with high rates of natural increase that are tempered only by emigration, where this is possible. Only four Pacific

---

630 Philip Martin, *Migration in the Asia-Pacific Region: Trends, Factors, Impacts*, UNITED NATIONS DEVELOPMENT PROGRAMME 1 (Aug. 2009), http://hdr.undp.org/en/reports/global/hdr2009/papers/HDRP_2009_32.pdf.

631 Martin, *supra* note 794, at 1.

632 Martin, *supra* note 794, at 1.

633 Martin, *supra* note 794, at 1.

634 Moore, E., and J. Smith. 1995. "Climate change and migration from Oceania: implications for Australia, New Zealand and the United States of America." *Population and Environment* 17(2):105–122.

635 Brian Opeskin & Therese MacDermott, *Enhancing Opportunities for Regional Migration in the Pacific*, PACIFIC INST. OF PUBLIC POLICY 1 (2009), http://www.pacificpolicy.org/wp-content/uploads/2012/05/D13-PiPP.pdf.

countries (Cook Islands, Niue, New Caledonia and Palau) have a rate of natural increase that is below the global average of 1.2 percent, and some (notably the Marshall Islands, Solomon Islands and Vanuatu) have rates that are among the highest in the world outside Africa (Population Reference Bureau, 2007). If these rates of natural increase were sustained over the long term, the populations of Solomon Islands, Marshall Islands, and Vanuatu would double in about 27 years, placing a substantial burden on each country's resources and social infrastructure.[636]

International mobility has had a substantial impact on the net population growth of many countries. Generally, in Polynesia migration has been a major check on population growth, resulting in only modest annual growth despite relatively high total fertility rates. In Melanesia, there is effectively zero net migration from the three countries that together account for 75 percent of Pacific peoples (Papua New Guinea, Solomon Islands, and Vanuatu). Finally, in Micronesia, the situation is different, with several countries (Northern Mariana Islands, Federated States of Micronesia and Marshall Islands) sharing the high net emigration experience of many Polynesian countries. Pacific states also face many common environmental challenges with respect to their limited land and marine resources. Two primary concerns are the depletion of natural resources and their degradation due to population pressures and over-exploitation.

Nauru is a telling example of the over-exploitation of a mineral resource. As one of the richest phosphate islands in the Pacific, it attracts the attention of developed states because phosphate is a prized ingredient in commercial fertilizer.[637] Around the year 2000, the primary deposits were substantially exhausted, and mining was ceased. The problems in Nauru extended well beyond the depletion of phosphate rock. The mining left a majority of the land wholly unusable for any other purpose, resulting in "near complete environmental devastation" (Gowdy and McDaniel, 1999: 333). Exhaustion of its most significant natural resource, coupled with gross mismanagement of the income derived from that resource has left Nauru with an uncertain economic future (Connell, 2006). The problems of resource depletion in Pacific countries are not confined to mineral resources. Over-exploitation of inshore marine resources has caused declines in

---

636 Opeskin, *supra* note 801, at 2; Dupont, A., and G. Pearman. 2006. *Heating up the Planet: Climate Change and Security*. Lowy Institute Papers No. 12. Lowy Institute for International Policy: Sydney.

637 Krishnan, V., P. Schaeffel, and J. Warren. 1994. *The Challenge of Change: Pacific Island Communities in New Zealand 1986-1993*.

coastal fish stocks, especially when combined with damaging fishing practices such as dynamiting (Cordonnery, 2003). Offshore waters may also be suffering from stock depletion because the developing states of the Pacific have wholly inadequate resources for surveillance of the licensed or illegal fishing operations conducted by foreign states in their maritime zones (Hanich et al., 2007).[638] Depletion of natural resources has been coupled with the degradation of land and sea resources, which is most pronounced where there are growing numbers of people (Boer, 1995).[639]

There is an emerging consensus among scientists that the world's climate system is warming, as evidenced by increases in average air and ocean temperatures, widespread melting of snow and ice, and rising average sea levels (Intergovernmental Panel on Climate Change, 2007). The principal international instrument regulating climate change—the UNFCCC1992—expressly recognizes that "low-lying and other small island countries...are particularly vulnerable to the adverse effects of climate change."[640] These effects include climate processes (e.g., rising sea levels, coastal erosion, salinization of agricultural land) and climate events (e.g., increased incidence of extreme weather such as tropical cyclones and tidal surges) (Zurick, 1995; Moore and Smith, 1995; Brown, 2008). Atoll states such as Tokelau and Tuvalu will have the distinction of being the first Pacific Island countries to be totally inundated by a sea level rise. A one-meter rise in sea level will submerge 80 percent of the Majuro atoll in the Marshall Islands and 12.5 percent of the landmass in Kiribati (Burns, 2000). Beyond the physical inundation of land, rising sea levels are likely to have a significant impact on the viability of coastal populations because key economic sectors—fishing, tourism, and agriculture—will all be affected (Leane, 2005). By 2050, periodic storm surges in South Tarawa, the most densely populated area in Kiribati, are predicted to cost the country 10–30 percent of annual GDP (Dupont and Pearman, 2006).[641]

Colonialism has left a complicated legacy of legal and political associations in the Pacific. The partitioning of the Pacific between colonial powers created

---

638 G. Leane and B. von Tigerstrom (eds). *International Law Issues in the South Pacific.* Pp 161-197. Ashgate: Aldershot.

639 Opeskin, *supra* note 801, at 2.

640 Moore, E., and J. Smith. 1995. "Climate change and migration from Oceania: implications for Australia, New Zealand and the United States of America." *Population and Environment* 17(2):105–122.

641 Opeskin, *supra* note 801, at 2; www.uneq.org

large administrative units from what had been just small tribal groupings. The new territorial boundaries were seen as a European artifact, much as they were in Africa (Naidu, 2003). Colonization undoubtedly placed significant restrictions on the movement of people between the islands of the Pacific. The same may be said of decolonization, which thrust the notion of the modern state, conceived as a territorially bounded entity, upon the newly independent states of the Pacific (Kratochwil, 1986). Yet in many cases colonialism was accompanied by new rights of citizenship and these selectively expanded, rather than diminished, the prospects of Pacific migration. The experience of Pacific islands has not been uniform in this respect and the position in New Zealand, the United States and France must again be contrasted with that of Australia and the United Kingdom. New Zealand fostered individual relationships with Polynesia. Tokelauans, Cook Islanders, and Niueans were granted New Zealand citizenship in what has been described as "possibly one of the most generous post-colonial arrangements in modern history" (Krishnan et al., 1994).[642]

Under the New Zealand Bill of Rights Act 1990, citizenship confers a right to enter and move freely within New Zealand, and thus to access the labor market, education and other governmental services. The impact has been dramatic. At the time of the 2006 census, there were 265,974 people of Pacific ethnicity living in New Zealand—6.4 percent of the New Zealand population (Statistics New Zealand, 2008). Not all of them are immigrants: Indeed, six out of ten were born in New Zealand. Nevertheless, the impact of a liberal citizenship regime is revealed by the fact that there are 14 times as many Niueans, six times as many Tokelauans, and three times as many Cook Islanders in New Zealand than in their home islands.[643]Australia has been indirectly affected by these policies because New Zealand citizens also have a right of access to Australia under conventional Trans-Tasman travel arrangements, thus facilitating stepwise migration.[644]

The United States has also facilitated migration between its affiliated Pacific islands and the mainland. Residents of the two unincorporated territories (Guam and American Samoa) are United States citizens whose freedom of movement within the United States is constitutionally protected. Likewise, residents of

---

642 Opeskin, *supra* note 801, at 2.

643 Moore, E., and J. Smith. 1995. "Climate change and migration from Oceania: implications for Australia, New Zealand and the United States of America." *Population and Environment* 17(2):105–122.

644 Opeskin, *supra* note 801, at 3.

Northern Mariana Islands are United States citizens under the Covenant of political union. France too adopted a generous attitude towards the citizenship of indigenous people of the Pacific. Under the 1946 Constitution of the French Republic, all inhabitants of French overseas territories were granted French citizenship, with the concomitant right to move freely among the regions, and between the territories and metropolitan France (de Deckker, 1994). In practice, there has been very little migration from French Pacific territories to France. On the contrary, there has been significant net migration to New Caledonia including both "Métros" from France and Polynesians from Wallis and Futuna, who have mostly outgrown the islands' limited resources.[645]

The approach of New Zealand, the United States, and France stands in contrast to the United Kingdom and Australia, which generally gave no automatic citizenship or rights of migration to Pacific populations over which they had exercised colonial authority. For the United Kingdom, citizenship was a political impossibility: not only were its Pacific possessions numerous (including Fiji, Kiribati, Solomon Islands, Tonga, Tuvalu and Vanuatu), but its situation was replicated in colonies in Africa, the Caribbean and the Indian subcontinent. These pragmatic concerns were also right of Australia's relations with Papua New Guinea, which was both proximate and highly populous: at independence in 1975, Papua New Guinea's population was 2.9 million, Australia's 13.6 million.[646]

Australia prides itself on immigration that is "selective, skilled and tightly managed," and designed for nation building rather than alleviating temporary shortages (Millbank, 2006). Pacific islanders are entitled to migrate to Australia only because they satisfy standard immigration criteria or because they are New Zealanders who enjoy the Trans-Tasman concessions. Over the past 20 years, a range of public inquiries in Australia has recommended special migration status for Pacific Islanders for a variety of reasons, including enhancing the effectiveness of overseas aid, safeguarding national security, and improving regional foreign relations (Millbank, 2006). So far these recommendations have not been adopted. Even the 2008 Port Moresby Declaration, proclaiming "a new era of cooperation with the island nations of the Pacific" is notably silent on the migration question. New Zealand has taken a very different approach based on a self-acknowledged "special relationship" with Pacific island states, especially

---

645 Opeskin, *supra* note 801, at 3.

646 Opeskin, *supra* note 801, at 3; Rumley, D., V. Forbes and C. Griffin (eds). 2006. Australia's Arc of Instability: The Political and Cultural Dynamics of Regional Security.

in Polynesia (Bedford et al., 2007).[647]In addition to granting citizenship to residents of the Cook Islands, Niue, and Tokelau, a number of other Pacific island countries have "preferential visa" access to New Zealand. Following the Treaty of Friendship that accompanied the independence of Samoa from New Zealand in 1962, in 2002, New Zealand established a new visa class—the Pacific Access Category (PAC)—for other Pacific countries with which New Zealand had close cultural and historical ties. The annual quota of 400 places[648] is currently allocated between Tonga (250), Tuvalu (75) and Kiribati (75). From 2003, Fiji was also included in the scheme with an annual allocation of 250 places, but participation was suspended following the 2006 coup.[649]

The Pacific has a long history of migration of unskilled laborers to fill the needs of neighboring countries in industries such as agriculture and mining. A recent incarnation is New Zealand's Recognised Seasonal Employer (RSE) scheme, which commenced in April 2007 and replaced country-specific work permit arrangements. The RSE scheme allows up to 8,000 overseas workers to be given limited purpose visas each year to work in New Zealand's horticulture and viticulture industries for up to nine months. In August 2008, the Australian government announced a similar pilot seasonal worker scheme. The proposal is to allow up to 2,500 seasonal workers (from Kiribati, Vanuatu, Tonga and Papua New Guinea) into Australia over a three-year period to work for up to seven months each year in the horticulture industry. To date, the scheme has made only a modest start.[650]

Migration from Pacific Islands to the Pacific Rim can be a powerful tool for promoting human development in the region. A recent report of the United Nations Development Programme documents substantial evidence that human mobility is strongly linked to, and has the potential to significantly reduce, spatial and national differences in well-being. Conversely, restrictions on human movement appear to be strongly related to disparities in human development (UNDP 2009: 7). The gains from migration come not only in the form of higher incomes but in better health, education, and empowerment, and are greatest for

---

647 Ware, H. 2005. "Demography, migration and conflict in the Pacific" Journal of Peace Research 42:435–454.

648 Statistics New Zealand. 2008. QuickStats about Pacific People. http:// www.stats.govt.nz

649 Opeskin, *supra* note 801, at 3.

650 Opeskin, *supra* note 801, at 2; Adams, Richard and John Page. 2005. Do International Migration and Remittances Reduce Poverty in Developing Countries? World Development Vol. 33. 1645-1669. October 2005.

those who move from the poorest to the wealthiest countries. On what basis should developed states of the Pacific Rim accept the notion that responsibility for further migration is theirs given the sizeable international community that now numbers more than 190 states? First, there are circumstances in which states owe obligations to correct injustices that arise from past or present wrongs. Colonial exploitation (phosphate mining, forced labor) and environmentally degrading practices (nuclear testing, excessive GHG emissions) are pertinent Pacific examples. Second, obligations of humanity and distributive justice provide an ethical foundation for giving international development assistance to alleviate human suffering and poverty (Opeskin, 1996).[651]

The United States, New Zealand, Australia and France fall far short of meeting the United Nations target of giving 0.7 percent of annual national income in official foreign aid. Yet labor migration can provide an effective alternative means of assisting Pacific peoples to develop sustainable livelihoods.[652] A third consideration underpinning the desirability of greater Pacific mobility is the self-interest of developed states. Demographic data support the view that migration has provided a safety valve for "social and economic discontents" in some Pacific microstates (Ware, 2005: 451). This has reduced the potential for internal conflict in Polynesia, where persistent high rates of natural population increase would otherwise have resulted in a "youth bulge," with few economic prospects, competing for limited resources. But the emigration safety valve has not been available uniformly across the Pacific.[653] In Melanesia, where there are very limited rights of access to neighboring developed states, political instability has been common, giving rise to the region's soubriquet as the "arc of instability" (Rumley et al., 2006).[654]

The arguments for more permeable borders do not affect all Pacific countries equally. The greatest priority should be to enhance labor mobility for countries facing a combination of ills that makes their circumstances especially challenging. Kiribati, Tuvalu, and Nauru have a particular need for a migration safety value. Melanesian countries are also deserving of heightened opportunities: their resource limitations are less severe, but they have large populations with very high rates of population growth and a near complete absence of other

---

651 Opeskin, *supra* note 801, at 3-4.

652 Borjas, George J. 1994. The Economics of Immigration. Journal of Economic Literature 32.

653 Idem.

654 Opeskin, *supra* note 801, at 4.

migration channels. Nor do the arguments for more permeable borders affect all Pacific Rim countries equally. Both New Zealand and the United States have been reasonably generous in granting citizenship or preferential visa status to countries within Polynesia and Micronesia, respectively.

More can still be done to extend the scope of their Pacific migration policies. New Zealand has commenced this process by including many Micronesian and Melanesian countries in its seasonal employment scheme.[655] It is Australia that stands out as the Pacific neighbor with the greatest capacity to develop new migration streams that recognize Australia's history as a colonizing power, its self-interest in promoting regional security, and the particular needs of some Pacific island countries. The seasonal worker scheme announced in 2008 takes a small but valuable step along this path. Finally, it would be naïve to suggest that all problems faced by Pacific countries can be addressed by opening the borders of neighboring states. Migration is one avenue for improving the position of Pacific Islanders, but must be considered alongside other policy initiatives.[656]

Most Asia-Pacific governments sending workers abroad have agencies charged with protecting migrants during recruitment and responding to those in need elsewhere. The effectiveness of these organizations is often a subject of dispute between local NGOs and governments, with NGOs often critical of government migrant-protection efforts, especially in migrant-sending countries such as Bangladesh and Indonesia. Piper (2007) argues that NGOs must pressure government agencies to fulfill their mandates.[657]

In some migrant-receiving countries in the Asia-Pacific region, migrants have formed organizations to protect their interests, notably Filipino domestic helpers in Hong Kong. However, in most Asia- Pacific countries, there are restrictions on the ability of foreign migrants to form advocacy organizations, so that NGOs led by citizens often take the lead in protecting migrants. These organizations are sometimes pressured by host-country governments.[658]

It should be noted that many residents of migrant-receiving countries in the Asia-Pacific region do not favor equal rights for migrants and want their

---

655 Borjas, George. 2003. The Labor Demand Curve is Downward Sloping. Quarterly Journal of Economics.

656 Opeskin, *supra* note 801, at 4.

657 Martin, *supra* note 794, at 63.

658 Martin, *supra* note 794, at 63; Abella, Manolo. 1995. Asian Migrant and Contract Workers in the Middle East in Cohen, Robin, Ed. Cambridge Survey of World Migrations, Cambridge University Press.

governments to do more to reduce illegal migration.[659]For example, there were competing demonstrations in Seoul, Korea in November 2008, as migrants and their allies denounced the raids mounted by the government to locate unauthorized foreigners while several Korean civic groups called for more government action against unauthorized migrants.[660]

There is less evidence of activism involving returned migrants. We found no political parties or other collective entities representing returned migrants that press for fundamental changes in government migration, economic or other policies in the major migrant-sending countries. For example, Filipino domestic helpers in Hong Kong are among the best-organized migrants abroad, and the organizations representing them have been very active in demanding changes in laws and regulations in both Hong Kong and the Philippines that affect women while they are migrants. Migrants settled abroad sometimes continue to participate in political affairs at home, which can speed or slow development and political change. One of the examples of a Diaspora accelerating political change at home involved the support of Filipino migrants for the removal of Ferdinand Marcos. Corazon Aquino, who replaced Marcos in 1986 as president, traveled to San Francisco soon after her inauguration and thanked Filipino-Americans for their contributions to the struggle for democracy.[661] The Philippines has established a relatively complex system of incentives for its Diaspora to remain engaged in the Philippine economy and society but does not have systems in place to evaluate their effectiveness.[662]

New Zealand and Australia have launched guest worker programs with Pacific island countries to fill seasonal farm jobs and to jump-start development in rural areas of small island economies. Under NZ's Recognized Seasonal Employers (RSE) scheme and Australia's Pacific Seasonal Workers Pilot (PSWP) scheme, poor residents of island nations are to be selected by employers or local governments to work seasonally in farm jobs, and government ministries devoted to development assistance are involved with labor and migration

---

659 An oft-cited example involves Irene Fernandez, director of the Malaysian migrant rights organization Tenaganita (www.tenaganita.net). Fernandez published a memo in 1995 on Abuse, Torture and Dehumanized Conditions of Migrant Workers in Detention Centers, charging that the Malaysian government did not protect unauthorized migrants while they were being detained before removal.

660 Martin, *supra* note 794, at 64.

661 Abella, Manolo, Philip Martin, and Elizabeth Midgley. 2004. Best Practices to Manage Migration: The Philippines. March. Mimeo.

662 Martin, *supra* note 794, at 64-65.

departments in program administration. The programs are too new to evaluate their development impacts but are significant for aiming to achieve the win-win-win outcomes sought by the GFMD. The New Zealand government on April 30, 2007, launched the Recognized Seasonal Employers (RSE) scheme to admit workers from Pacific islands to fill seasonal farm jobs. The RSE began with workers from five islands, and was extended to include the Solomon Islands in 2008; up to 8,000 foreign workers can be admitted under the RSE in the year ending 31 March 2009.[663]

"The purpose of the RSE is to fill seasonal jobs in New Zealand and to promote development in the Pacific islands, generating the win-win-win outcomes for migrants, sending- and host-nations fostered by the Global Forum on Migration and Development."[664] "The Pacific islands are inhabited by small populations, have high fertility rates and not many natural resources. On average, women give birth to 3.7 children in Tonga, and over a third of residents are under 15."[665] "Originally, six islands were included—Samoa, Tonga and Tuvalu in Polynesia, Kiribati in Micronesia, and Fiji and Vanuatu in Melanesia."[666] "As part of the sanctions against Fiji after a military coup in December 2006, Fiji was dropped from the list."[667] "New Zealand's immigrant selection system uses points to assess those wanting to migrate for employment; low-skilled workers willing to fill seasonal jobs tend to be excluded."[668]

The New Zealand horticultural industry exports almost half of its NZ$5 billion in annual output with the help of a peak 40,000 seasonal workers in March-April; 60 percent are hired in the Hawke's Bay and Bay of Plenty region.[669] Employers who have been relying on the un- and under-employed, students, and working holidaymakers have been complaining of labor shortages as the horticultural industry expanded amidst a boom that reduced the supply of workers available to fill seasonal jobs. Employers complained of high turnover among too few workers, which led to losses from unpicked crops and

---

663 Martin, *supra* note 794, at 66.

664 Martin, *supra* note 794, at 66; www.gfmd2008.org

665 Martin, *supra* note 794, at 66 n.79.

666 Martin, *supra* note 794, at 66 n.80.

667 Martin, *supra* note 794, at 66 n.80.

668 Martin, *supra* note 794, at 66 n.81.

669 www.hortnz.co.nz/activityareas/seasonalwork.html

discouraged the investment in worker training needed to raise productivity. A 2005-2006 Seasonal Work Permit pilot program allowed visitors in NZ from visa-waiver countries to work up to nine months in areas with government-determined labor shortages.[670]

Under the RSE, New Zealand employers must try and fail to recruit local workers before obtaining permission to hire guest workers from the Pacific Islands, pay half of the cost of a return ticket for Pacific Island migrants, guarantee them work for at least 240 hours and 30 hours a week at the minimum wage of NZ$12.10 (US$7) an hour, and provide them with housing, health insurance and pastoral care, such as transportation for banking and religious services. Guest workers must have passports, health checks, and police clearances and undergo pre-departure orientation before departing for New Zealand, where they can remain up to seven months (nine months from Kiribati and Tuvalu because of higher travel costs).[671]

New Zealand employers can recruit Pacific island workers directly, usually with the help of recruitment agents, or select workers from lists prepared by local governments. For example, the Tongan government used village committees to rank the work-ready men and women who wanted to work in New Zealand by criteria such as honest and hard-working and with some English (Gibson, et al., 2008).[672] About 5,000 of Tonga's 67,000 working-age adults registered to work in New Zealand in 2008, representing 20 percent of Tongan men between 20 and 60.[673]

Tonga had about 117,000 residents in 2007 when there are about 22,000 Tonga-born persons living in New Zealand. McKenzie surveyed Tongans selected by lottery to move to New Zealand between 2002 and 2005 and found that those selected better off, but not their relatives who remained behind in Tonga.[674]

Some 600 Tongans were in New Zealand in March 2008. Most were satisfied, but almost 10 percent left their jobs before the end of their contracts because there was not sufficient work. One reason is that many New Zealand employers

---

670 Martin, *supra* note 794, at 67.

671 Martin, *supra* note 794, at 67.

672 Castles, Stephen and Mark Miller. 2003. The Age of Migration. International Population Movements in the Modern World. Palgrave Macmillan.

673 Martin, *supra* note 794, at 67.

674 Martin, *supra* note 794, at 67 n.82.

are accustomed to hiring working holidaymakers, young people earning money while touring New Zealand, underestimated the productivity of Tongan workers and requested too many, and some of the Tongans who expected to work six days a week left early when work slowed and they were obtaining only three to four days of work a week. There is a significant Tongan community in New Zealand, and if a Tongan seasonal worker does not return by the end of the contract, that village is blacklisted and unable to send seasonal workers to New Zealand in the future.[675]

In Vanuatu, many New Zealand employers used private agents to recruit seasonal workers rather than relying on local government lists (McKenzie, et al., 2008). Most of those who came to New Zealand from Vanuatu were subsistence farmers with less than ten years of schooling who had better-than-average English and more wealth. Thus, first reports suggest that the RSE is targeting the poorest in Tonga more successfully than in Vanuatu. By mid-June 2008, some 5,100 RSE migrants were in New Zealand; almost 75 percent were in the Hawke's Bay and Bay of Plenty areas. The largest employer was approved to hire over 400 RSE migrants, but a third of the 75 farmers requested five or fewer RSE migrants (Ramasamy et al., 2008, 182).[676]

"Evaluations suggest the RSE is successful in filling New Zealand jobs, although there have been complaints of workers incurring living costs when there is no work and some employers setting piece rates so low that workers earn only the minimum wage rather than more."[677] "Piece-rate workers normally earn more than the minimum wage, giving them an incentive to work faster, but some New Zealand employers had to raise piece rates so that RSE workers received, at least, the minimum wage."[678] "The development impacts of the RSE are less clear. In Tonga, workers selected to go to New Zealand under the RSE were from poorer rural households who did not have" a wage.[679] "Tonga has 17 districts, and there were reported, at least, two RSE workers from every Tongan

---

675   Martin, *supra* note 794, at 68; Chalamwong, Yongyuth. 2006. The Economy, Labor Market and International Migration in Thailand, 2005.

676   Martin, *supra* note 794, at 68; www.gfmd-fmmd.org

677   Martin, *supra* note 794, at 68.

678   Martin, *supra* note 794, at 68.

679   Martin, *supra* note 794, at 68.

district; 71 percent from Tongatapu, the island" on "two-thirds of all Tongans" live.[680]

"Air travel costs between Tonga and New Zealand have dropped to a very low price, and some Tongans went home at their own expense when work slowed down returning to New Zealand when there was more work."[681] "In September 2008, the New Zealand government announced that RSE migrants would be able to change employers while in New Zealand."[682] "One survey found that RSE migrants averaged 17 weeks of work in New Zealand and had average net earnings of NZ$5,700 ($3,400) after paying for half of the airfare and their living expenses in New Zealand."[683]

The RSE was launched with the support of the World Bank, which urged Australia and New Zealand to develop temporary worker programs that include having employers and migrants share the cost of recruitment and travel, target selection in sending countries on the low-skilled people, find the balance between a sufficient time abroad for migrants to achieve significant savings but not so long that they settle, and guarantee migrants who are good workers and obey program rules the right to participate in the future.[684]

Australia plans its own Pacific Seasonal Workers Pilot Scheme. The government announced in August 2008 that up to 2,500 guest workers from Kiribati, Tonga, Vanuatu and Papua New Guinea could be employed to pick fruit in Victoria's Swan Hill region and New South Wales' Riverina region for up to seven months a year. As in NZ, farm employers will pay half of the workers' round-trip transportation during the three-year trial. Farmers, who say they need 22,000 more seasonal workers, argue that up to AU$700 million in fruit rots each year for lack of labor to pick it.[685]

"With the PSWP, Australia will have a more diverse seasonal hired farm workforce, including foreign working holidaymakers and students as well as recent immigrants and Australians."[686] "Reports from the Swan Hill area suggest

---

680 Martin, *supra* note 794, at 68 n.83.

681 Martin, *supra* note 794, at 68 n.84.

682 Martin, *supra* note 794, at 69.

683 Martin, *supra* note 794, at 69.

684 Martin, *supra* note 794, at 69.

685 Martin, *supra* note 794, at 69.

686 Martin, *supra* note 794, at 69.

that contractors match many foreign-born workers with jobs and that some take advantage of workers who do not understand their rights."[687] "The minimum wage in the area for farm workers is supposed to be AU$17, but many contractors reportedly pay AU$12 and charge workers for housing and rides to work. Most contractors officially receive a five percent commission from the farms to which they supply workers, but many augment this commission with other charges levied on workers."[688] "Local reports say that larger farms run by investment partnerships are most likely to use reputable contractors."[689]

Almost 135,000 temporary working visas were issued in 2006-2007, along with 250,000 visas to students coming from other countries, (however allowed to work 20 hours per week while schooling). Working holidaymakers are young people in general (18 to 30 years old) from developed countries who work up to 6 months for one employer in Australia (not exceeding 12 months of overall stay, with the possibility to extend for another 12 months only if they work at least 3 months in agriculture or construction in rural areas (regional Australia), which 8,000 did in 2006-2007.[690]

The New Zealand and Australian programs are quite recent in order to assess their development impacts. Sending and receiving governments apparently hope that these programs will provide jobs, savings and potentially investment to Pacific Islands while obtaining seasonal work in countries that need extra labor force during high productive seasons. One concrete outcome of these programs is a reduction in capital transfer costs, which were at least 15 percent of the amount transferred before the programs began. The money transfer costs have been reduced as governments requested bids for banks to offer dual ATM systems. In such a way, deposits made in New Zealand could be withdrawn in Tonga and elsewhere in local currency at low cost.[691]

There are development agencies and nonprofit employer agencies involved in contracting Pacific island workers, which could increase the development impacts of remittances and avoid turning labor contracting into a profit center.

---

687   Martin, *supra* note 794, at 69 n85.

688   Martin, *supra* note 794, at 69 n.85; Hamilton, Bob and John Whalley. 1984. Efficiency and Distributional Implications of Global

Restrictions on Labor Mobility. Journal of Development Economics, 14:61-75.

689   Martin, *supra* note 794, at 69 n.85.

690   Martin, *supra* note 794, at 70.

691   Martin, *supra* note 794, at 70.

Matching remittances that are invested could help to create jobs that lead to private development in migrant areas of origin. The largest New Zealand contractor, Seasonal Solutions Central Otago[692] is an employer coop that can act as an employer of seasonal workers and transfer them from farm to farm, reducing downtime for migrants.[693]

There are also risks. The RSE and PSWP are structured to foster long-term relationships between farm employers and Pacific Island migrants who gain training and experience in seasonal farm work. Newspapers report that some working holidaymakers do not do three months of farm work, and instead, pay farmers to sign a form saying they have worked for the required three months.[694]

Island workers prepare to go abroad. Wages are at least ten times higher in Australia and New Zealand than at home and returned workers may rest and wait for the next opportunity to earn high wages abroad rather than work at home, minimizing development. Finally, families who depend on remittances may reduce work efforts.[695]

Most economic research on the impacts of migrants on labor markets and domestic economies focused on developed countries, in particular, wide receivers such as the US, which has about 20 percent of the world's over 200 million migrants.[696]

In a simple two-factor production function with homogeneous labor and constant returns to scale, adding immigrants reduces wages in the short term (assuming full employment), but there is no change in the long-term return to labor and capital. If labor is "heterogeneous", the arrival of immigrants has long-run distributional consequences, helping complementary workers and hurting those who are substitutes. Studies of the impacts of migrants on receiving-area labor markets began with efforts to compare wage and unemployment rates in cities with more and fewer migrants. The hypothesis was straightforward: if adding more workers via migration puts downward pressure on wages, upward pressure on unemployment rates or both, cities with more migrants should have lower wages or higher unemployment rates, especially for workers most similar

692 www.jobscentral.co.nz

693 Martin, *supra* note 794, at 70.

694 Martin, *supra* note 794, at 70.

695 Martin, *supra* note 794, at 71.

696 Martin, *supra* note 794, at 75; Hugo, Graeme. 2008. Best Practice in Temporary Labor Migration for Development. Prepared for the Global Forum on Migration and Development. Manila.

to the migrants. However, Card's study (1990) which focused on the Miami labor market after the 1980 Mariel boatlift found that the unemployment rate in Miami rose slower between 1979 and 1981 despite the sudden eight percent jump in the labor force. This was examined in comparison to the cities that did not attract additional migrant workers.[697]

Three explanations were offered for the apparent gap between the theory that adding to the supply of labor puts downward pressure on wages and empirical studies that could not find migrant-depressing wage effects. First, migrants are mobile. If they move to cities that are adding jobs, then immigration, employment, and wages can rise together even if, e.g., wages would have risen even faster in the absence of immigration. Second, US workers may move away from migrant cities or not move to them, spreading any adverse effect of migrants on wages throughout the US labor market and making it hard to measure migrant effects in cities with high shares. Third, there may be measurement errors in city comparisons. For example, many of the studies focus on the wages or unemployment rates of Black workers, who in migrant cities may be disproportionately employed by the government, sheltering their wages from immigrant competition.[698]

Borjas (2003) emphasized that adding to the supply of labor puts downward pressure on wages, following traditional comparative statics analysis. Because of US worker mobility, Borjas believes that migrant impacts on local workers must be assessed at the national level rather than in comparisons of cities with more and fewer migrants. Using a three-level CES production function, Borjas grouped workers into four education and eight work experience groups, viz, less than high school, high school graduate, some college, and college graduates, with work experience measured in five-year increments. Borjas estimated that the wages of all US workers fell about 3.4 percent between 1980 and 2000 as a result of immigration in the short run, but only high school dropouts experienced significant wage drops in the long run, down almost five percent, even after capital adjusted to the larger labor force (Borjas and Katz, 2005).[699]

---

697   Martin, supra note 794, at 75; Huguet, Jerrold. 2008. Migration & Development: The global discourse and its implication in the Mekong. Mekong Migration Center. July 15-16.

698   Martin, *supra* note 794, at 76.

699   Martin, *supra* note 794, at 76;

www.ilo.org/global/What_we_do/Publications/ILOBookstore/Orderonline/Books/lang--en/docName--WCMS_PUBL_9221130436_EN/index.htm

Other researchers have extended this approach of grouping workers by their education and work experience to estimate the impacts of migrants on local workers in particular age and experience groups. The first phase of US studies about the effects of migration labor markets involved comparisons of cities with more and fewer migrants, with results that showed there were few negative effects of immigrants on US-born workers. The current phase involves separating the US- and foreign-born workers within education and experience cells and estimating the effects of foreign-born on US-born workers. If US- and foreign-born workers are assumed to be substitutes and if capital is assumed to be fixed, there are signification negative wage effects. However, if foreign-born workers are complements to US-born workers, and if capital is allowed to adjust to the larger labor force, the wages of US-born workers will rise in most education-experience cells, but there are significant drops in immigrant wages as immigrants compete with each other.[700]

Thailand has the problem of managing migrant workers because its economic success enabled internal migrants who once filled low-skill jobs to find better opportunities in Thailand or abroad. Thai employers turned to migrants from Myanmar, Laos and Cambodia to replace previous internal migrants as well as to fill newly created jobs in Thailand's expanding economy. Thailand's migrant worker policies assumed that the need for migrants would be short-lived despite periodic re-registrations of migrants that demonstrated that some occupations, industries, and areas had become structurally dependent on migrants.[701]

The number of international migrants—people living outside their country of citizenship—reached 191 million in 2005, meaning that three percent of the world's people had left their country of birth for a year or more. The number of migrants will probably keep increasing because of demand-pull factors in receiving countries, supply-push factors in sending countries and networks that create communications and transportation infrastructures that allow migrants to learn about opportunities abroad and to take advantage of them. Trying to manage migration by adjusting migrant rights, as when governments make it harder to apply for asylum or restrict migrant access to welfare benefits, can

---

700 Martin, *supra* note 794, at 77.

701 Martin, *supra* note 794, at 78; Martin, Philip L. 2003. Thailand: improving the management of foreign workers. Bangkok: ILO and IOM. www.ilo.org/asia/whatwedo/publications/lang--en/docName--

violate fundamental human rights and encourage smuggling and trafficking in people.[702]

Every one of the world's 200 countries participates in the international migration system as a destination for migrants, a country through which migrants transit, or an area of origin—many participate in all three ways.[703]Martin argues that most migrants do not move far from home, and each of the world's continents has a migration system with unique characteristics, including the large number of unauthorized migrants in the US, the unexpected settlement of guest workers in Europe, and the very high shares contract foreign workers in private sector labor markets of the oil-exporting countries in western Asia.[704]

Human mobility in the Asia-Pacific region is unique in many respects. Firstly, low in numbers compared with other areas of the world (e.g.: Europe, North America), reflecting the fact that most destination countries are not open to immigrants and that in very large states what may be international migration elsewhere is internal migration, as in China.[705] Second, Asian labor receiving countries have very different policies toward low-skill migrants, ranging from Singapore's strict regulation of low-skill migrants considered to be workers while employed in the country to Japan's use of foreign trainees to the Gulf countries' reliance on local sponsorship and contracts to rotate migrants in and out of destination areas. Third, the major labor-sending countries seek to send more skilled migrants to destinations outside Asia in a bid to improve protections and increase remittances.[706]

Migration is usually done in search of better economic opportunities. The higher earnings achieved by most Asian migrants are generally positive for human development, enabling individuals and their families to improve their housing and levels of consumption as well as to invest in the health and education of their children. Women are the majority of migrants leaving many Asian nations, and their foreign earnings often empower them in traditional rural

---

702 Martin, *supra* note 794, at 82.

703 Massey, Douglas S., Joaquin Arango, Graeme Hugo, Ali Kouaouci, Adela Pellegrino, and J. Edward Taylor. 1998. Worlds in Motion: Understanding International Migration at the End of the Millennium. New York. Oxford University Press.

704 Martin, *supra* note 794, at 82.

705 Stark, Oded and J. Edward Taylor. 1989. Relative Deprivation and International Migration. Demography Vol 26. pp1-14.

706 Martin, *supra* note 794, at 83; Sussangkarn, Chalongphob. 1996. Macroeconomic Impacts of Migrant Workers: Analyzes with a CGE Model.

societies. However, returned migrants rarely form political organizations that advocate changes that may make migration unnecessary in the future. Instead, movement acts more often as a safety valve in labor-sending countries.[707]

This means that destination governments that acknowledge migrants are likely to continue to be employed in the medium term and create mechanisms to involve the social partners in the development of a transparent migrant worker policy and promote cooperation with migrant countries of origin are most likely to reap the benefits of migration while protecting the rights of migrants and local workers. In labor-sending countries, governments that aim to protect their nationals during recruitment and while abroad from unscrupulous agents and employers, and cooperate to reduce the cost of remittances, can help to maximize the human development impacts of the window of opportunity opened by migration.[708]

---

707 Martin, *supra* note 794, at 83.

708 Martin, *supra* note 794, at 83-84.

CHAPTER FOUR

THE HUMAN RIGHTS PERSPECTIVE

4.1. INTERNATIONAL HUMAN RIGHTS LAW

4.1.1. Human Security

Human security is an emerging paradigm for understanding global vulnerabilities, one that goes against the traditional definition of national security by focusing on the concept of security as it relates to the individual rather than the state. This paradigm considers that human security is crucial for national, regional and global stability.

According to James Ohwofasa Akpeninor, this paradigm "emerged from a post-cold war, multidisciplinary understanding of security involving a number of research fields, including development studies, international relations, strategic studies and human rights."[709] The United Nations Development Programme's 1994 Human Development Report[710] Is considered a milestone publication in the field of human security, with its argument that ensuring "freedom from want" and "freedom from fear" for all persons is the best path to tackle the problem of global insecurity.

The emergence of the human security concept occurred at the end of the cold war. The rapid pace of globalization, the reduced threat of nuclear war between the superpowers, the rise of global democracy and international human

---

709 James O. A. (2013). *Modern concepts of security.* Bloomington, IN: AuthorHouse

710 United Nations Development Programme (1994): Human Development Report.

rights allowed for concepts of "development" and "security" to be reconsidered. According to the UNDP's 1994 Human Development Report, the scope of global security should be expanded to include economic, food, health, environmental, personal, community and political security.

Economic security requires an assured basic income for individuals. Currently, only about a quarter of the world's people are economically secure. While economic security is a constant struggle in developing countries, it is also a problem that arises in developed countries. Unemployment accounts for a lot of ethnic violence and political instability.

Food security requires all people to have both physical and economic access to basic food. According to the United Nations, it is not the overall lack of food that is a problem, but rather a problem that lies in the poor distribution of food as well as a lack of purchasing power. In the past, UN officials have advised to tackle issues relating to access to assets, work and assured income (related to economic security), which would, in turn, tackle food security, issues.

Health Security aims to protect all people from diseases and unhealthy life-styles. In developing countries, the major causes of death traditionally were infectious and parasitic diseases, whereas, in industrialized countries, they were diseases of the circulatory system. Today, lifestyle-related chronic diseases are leading killers worldwide, with 80 percent of deaths occurring in low- and middle-income countries.[711] According to the United Nations, in both developing and industrial countries, threats to health security are usually greater for poor people in rural areas, particularly children. This is due to malnutrition and insufficient access to health services, clean water, and other essential needs.

Environmental security intends to protect people from air pollution, lack of access to clean water, and other threats in nature as well as deterioration of the natural environment. Global warming, caused by the emission of GHGs, is another environmental security issue.

Personal security aims to protect people from physical violence, whether from the state or external sources, violent individuals, and domestic abuse. For many, violent crime represents the greatest source of anxiety.

Community security strives to protect people from the loss of traditional relationships and ethnic violence. Ethnic groups are often threatened and feel violated. The United Nations declared 1993 the Year of Indigenous People to

---

[711] Tadjbakhsh, Shahrbanou & Chenoy, Anuradha M. *Human Security: Concepts and Implications*, London: Routledge, 2006.

bring awareness to the continuing violence of the 300 million aboriginal people in 70 countries.

Political security is concerned with whether people live in a society that honors their fundamental human rights. Human rights violations commonly occur during periods of political unrest. Along with repressing individuals and groups, governments may try to exercise control over ideas and information.

In an ideal world, each of these seven categories would receive adequate global attention and resources. Yet attempts to implement this human security agenda have led to the rise of two major schools of thought on how to best practice human security—"Freedom from Fear" and "Freedom from Want." The former aims to protect individuals from violence while recognizing that violent threats arise from poverty and other forms of inequities. This school of thought argues that limiting the focus to only violence is a realistic and feasible approach towards Human Security. Emergency assistance, conflict prevention and resolution, and peace building are the primary concerns of this approach. Canada was one of the countries to incorporate "Freedom from Fear" as part of its foreign policy during its efforts to ban landmines. And yet, whether such a "narrow" approach can actually serve its purpose in guaranteeing more fruitful results remains to be an issue.

The latter school of thought, "Freedom from Want," argues that the agenda should be broadened to include hunger, disease and natural disasters because they are inseparable concepts in addressing the root of human insecurity, and they kill far more people than war, genocide and terrorism combined.[712] Unlike "Freedom from Fear," it focuses on more than just violence with an emphasis on development and security goals.

Human security is indebted to the human rights tradition (the ideas of natural law and natural rights). The development of the human security model can be seen to have drawn upon ideas and concepts fundamental to the human rights tradition. Both approaches use the individual as the central referent, and both argue that a broad range of issues (i.e., civil rights, cultural identity, access to education and health care) is fundamental to human dignity. A significant difference between the two models is in their approach to addressing threats to human dignity and survival. While the human rights framework takes a legalistic approach, the human security framework, by utilizing a diverse range of

---

712 Human Security Centre. "What is Human Security." Retrieved on 19 April 2008.

actors, adopts flexible and issue-specific strategies, which can operate at local, national or international levels.

The nature of the relationship between human security and human rights is contested among human security advocates. Some human security advocates argue that the goal of human security should be to build upon and strengthen the existing global human rights legal framework.[713] However, other advocates view the human rights legal framework as part of the global insecurity problem and believe that a human security approach should propel us to move above and beyond this legalistic approach to get at the underlying sources of inequality and violence which are the root causes of insecurity in today's world.[714]

4.1.2. Documents

4.1.2.i. United Nations Charter

The Charter of the United Nations is the foundational treaty of the international organization called the United Nations. On June 26, 1945, 50 of the 51 original counties signed it at the San Francisco War Memorial and Performing Arts Center. The treaty entered into force on 24 October 1945, after being ratified by the five permanent members of the Security Council and a majority of the other signatories. There are currently 193 member states in the United Nations.

Since it is a constituent treaty, its articles bind all member states. Furthermore, the Charter states that obligations to the United Nations prevail over all other treaty obligations. Most countries in the world have now ratified the Charter. One notable exception is the Holy See, which has chosen to remain a permanent observer state and, therefore, is not a full signatory to the Charter.[715]

---

713 S Tadjbakhsh, "Human Security," Human Development Insights Issue 17, New York: UNDP HDR Networks.

714 Hampson, F., Madness in the Multitude: Human Security and world disorder, Ontario: Oxford University Press, 2002.

715 United Nations, Introductory Note. Retrieved from http://www.un.org/en/documents/charter/

4.1.2.ii. United Nations International Covenant on Civil and Political Rights

The International Covenant on Civil and Political Rights (ICCPR) is a multilateral treaty adopted by the United Nations General Assembly on December 16, 1966, and which has been in force from March 23, 1976. It commits its parties to respect the civil and political rights of individuals, including the right to life, freedom of religion, freedom of speech, freedom of assembly, electoral rights and rights to due process and a fair trial. As of March 2012, the Covenant had 74 signatories and 167 parties.[716]

The ICCPR is part of the International Bill of Human Rights, along with the International Covenant on Economic, Social and Cultural Rights (ICESCR) and the Universal Declaration of Human Rights (UDHR).[717] The ICCPR evolved from the same process that led to the Universal Declaration of Human Rights.

Article 1 of the ICCPR recognizes the right of all people to self-determination, including the right to "freely determine their political status", pursue their economic, social and cultural goals, and manage, and dispose of their resources.[718]

Although it has 167 states parties, the covenant is not enforceable in Australia. In New Zealand ICCPR has not yet been made part of the law, but the country did take measures to give effect to many of the rights contained in the ICCPR by passing the New Zealand Bill of Rights Act in 1990."

The United States ratified the ICCPR in 1992, with five reservations, five understandings, and four declarations. Senate's ratification included the statement that "the provisions of Article 1 through 27 of the Covenant are not self-executing."[719] If a treaty or covenant is not self-executing, and Congress has not implemented the agreement through legislation, the ratification will not create a private right of action within the US judicial system.

Therefore, even though the ICCPR is *allegedly binding upon the United States as a matter of international law, it is not part of the nation's domestic law. As a reservation that is "incompatible with the object and purpose" of a treaty, it is void as*

---

716 Sieghart, Paul (1983). The International Law of Human Rights. Oxford University Press. p. 25.

717 "Fact Sheet No.2 (Rev.1), The International Bill of Human Rights." United Nations OHCHR. June 1996. Archived from the original on 2008-03-13. Retrieved 2008-06-02.

718 International Covenant on Civil and Political Rights art 1, Dec. 16, 1966, S. Treaty Doc. No. 95-20, 6 I.L.M. 368 (1967), 999 U.N.T.S. 171 [hereinafter ICCPR].

719 S. Exec. Rep. No. 102-23 (1992).

a matter of the Vienna Convention on the Law of Treaties and international law.[720]
As a result, it's questionable whether the non-self-execution declaration is even
legal under domestic law.

The United States has not yet accepted any of the obligations required under
the Covenant. It has not changed its domestic law to comply with the Covenant.
Therefore, the Covenant has become ineffective, with the United States officials'
insistence upon preserving a vast web of sovereign, judicial, prosecutorial and
executive branch immunities that often deprive its citizens of the "effective
remedy" under the law the Covenant is intended to guarantee.

4.1.2.iii. United Nations International Covenant on Economic, Social, and Cultural Rights

The ICESCR is a multilateral treaty adopted by the United Nations General
Assembly on 16 December 1966, and entered into force on 3 January 1976.[721] It
commits its parties to work towards achieving economic, social and cultural
rights (ESCR) for individuals. These also include labor rights, the right to health
and education, and the right to an adequate standard of living. As of July 2011,
the Covenant had 160 parties.[722]

Article 1 recognizes the right of all peoples to self-determination, including the right to "freely determine their political status, pursue their economic,
social and cultural goals, and manage and dispose of their own resources."[723]
It recognizes a negative right of a people not to be deprived of its means of
subsistence and imposes an obligation on those parties still responsible for non-
self-governing and trust territories (colonies) to encourage and respect their
self-determination.[724]

---

[720] Vienna Convention on the Law of Treaties art. 18, May 23, 1969, 1155 U.N.T.S. 331.

[721] *United Nations Treaty Collection: International Covenant on Civil and Political Rights,* UNITED NA-
TIONS (last viewed Feb. 25, 2009), http://treaties.un.org/Pages/ViewDetails.aspx?mtdsg_no=IV-
3&chapter=4&lang=en

[722] *Id..*

[723] International Covenant on Economic, Social, and Cultural Rights, Dec. 16, 1966, S. Treaty Doc. No.
95-19, 6 I.L.M. 360 (1967), 993 U.N.T.S. 3 [hereinafter ICESCR].

[724] ICESCR, *supra* note 899, at art. 1.3.

Articles 2–5 establish the principle of "progressive realization."[725] This principle requires the rights be recognized "without discrimination of any kind as to race, color, sex, language, religion, political or other opinion, national or social origin, property, birth or other status."[726] The rights can only be limited by law, in a manner compatible with the nature of the rights, and only for the purpose of "promoting the general welfare in a democratic society."[727]

Progressive realization differs from ICCPR, which obliges parties to "respect and to ensure that all individuals within its territory and subject to its jurisdiction." However, that does not make the Covenant meaningless. The requirement to "take steps" imposes a continuing obligation to work towards the realization of the rights.[728] The CESCR General Comment 3 points out that the Committee on Economic, Social, and Cultural Rights also interprets the principle as imposing minimum core obligations to provide, at the least, minimum essential levels of each of the rights. If resources are highly constrained, this should include the use of targeted programs aimed at the vulnerable.[729]

The right to adequate food also referred to as the right to food, is interpreted as requiring "the availability of food in quantity and quality sufficient to satisfy the dietary needs of individuals, free from adverse substances, and acceptable within a given culture."[730] This must be accessible to all, implying an obligation to provide special programs for the vulnerable. The right to adequate food also implies a right to water.[731]

Article 12.2 requires parties to take concrete steps to improve the health of their citizens, including reducing infant mortality and improving child health, improving environmental and workplace health, preventing, controlling and

---

725 The principle of "progressive realization" acknowledges that some rights (for example, the right to health) may be difficult in practice to achieve in a short period, and that states may be subject to resource constraints, but requires them to act as best they can within their means.

726 ICESCR, *supra* note 899, at art. 2.2.

727 ICESCR, *supra* note 899, at art. 4.

728 U.N. Committee on Economic, Social and Cultural Rights [hereinafter CESCR], General Comment 3: The Nature of States Parties Obligations (Art. 2, Para. 1 of the Covenant), 5th Sess., para. 9, U.N. Doc. E/1991/23 (1990)

729 CESCR General Comment 3, *supra* note 904, at para. 12.

730 CESCR, General Comment 12: The Right to Adequate Food (Art. 11 of the International Covenant on Economic, Social, and Cultural Rights), 20th Sess., para. 8, U.N. Doc. E/C.12/1999/5 (1999).

731 CESCR, General Comment No. 15: The Right to Water (Arts. 11 and 12 of the International Covenant on Economic, Social, and Cultural Rights), 29th Sess., para. 3, UN Doc. E/C 12/2002/11 (2003).

treating epidemic diseases, and creating conditions to ensure equal and timely access to medical services for all. These are considered to be "illustrative, non-exhaustive examples," rather than a complete statement of parties' obligations.[732]

4.1.2.iiii. Regional Human Rights conventions and bodies

According to the United Nations Office of the High Commissioner for Human Rights (OHCHR), the Pacific region, compared with other regions of the world, has ratified the fewest number of core international human rights treaties, while at the same time nearly every Pacific island country guarantees basic civil and political rights through its constitution.[733]Ratification and implementation of those treaties are widely recognized as an essential requirement for promoting and protecting human rights on the national level. The treaties oblige States Parties to take measures to ensure that their domestic legislation and policies conform to international standards. For States Parties in the Pacific region, human rights treaties offer an added value: they provide a legal basis and structure to support internationally agreed development goals, most of which are included in regional and national development strategies.[734]

Over the past two decades, economic growth and development in the Pacific region have been relatively slow. Growing poverty and a lack of sustainable livelihood opportunities are evident in many Pacific countries. Lack of access to the benefits from and control over natural resources is linked to rising disparities in income, social tension, and political instability. For small island economies, the result of globalization is all too often human rights violations, particularly in the economic and social sphere. In October 2005, Pacific Island Forum leaders adopted the Pacific Plan of Action for Strengthening Regional Cooperation and Integration (the Pacific Plan). The Pacific Plan aims to develop a region that supports the sustainable management of its resources, democratic values, and

---

732 CESCR, General Comment 14: The Right to the Highest Attainable Standard of Health (Article 12 of the International Covenant on Economic, Social, and Cultural Rights), 22d Sess., para. 7, U.N. Doc. E/CN.12/2000/4 (2000).

733 United Nations Office of the High Commissioner for Human Rights (2009). *Ratification of International Human Rights Treaties: Added Value for the Pacific Region.* Pacific Islands Forum Secretariat. Retrieved from

http://pacific.ohchr.org/docs/RatificationBook.pdf

734 *Pacific Islands Forum Secretariat,* UNITED NATIONS OFFICE OF THE HIGH COMMISSIONER FOR HUMAN RIGHTS vii (July 2009), http://pacific.ohchr.org/docs/RatificationBook.pdf.

respect for human rights. Initiative 12.5 of the Pacific Plan explicitly promotes the ratification and implementation of international human rights treaties. In addition, all members of the Pacific Island Forum have committed themselves to achieving all eight Millennium Development Goals (MDG) by the year 2015.[735]

The links between the MDGs and the Strategic Objectives of the Pacific Plan are visible. What might seem less clear is how these development goals are related to international human rights instruments. As UNDP noted in its Human Development Report 2000: "a decent standard of living, adequate nutrition, healthcare, education and decent work and protection against calamities are not just development goals—they are also human rights." Thus, the poor not only have needs, but they also have rights. Therefore, duty-bearers, that is to say, states, have legal obligations to fulfill. These legal requirements, as set out in the core international human rights instruments, underpin both the MDGs and the Pacific Plan's Strategic Objectives. Despite their commitment to these development goals, not all countries in the Pacific region have made a similar commitment to adherence to the essential international treaties on which sustainable development must be built. While the link between human rights and development should now be clear, there are also some less obvious benefits, or added value, for Pacific island states in ratifying these core human rights treaties.[736]

Some States argue that they are, in one way or another, ill-equipped to assume the legal obligations imposed by international human rights treaties. They cite lack of financial resources, the existence of customary practices that might conflict with human rights principles, the idea (which is not entirely correct) that the state must be in full compliance with the treaty before it can ratify the treaty, and the demands of the treaty reporting process. In fact, all of these concerns can be allayed with the assistance of civil society, the support of the international community and the political will of governments. Many United Nations agencies and other regional and international organizations provide support for treaty ratification, implementation, and reporting. National human rights institutions, which serve as a bridge between civil society and the government, can also play a vital role in raising public awareness about the need to ratify these treaties. Most Pacific island countries have a bill of rights enshrined in their constitutions; most have also already ratified the Convention on the Rights of the Child and the Convention on the Elimination of All Forms of

---

735 *Pacific Islands Forum Secretariat, supra* note 909, at vii.

736 *Pacific Islands Forum Secretariat, supra* note 909, at vii.

Discrimination against Women, two of the core international human rights treaties. Given this rights-based foundation, the Pacific region is primed to commit itself more completely to the international human rights system. Increasing the levels of ratification, with the aim of ratifying and implementing all the core human rights treaties would demonstrate to the world that Pacific island countries are prepared to make that commitment.[737]

Nearly every Pacific island country guarantees basic civil and political rights through its constitution. A few countries in the region also provide for some economic, social and cultural rights. Yet, compared with other areas of the world, the Pacific region has ratified the fewest number of core international human rights treaties. Ratification and implementation of those treaties are widely recognized as a primary requirement for promoting and protecting human rights on the national level, as these agreements establish measures that States Parties must take to ensure that their domestic legislation and policies conform to international standards. Human rights treaties offer an added value to States Parties in the Pacific region: they impose legal obligations that underpin internationally agreed development goals, most of which are mirrored in regional and national development strategies.[738]

Most observers agree that over the past two decades, economic growth and development in the Pacific region have been relatively disappointing. Reports issued by the Asian Development Bank and the United Nations Development Programme (UNDP) have repeatedly attributed the lack of progress to various factors, including poor governance. Growing poverty and a lack of sustainable livelihood opportunities are evident in many Pacific countries. Lack of access to the benefits from and control over natural resources is linked to rising disparities in income, social tension, and political instability. Often, the impact of globalization on small island economies is made manifest in human rights violations, particularly of economic, social and cultural rights. In October 2005, Pacific Island Forum leaders adopted the Pacific Plan of Action for Strengthening Regional Cooperation and Integration (the Pacific Plan). The Pacific Plan aims to develop a region that is "respected for the quality of its governance, the sustainable

---

737 *Pacific Islands Forum Secretariat, supra* note 909, at viii. A regional human rights mechanism for the Pacific? Lessons learned from developments in other regions. Retrieved from www.ishr.ch

738 *Pacific Islands Forum Secretariat, supra* note 909, at iii-1.

management of its resources, the full observance of democratic values, and for its defense and promotion of human rights."[739]

The link between the Plan's 15 Strategic Objectives and the need to protect and promote human rights is explicitly stated. Indeed, the goals to reduce poverty (4), improve health (6), improve education and training (7), improve gender equality (8), recognize and protect cultural values, identities and traditional knowledge (11), improve transparency, accountability, equity and efficiency in the management and use of resources (12), improve political and social conditions for stability and safety (13) and increase national ownership and commitment to regional approaches, plan, policies and programs (14) are all directly connected to provisions contained in the principal international human rights treaties. These links are recognized further in initiative 12.5 of the Plan, which explicitly promotes the ratification and implementation of international human rights treaties by PIF countries. In addition, all members of the Pacific Island Forum have committed themselves to achieving the Millennium Development Goals (MDGs) by 2015. These goals are: eradicate extreme poverty and hunger, achieve universal primary education, promote gender equality and empower women, reduce child mortality, improve maternal health, combat HIV/AIDS, malaria and other diseases, ensure environmental sustainability, and develop a global partnership for development.[740]

ICESCR in the Pacific

Around 25 percent of the region's populations live in poverty. None of the countries in the region provides access to potable water to its entire population; in some rural communities, only 20 percent of the residents have access to safe drinking water. While expenditure on education has increased, schools in rural areas and on outer islands frequently lack books and other teaching materials, according to a study published by the Asian Development Bank (*Hardship and Poverty in the Pacific*, by David Abbott and Steve Pollard). The ICESCR directly addresses these issues, covering the rights to education, health, and work and

---

[739] *Pacific Islands Forum Secretariat, supra* note 909, at 1; http://www.hurights.or.jp/archives/focus/section1/pdf/focus49.pdf

[740] *Pacific Islands Forum Secretariat, supra* note 909, at 1; http://www.spc.int/fpocc/index2.php?option=com_content&do_pdf=1&id=333

the right to an adequate standard of living, including food, clothing and housing. It is the human rights treaty that links sustainable development to human rights.[741]

ICCPR in the Pacific

The Several Pacific States have faced governance challenges since their independence, including political and civil instability. As the Asian Development Bank's study, Hardship and Poverty in the Pacific, acknowledges, good governance is the key to fighting poverty, and good governance is not possible without respecting the civil and political rights enshrined in the ICCPR. These rights include freedom of expression, movement, thought, conscience and religion, the right to vote and to stand in elections, and the right to life.[742]

International Convention on the Elimination of All Forms of Racial Discrimination (ICERD) in the Pacific

Virtually all Pacific island countries have specific provisions in their constitutions that prohibit discrimination based on race, but they do not provide adequate explanations or definitions as to what constitutes racial or ethnic discrimination. While the ICERD focuses on racial discrimination perpetrated by the State against an individual or group of people, it also establishes responsibility for preventing private actors from discriminating by race in all areas, including the workplace and the media. While the issue of racial discrimination is not specifically addressed in the Pacific Plan, harmonization of legislation with the ICERD is one of the targets of the good governance Strategic Objective for the first three years of the Plan (2006-2008).[743]

---

741 *Pacific Islands Forum Secretariat, supra* note 909, at 4.

742 *Pacific Islands Forum Secretariat, supra* note 909, at 4.

743 *Pacific Islands Forum Secretariat, supra* note 909, at 4-5. Retrieved from
     http://www.int-erd.org/index.php?option=com_content&view=article&id=83&Itemid=85

Convention against Torture and Other Cruel, Inhuman or Degrading
Treatment of Punishment (CAT) in the Pacific

By promoting minimum standards for interrogations, investigations, custody
and treatment of persons subjected to any form of arrest, detention or imprison-
ment, CAT aims to protect individuals from harm caused by a state or its agents,
including the police. The Pacific region is not immune to the brutality of law
enforcement officials, and such cruelty leads to public mistrust of these staff
members. Implementation of the CAT would result in improved performance of
law enforcement officials and, therefore, better community relations with these
staff members. Improving safety and security, a flow on effect to promote better
relations and trust between law enforcement officials and communities, is one
of the main objectives of the Pacific Plan; yet Australia and New Zealand are the
only countries in the region that have ratified CAT.[744]

Convention on the Elimination of All Forms of Discrimination against
Women (CEDAW) in the Pacific

While women make up 50 percent of the Pacific's population, they represent only one-third of the formal, paid workforce and, within that, hold only 10
to 20 percent of managerial positions. Pacific island countries have the lowest
number of women parliament members out of all the regions of the world, with
a regional average of just 4.5 percent. Yet, CEDAW is the second most ratified
international human rights treaty in the Pacific. CEDAW calls for State Parties
to change laws and policies that have a detrimental impact on women. Studies
have shown that when the lives of women are improved, their families and communities also benefit from the improvements.[745]

Convention on the Rights of the Child (CRC) in the Pacific

The Convention on the Rights of the Child (CRC) protects the rights of
all children less than 18 years of age by setting standards for their civil rights
and freedoms, health care, education, legal, public and social services, juvenile
justice, and economic and other forms of exploitation. All of these issues are

---

744 *Pacific Islands Forum Secretariat, supra* note 909, at 5.

745 *Pacific Islands Forum Secretariat, supra* note 909, at 5; http://www.un.org/womenwatch/daw/cedaw/

addressed in the Pacific Plan—and every Pacific Island country has ratified, although not yet fully implemented, this treaty.[746]

International Convention on the Protection of the Rights of All Migrant Workers and Members of their Families[747] in the Pacific

The United Nations estimates that around three percent of the world's population, or 175 million people, are migrants. For many years, Pacific Islanders have migrated for better salaries and living conditions. More recently, however, skilled migrants from other countries have been coming to the region as well. Remittances are the largest source of income for some Pacific Island countries. Since the primary objective of the International Convention on the Protection of the Rights of All Migrant Workers and Members of their Families (ICRMW) is to protect migrant workers and their families from exploitation and violation of their fundamental human rights, ratification of the treaty is a significant step toward protecting the rights of migrant workers in the region and of those from the region who work abroad. That protection, in turn, supports the region's social and economic development.[748]

International Convention for the Protection of All Persons from Enforced Disappearance in the Pacific

This Convention is not yet in force. It will go into force after twenty states have ratified or acceded to it. Currently, there are 81 signatories and seven state parties to the Convention. This convention aims to bring about a strong international consensus against human rights violations such as enforced disappearances. [749] An enforced disappearance is a practice that affects men, women, and children from all parts of the globe. It involves the arrest, detention or abduction of persons by state officials without their fate or whereabouts being acknowl-

---

746 *Pacific Islands Forum Secretariat, supra* note 909, at 6.

747 The Committee on Migrant Workers (1990). *Claiming Human Rights.* Retrieved from http://www.claiminghumanrights.org/icrmw.html

748 *Pacific Islands Forum Secretariat, supra* note 909, at 6.

749 *Pacific Islands Forum Secretariat, supra* note 909, at 7; http://www.islandsbusiness.com/islands_business/index_dynamic/containerNameToReplace=MiddleMiddle/focusModuleID=20006/overideSkinName=issueArticle-full.tpl

edged. The victims include human rights defenders, religious leaders, and people belonging to different ethnic and indigenous groups. By joining this Convention, Pacific island states can help reinforce the international consensus against such crimes and violations.

Advantages of Ratification and Implementation

The link between human rights—and the international human rights framework—and development should now be clear. But there are also some less obvious benefits for Pacific island states in ratifying these core human rights treaties:

- Ratification provides a legal regime of accountability

International human rights treaties set a legal system of obligation and responsibility that can complement and reinforce the implementation of national and regional plans while, at the same time, help to measure progress in development. The mechanism of treaty monitoring and reporting allows for the periodic review of national policies and practices that are then measured against international standards. Ratification of a treaty enables a State Party to ask for assistance in complying with its treaty obligations.[750]

- Ratification enables the realization of human rights and strengthens adherence to the rule of law

Ratification and implementation of human rights treaties indicate a commitment to strengthening the protection and promotion of human rights nationally and to promoting respect for social justice, the rule of law and democracy. International human rights treaties offer a common language and a clear set of norms and standards. Using the language of rights as a common language allows for broad international consensus and international collaboration. It helps to demonstrate the strong international consensus, by defending certain rights or combating certain abuses.[751]

---

750 *Pacific Islands Forum Secretariat, supra* note 909, at 8. Retrieved from http://www.iwraw-ap.org/resources/human_rights.htm

751 *Pacific Islands Forum Secretariat, supra* note 909, at 8.

- Ratification provides an opportunity to strengthen intra-government cooperation

With the commitment to promote and protect human rights implied in ratification and implementation, government agencies are more likely to work together on crosscutting issues. Greater cooperation between national and local authorities can mean more efficient implementation of the Pacific Plan. Through lessons-learned and model legislation, cooperation can be exported not just from agency to agency, but also from country to country within the region.[752]

- Ratification improves the public profile of Pacific Island countries and their governments

"Ratification and implementation of these treaties demonstrate good will and the political intention of the ratifying state to comply with international norms and standards. It also shows international solidarity and cooperation and, for Pacific island countries, a willingness to improve the lives of their populations."[753]

- Ratification involves meaningful participation of civil society in the development process

The provisions contained in human rights treaties assume that their beneficiaries are not passive recipients, but active rights-holders who can claim their rights. Thus, civil society becomes a partner of the state in implementing the treaty. The treaty reporting process, in particular, encourages constructive collaboration between state entities and members of civil society. These efforts can, in turn, lead to greater participation by and support from civil society in the development activities elaborated in the Pacific Plan.[754]

- Ratification encourages a fairer system of aid, technical support, and global justice

---

752 *Pacific Islands Forum Secretariat, supra* note 909, at 8.

753 *Pacific Islands Forum Secretariat, supra* note 909, at 8.

754 *Pacific Islands Forum Secretariat, supra* note 909, at 8.

In recent years, a significant number of donor agencies, including many that are active in the Pacific region, have mainstreamed human rights into their aid policies. Ratification and implementation of international human rights treaties reassure donors that the state Party will use donor funds toward equitable and just practices, thus building confidence that could perhaps lead to greater support. In addition, development agencies often use the treaty-reporting process as an opportunity to assess national strengths and weakness and to discuss with state officials, national human rights institutions, civil societies and United Nations entities possible new or continued programming. Ratification and implementation thus open possible channels for international aid and technical support.[755]

4.1.3. Office of High Commissioner for Human Rights

The Office of the United Nations High Commissioner for Human Rights (OHCHR) is a United Nations agency that works to promote and protect the human rights and human dignity that are guaranteed under international law and in the Universal Declaration of Human Rights of 1948. The office was established by the United Nations General Assembly on 20 December 1993[756] and is headed by the High Commissioner for Human Rights, who co-ordinates human rights activities throughout the United Nations System and supervises the Human Rights Council in Geneva, Switzerland.

The mandate of the Office of the United Nations High Commissioner for Human Rights derives from Articles 1, 13 and 55 of the Charter of the United Nations, the Vienna Declaration and Program of Action and General Assembly resolution 48/141 of December 20, 1993. In connection with the programmed for reform of the United Nations (A/51/950, para. 79), on September 15, 1997, the Office of the United Nations High Commissioner for Human Rights and the Centre for Human Rights were combined into one Office of the United Nations High Commissioner for Human Rights.[757]

---

755 *Pacific Islands Forum Secretariat, supra* note 909, at 9; http://www.hrlrc.org.au/files/Policy-Paper-Asia-Pacific-and-Human-Rights.pdf

756 United Nations Office of the United Nations High Commissioner for Human Rights, Who We Are (2015). Retrieved from http://www.ohchr.org/EN/AboutUs/Pages/BriefHistory.aspx

757 *Id.*

Section two from the Terms of Reference states that the Office of the United Nations High Commissioner for Human Rights has the following functions:

- Promotes universal enjoyment of all human rights by giving practical effect to the will and resolve of the world community as expressed by the United Nations.

- Plays the leading role on human rights issues and emphasizes the importance of human rights at the international and national levels.

- Promotes international cooperation for human rights.

- Stimulates and coordinates action for human rights throughout the United Nations system.

- Promotes universal ratification and implementation of international standards.

- Assists in the development of new norms.

- Supports human rights organs and treaty monitoring bodies.

- Responds to grave human rights violations.

- Undertakes preventive human rights action.

- Promotes the establishment of national human rights infrastructures.

- Undertakes human rights field activities and operations.

- Provides education, information advisory services and technical assistance in the field of human rights.

4. 2.1 Pacific States Identity Rights

4.2.1.i. Geopolitical Rights

Lying below sea level does not necessarily mean the end of state, livelihood or culture, as the Netherlands represents. Half of the country lies just one meter above the sea's surface, while a quarter of the state's territory lies below sea level, including 21 percent of the population living there.[758]

The differences between the Netherlands and the Pacific islands are primarily the financial resources and infrastructure to help implement coping mechanisms. Especially after the devastating floods in the 1950s, the European country built a sophisticated dike system over decades, with a large number of locks and a network of reservoirs and sewage pipes.[759]

"You will find that the range of options to adapt is wide. Some of them are expensive, some are cheap, and some are out of this world and you can only dream of. Many, though, cannot immediately be implemented, because the people of the Pacific lack resources and capacity to carry them out," said Peniamina Leavai of the Pacific Adaptation to Climate Change Project.[760]

The possibilities for mitigating climate change's adverse impacts on people's livelihoods range from migration and infrastructural change to investing in nature-based assets to climate-sensitive policymaking.[761]

Migration can include relocating to other islands, from the coastline inland, or to developed countries or other Pacific island regions. Infrastructural change can take the form of reinforcing homes to withstand cyclones and surges as well

---

758 Rousbeh Legatis, *Climate Change: A Rising Sea Threatens Pacific Islands*, INTER PRESS SERVICE (Nov. 15, 2011), Retrieved from http://www.ipsnews.net/2011/11/climate-change-a-rising-sea-threatens-pacific-islands/.

759 Legatis, *supra* note 934.

760 Legatis, *supra* note 934.

761 Legatis, *supra* note 934.

as redesigning water storage and supply technology to manage inundation and seawater intrusion.[762]

Coral reefs and mangroves can act as natural sea defenses and fish nurseries. Increased investment in these resources would bolster already existing naturally resilient structures. Finally, political steps, at the local and regional as well as international levels, can raise awareness about the impact of certain lifestyles on the environment.[763]

According to Penjamina Leavai of the Pacific Adaptation to Climate Change Project (PACC), long before Small Island States might find themselves submerged, another possible outcome of rising sea levels is that islands "are left barren, (or) uninhabitable." [764]

The situation and living conditions of inhabitants of the Pacific islands vary considerably across the region, as they are shaped by the financial resources' availability, geography, technology and the affluence of the population.[765] Rousbeh Legatis of Inter Press Service states that "the rate at which these affected areas become uninhabitable will also fall in a broad range, from already happening now to happening in a couple of months, years, and in 20 years' time and more."[766] Yet environmental changes, accelerated by climate change, already severely affect the livelihoods of people in the Pacific.

A Council of Elders member Ursula Rakova states that "high tides are frequent and continue to wash away the shorelines" There are currently about 2,700 families living on the Carteret Islands, 86 kilometers away from Papua New Guinea's main island Bougainville, who are affected by these high tides. She told IPS that her biggest concern, as well as that of her community, is that one day, a tide of massive proportions will simply sweep over the islands and most or all people will be washed away without any trace. That is a valid concern since one of the islands in the region has already been divided in half by rising waters.

Due to these circumstances, locals have found it hard to adapt to the changed environmental conditions, especially since a significant area of arable land has been lost. This is a huge problem due to the fact that people's livelihoods are

---

762 Legatis, *supra* note 934.

763 Legatis, *supra* note 934.

764 Legatis, *supra* note 934.

765 Legatis, *supra* note 934.

766 Legatis, *supra* note 934.

based on fishing and harvesting natural crops. That is why the Council of the Elders developed and implemented what is called an autonomous adaption strategy by relocating and resettling their Islanders in safer grounds. Rakova founded the organization Tulele Peisa, which means "sailing the waves on our own," for this purpose. The group coordinates the relocation of the Islanders to host communities.

Since the relocation started, only a few families have resettled to PNG's Marau islands. While the international community is responding positively to their cause, Rakova emphasized that the government's reaction remains "very slow and does not set its priorities right."[767] Moreover, the international community also needs to act to reduce GHG emissions to keep a likely 21st-century temperature rise below 2 degrees Celsius and perhaps as low as 1.5 degrees."[768] Finally, of particular importance is a socio-ecological approach involving the entire island to strengthen people's resilience against the adverse impacts of climate change. The approach must consider the unique traditional cultural-environmental relationship that the people have with their environment.

Meanwhile, Tokelau, Tuvalu, and the Cook Islands have been suffering from drought conditions constituting a state of emergency. Experts have been working intensively for decades to confront adverse consequences of climate-induced changes in the Pacific region.[769] They warn that the situation will only worsen if global climate policymaking follows a business-as-usual approach. In Tuvalu, where groundwater is unsafe due to high salinity and pollution, the drinking water scarcity could be further aggravated. There, rainfall is a primary natural source for reservoirs, while increased sea level rise could cause the intrusion of seawater. This situation could easily result in social tensions between the affected population living on the Main Island, Funafuti, and islanders seeking drinking water who have migrated to Tuvalu's capital.[770]

More extreme and unusually frequent weather events like cyclones or tidal surges, driven by increased sea level rise, cause coastal erosion and force people to move inland to find new sources of livelihood. Samoa's coastlines, for

---

767 Legatis, R. Rising sea threatens the Carteret Islands. Retrieved from http://asopa.typepad.com/asopa_people/2011/11/rising-sea-threatens-the-carteret-islands.html

768 Gibson, J (2006). Are Pacific Island Economies Growth Failures? Geo-Political Assessments and Perspectives. Retrieved from http://ips.ac.nz/events/completed-activities/Pasifika%20project/Gibson%20Pacific%20Economies.pdf

769 Id.

770 Id.

example, have eroded from a few to 80 meters, and people have relocated inland where territory is already partitioned. Disputes over customary lands will likely intensify. Recently, in what was supposed to be monsoon season with typical knee-high flooding, some islands instead found themselves in a drought season.

In the face of these changes, local and regional response strategies have been formulated over time, and policy and decision-makers have been provided with information from lessons learned on the ground. But despite these very visible consequences of climate change in the Pacific, international development partners and donor countries have proven to be slow in increasing their efforts to finding a global solution to this world problem.

4.2.1.ii. Administrative Rights

Tuvalu consists of nine low-lying atolls totaling around 26 square kilometers, and in the past few years, the "king tides" that peak in February has been rising higher than ever. The government and many experts already assume the worst: Sometime in the next 50 years, if rising sea-level predictions prove accurate, the entire 11,800-strong population will have to be evacuated.[771]

The ocean could swallow Tuvalu as a whole, making it the first country to be wiped off the map by global warming. But in one respect, the Tuvaluans may be the lucky ones—at least compared with some of their Pacific island neighbors. The New Zealand government already takes in a quota of Tuvaluans every year, many of which have found jobs in the strawberry fields and packing plants around Auckland. And it has assured Tuvalu that it will absorb the entire population if the worst-case scenario becomes reality. That is a lifeline that many similarly threatened island nations—including Kiribati, Vanuatu, the Marshall Islands, the Cook Islands, Fiji and the Solomon Islands—do not yet have.

While their stories may not be as compelling as Tuvalu's, such nations include atolls that may also vanish. And they depend on vulnerable, low-lying coastal areas for living space, cropland, and tourism. For them, even conservative estimates of rising waters look set to make life on once-idyllic islands increasingly nasty, crowded and very, very wet.[772] The region already faces a

---

771 Adams, J. (2012). Rising sea levels threaten small Pacific island nations. *The New York Times - Breaking News, World News & Multimedia.* Retrieved from http://www.nytimes.com/2007/05/03/world/asia/03iht-pacific.2.5548184.html.

772 Sea level rise (2012). *Greenpeace.* Retrieved from

http://www.greenpeace.org/international/en/campaigns/climate-change/impacts/sea_level_rise/

witches' brew of problems that environmentalists say are being worsened by climate change: coastal erosion, saltwater intrusion onto taro cropland and tourist sites, shortages of potable water, anemic economies propped up by foreign aid, disease, and dependence on sugar-packed, processed food imports. And there are health problems like obesity and diabetes exacerbated by such food imports. A recent World Health Organization survey found that the South Pacific was the world's most overweight region.[773]

There is a concern that, ultimately, these issues will combine to power a wave of emigrants fleeing the Pacific islands. Indeed, there are already signs of flight: according to a study by the Australian government, applications for New Zealand residency from eligible Pacific Island nations shot up sharply in 2005 and 2006, compared with 2003. Some countries' economies already depend on remittances from islanders who have gone abroad to find jobs, and climate change could swell those numbers. Meanwhile, villages have already been evacuated from low-lying areas in Vanuatu and the Carteret Islands of Papua New Guinea.

Ben Namakin, an environmentalist, and native of Kiribati says that, in his homeland, saltwater intrusion is already ruining taro patches and spoiling well water, houses are being flooded, coastlines are receding, and a causeway whose beauty he had appreciated since he was a child collapsed in 2006.[774]

And, as in many such Pacific island nations, there is little higher, habitable land for people to move to. Namakin further states that there will likely be increased demands for migration, as people look for economic opportunities.

If a mass exodus occurs, countries like Tuvalu, which have contingency plans and close relations with a developed country partner like New Zealand, will have an advantage. The Marshall Islands and the Federated States of Micronesia, for example, could benefit from closer historical ties with the United States (both are former US-administered trust territories). The biggest losses will be experienced by the unskilled, poor islanders who cannot easily emigrate—especially in politically unstable states like the Solomon Islands.[775]

---

773 *Id.*

774 Namakin, B. (2007). Climate Witness: Kiribati and Micronesia. *WWF Global*. Retrieved from http://wwf.panda.org/about_our_earth/aboutcc/problems/people_at_risk/personal_stories/witness_stories/?uNewsID=100800

775 Farrell, B. (2009). Pacific Islanders face the reality of climate change and relocation. UNHCR. Retrieved from http://www.unhcr.org/4b264c836.html

Environmentalists like Namakin are focused on fight over flight, drawing up adaptation plans and continuing to urge countries like the United States and Australia to take the lead in cutting emissions. His initiatives are meant to give more hope for a better and brighter future instead of only leaving. [776] The Pacific Regional Environment Program has joined other groups in the region to start a $34 million adaptation effort that includes preparing roads for flooding in the Federated States of Micronesia; improving seawalls and drainage systems in the Cook Islands; and relocating gardens, planting salt-resistant crops and reviving the fishing industry in Solomon Islands atolls.

4.2.2. Environmental Rights

Pacific islanders have lived in close harmony with their island environments for thousands of years and are well aware of the importance of environment protection to their way of life. Pacific people face the complex challenge, in common with other countries of the world, of integrating economic development with the need to protect the environment. The Legal Reviews are a vital step along the road to improved environmental management and the achievement of sustainable development in the Pacific region.[777]

"Environmental changes due to global warming are also affecting the number and distribution of species that would traditionally be hunted."[778] "Increased sea levels and storm surges are forcing whole communities to move inland while rising temperatures are creating new health risks through spread of previously uncommon diseases."[779]

Closer to Australia, Small Island Developing States in the Pacific, as well as communities in the Torres Strait, are also experiencing environmental changes

---

776 Kropp, R. (2012). Climate change poses growing flood risks to US Coastal cities. Retrieved from http://www.greenbiz.com/blog/2012/03/22/climate-change-poses-growing-flood-risks-US-coastal-cities

777 Vili Fuavao, *Foreword* to The World Conservation Union, Environmental Law in the South Pacific: Consolidated Report of the Reviews of Environmental Law in the Cook Islands, Federated States of Micronesia, Kingdom of Tonga, Republic of the Marshall Islands and the Solomon Islands, at ix (Ben Boer, ed., 1996); Intergovernmental Panel on Climate Change, "Summary for Policymakers" (Intergovernmental Panel on Climate Change, 2007).

778 Bridget Lewis, *Human Rights and Climate Change,* 14 Queensland Envt'l. Practice Reporter 185, 185 (2009), *available at* http://eprints.qut.edu.au/29510/2/29510.pdf.

779 Lewis, *supra* note 957, at 1; Martin Wagner, The Right to Be Cold: Global Warming and Human Rights. In: *Human Rights 2007: The Year in Review,* Marius Smith, and Erica Contini eds, (2008) 73.

due to climate change. Communities that rely on subsistence farming as their primary source of food and income are experiencing a shortage of arable land due to contamination of soil and water table from salt-water inundation. Inundation in some Torres Strait communities has become so common that they have been forced to raise their houses on stilts or move further away from the coast.[780]

Rising temperatures and changing precipitation patterns are likely to cause an increase in the incidence of water-borne and mosquito-borne diseases, as well as exacerbating other health problems. Fish stocks, an important source of food and income, have decreased due to changes in ocean salinity, temperature, and currents. For people in the Torres Strait, populations of important totemic species such as dugong and sea turtles have diminished due to decreased availability of sea grass beds and nesting beaches.[781]

The impacts of climate change on these communities are clearly severe, threatening their ability to sustain themselves and to enjoy their traditions and customs. In some places, whole communities are likely to see their homes vanish beneath the ocean, forcing them to uproot and move elsewhere. These consequences are made all the more devastating by the fact that climate change involves an inherent injustice—the communities who are suffering (and who will suffer) most are the ones who have contributed least to the problem. Around the world, the countries that are going to be worst affected by climate change are those who make the lowest contribution to GHG emissions.[782]

4.2.3. Socio-cultural Identity Rights

Within the African regional human rights system, the original instrument is the *African Charter on Human and Peoples' Rights* (*'African Charter'*), 45 that covers civil and political as well as economic, social and cultural rights within the same context, and with equal force. It has been pointed out that the African model represents a significantly new and challenging normative framework for the implementation of economic, social and cultural rights, placing the

---

780 Lewis, *supra* note 957, at 1; Sheila Watt-Cloutier, Testimony Presented at the Inter-American Commission on Human Rights (1 March 2007).

781 Lewis, *supra* note 957, at 1; United Nations Framework Convention on Climate Change, "Climate Change: Small Island Developing States" (Climate Change Secretariat [UNFCCC], 2005).

782 Lewis, *supra* note 957, at 1.

implementing institutions of the *African Charter* and human rights advocates in a position to pioneer imaginative approaches to the realization of these rights.[783]

While the preceding discussion reveals varied approaches to economic, social and cultural rights by the existing regional human rights system, the moral it portends for the conceptualization of human rights in any future regional human rights system for the South Pacific must not be overlooked. In the ongoing political and scholarly discourses on the establishment of either a Pacific or an Asia-Pacific charter-based regional human rights system, the spotlight should shift towards integrating all human rights into a single instrument. The effectiveness that such an approach has facilitated in building a body of jurisprudence on these rights within the existing regional human rights systems makes this a viable option for the South Pacific.[784]

Defining, or "exploring" cultural rights in the Pacific was the object of a colloquium organized in October 1998 by UNESCO (Pacific office), with the Centre for New Zealand Jurisprudence of the School of Law of the University of Waikato (Wilson and Hunt, 2000). This colloquium came on the heels of an August 1998 Collective Human Rights of Pacific Peoples Conference held at the University of Auckland (Tomas 1998). Both meetings took place during the 50th anniversary of the UDHR23, and both meetings sought to understand and define human rights in a Pacific context and to examine the interaction between culture, cultural rights, and human rights. Before and since these meetings there has been a lack of concerted reflection on cultural rights and the relationship between cultural and human rights in the Pacific. The exception has been work carried out by the legal community, and particularly the recent workshop held by the New Zealand Law Commission as part of its study on "Custom and Human Rights in the Pacific."[785]

Discussions about human rights in the region have often been a "dialogue of the deaf" between the advocates of human rights and the proponents of culture. It has been difficult to find common ground. Many of the latter consider human rights an imposition that 1) emphasizes individual rights to the detriment

---

783 Dejo Olowu, *Invigorating Economic, Social and Cultural Rights in the South Pacific: A conceptual approach*, 7 Queensland U. Tech. L. & Just. J. 71, 82 (2007);

http://www.hrcr.org/docs/Banjul/afrhr.html

784 Olowu, *supra* note 963, at 82; C Tremewan, Human Rights in Asia. (1993) 6 *Pacific Review* 17, 27.

785 Elise Huffer, *Cultural Rights in the Pacific – What They Mean for Children*, UNICEF 4 (Oct. 30, 2006), *available at* http://www.unicef.org/eapro/Cultural_rights_in_the_Pacific_-_what_this_means_for_children.pdf.

of collective rights and duties and obligations, and, 2) seeks to undermine culture. And because internationally there has been a lack of emphasis on cultural rights, most people in the Pacific are not aware of the benefits that a stronger focus on cultural rights, in all their dimensions, collective as well as individual, could provide. Pacific countries have had little interest in ratifying international conventions, particularly the first generation ones, for political, economic and cultural reasons.[786] Only Solomon Islands (1982) has acceded to (but not ratified) the CESCR. And although all Pacific countries have ratified the CRC, all are behind in their reporting. It is possible, however, that the eventual adoption of the United Nations Declaration on the Rights of Indigenous Peoples by the General Assembly will change the general perception of rights in the Pacific.[787]

There is, therefore, no single definition of cultural rights in the Pacific, but they are understood as the right to cultural identity; that is the "right to maintain and develop [a group's] distinct culture" (Stavenhagen, 1998: 7). This view derives from an understanding of culture as a "total way of life" or as Konai Thaman (2000: 1) puts it: "as a shared way of living of a group of people, which includes their accumulated knowledge and understandings, skills and values, and which is perceived by them to be unique and meaningful." In this sense, cultural rights are the "collective rights of a (cultural) group" (Thaman, 2000: 3).[788]

How to advance and promote cultural rights in the Pacific is the objective of the UNESCO Colloquium Agreed Statement (October 1998). The Statement lists six categories through which UNESCO can help achieve this goal: language; cultural values; education; media; international instruments and institutions, and family and community relationships. Although none of the proposed measures seem to have been (systematically) taken up since then (and one should ask why this is the case), the document makes some useful suggestions under each of these categories, particularly:

"Custom and human rights both concern rights. Human rights are understood
to be the rights that are innate and inherent to each of us as individuals.
Customary, traditional and cultural rights relate to our social mores as a distinct
people of community. They include the ownership of land and natural resources,

---

786 I Jenning, *The Commonwealth in Asia*, Oxford Clarendon Press, 1951. 57-61.

787 Huffer, *supra* note 964, at 5.

788 Huffer, *supra* note 964, at 5; UNDP, *Human Development Report 2005, International Cooperation at Crossroads: Aid, Trade and Security in an Unequal World* (2005).

folklore, traditional knowledge and social systems. Both these species of rights
belong to us by virtue of who and what we are. It follows that we will need to
balance them with each other, if we wish to derive benefit from both...."

His Excellency, Ratu Joni Madraiwiwi, 2006.[789]

4.2.4. Draft Pacific Charter on Human Rights

Pacific nations have a low level of engagement in the international human rights
treaty system. Even where treaties have been ratified most Pacific nations have
failed to meet the reporting requirements of such agreements. While the Law
Association for Asia and the Pacific (LAWASIA) contends that Pacific countries have relatively good human rights records, it concedes that problems still
exist in some areas. These include the status of women, the rights of indigenous
peoples and the rights of minorities. Conversely, Dejo Olowu, an independent
legal science researcher from Northwest University, contends that there is not
a "vibrant culture of human rights protection in the Pacific." Olowu argues that
the Pacific should not be insulated from international human rights protections,
and should proceed to ratify all international human rights treaties.[790]

There are many explanations for the perceived indifference of the Pacific
nations towards international human rights treaties. The primary reason given
for low levels of ratification is that many human rights norms are already constitutionally entrenched. The lack of economic, technical, human and institutional capacity to fulfill the commitments of international treaties is also seen
as a significant reason for low levels of ratification and reporting. Finally,
international human rights treaties are perceived as a form of neo-colonialism,
whereby former colonial powers and other Western nations force Pacific nations
to comply with instruments that have been principally designed by the West.[791]
This last point highlights the importance of designing a charter that reflects

---

789   Huffer, *supra* note 964, at 5; P Imrana Jalal and J Madraiwiwi, *Pacific Human Rights Law Digest Vol-
      ume I* (Pacific Regional Rights Resource Team, 2005)

790   Kelly Haines-Sutherland, *Balancing Human Rights and Customs in the Pacific Region: A Pacific Char-
      ter of Human Right?*, 2 ANU Undergraduate Research Journal 125, 134 (2010), *available at* http://
      eview.anu.edu.au/anuuj/vol2_10/pdf/ch08.pdf; Law Association for Asia and the Pacific, "Report on
      a proposed Pacific Charter of Human Rights prepared under the auspices of LAWASIA, May 1989"
      in Victoria.

791   A. H. Angelo, "Lo Bilong Yumi Yet" in Victoria University of Wellington (ed), *Essays and Documents
      on Human Rights in the Pacific* (1992) 33, 40.

the customs and culture of the Pacific so that, the people of the Pacific have a sense of ownership of towards the charter and are not reluctant to implement its provisions.[792]

Most Pacific constitutions contain clauses that protect human rights. Accordingly, many human rights norms are already encapsulated in Pacific law. Most Pacific constitutions also recognize customary law. However, the recognition of custom is often limited by Pacific constitutions to the extent that it conforms to human rights or the protection of justice. For example section, 100(3) of the Constitution of Fiji 1997 provides that custom will apply unless "inconsistent with a provision of this constitution or a statute, or repugnant to the general principles of humanity." Furthermore, there is evidence that Pacific courts and legislatures are adjusting the law so that discriminatory customary practices are made illegal. For example, the decision in 1994 of *Noel v Toto* in Vanuatu outlawed any discriminatory customs. These examples suggest that national courts and legislatures are favoring human rights over customary law when engaging in law reform and dispute resolution.[793]

The current system has not reconciled custom and human rights to ensure that both are consistently protected. Epeli Hau'ofa characterizes life in the Pacific as occurring at two different levels, the national level of government occurring in capital cities, and that of the ordinary people who "tend to plan and make decisions about their lives independently."[794] Courts at the national level (which are often comprised of expatriate judges) are reluctant to use custom in their decisions because judges are unfamiliar with Pacific customs, and find it difficult to apply unwritten law. Therefore, human rights are given more attention by the judiciary, and customary law is often excluded from consideration. However, the majority of disputes in Pacific nations does not reach the national level of Pacific legal systems and are instead presided over by chiefly authorities and governed by customary law. Constitutional protections and human rights are not applied in traditional dispute resolution. A fundamental question in creating a Pacific Charter of Human Rights is how a regional charter could be effective in addressing this inconsistency in the application of human rights and

---

792 Haines-Sutherland, *supra* note 969, at 134.

793 Haines-Sutherland, *supra* note 969, at 134-35; A. H. Angelo, "The Niue Constitution" (2009) 15 Revue Juridique Polynesienne 157, 177.

794 Idem.

custom, and whether it would impact on traditional dispute resolution where human rights are most likely to be infringed.[795]

The Law Association for Asia and the Pacific prepared a Draft Pacific Charter in 1989, following the Pacific context and encompassing cultural rights, group rights, and duties. It was hoped that governments of the Pacific would subsequently implement a mechanism based on the document prepared by LAWASIA. However, Pacific governments are yet to engage actively or comprehensively in the creation of a Pacific Charter of Human Rights.[796] This may be attributable to the criticism of the draft charter by academics such as Thaman as "still very much a European document." LAWASIA are currently revising the 1989 Draft Pacific Charter and are advocating for Pacific governments to agree to a basic set of human rights principles that can be applied in the Pacific context. However, the reluctance that has been demonstrated towards the LAWASIA draft charter begs the question of whether there is sufficient enthusiasm in the Pacific for a regional charter.[797]

4.2.5. International Human Rights Impact

Both environmental law and environmental human rights can be part of the law of nations. Each has its own body of international law supporting it, and each may rise to a level sufficient to be recognized as part of the law of nations under the ATCA. Because no case arguing a violation of international environmental law has been successful under the ATCA, the Pacific Island nations may be more successful alleging a violation of environmental human rights. As other human rights claims have been successful, combining an environment protection claim with a human rights claim might have the greatest chance of success.[798]

---

795 Haines-Sutherland, *supra* note 969, at 135; Caren Wickliffe, "Culture Rights, Culture and Human Rights Education" in Margaret Wilson and Paul Hunt (eds), Culture, Rights and Cultural Rights: Perspectives from the South Pacific (2000).

796 Law Association for Asia and the Pacific.

797 Haines-Sutherland, *supra* note 969, at 136; Retrieved from
    http://www.cla.asn.au/Article/2009/Paper%20Kelly%20HS%200912.pdf

798 RoseMary Reed, *Rising Seas, and Disappearing Islands: Can Island Inhabitants Seek Redress Under the Alien Tort Claims Act?*, PACIFIC RIM LAW AND POLICY JOURNAL (2002), *available at*
    http://www.vanuatu.usp.ac.fj/sol_adobe_documents/usp%20only/Pacific%20law/Reed.htm.

CHAPTER FIVE

THE INTERNATIONAL LAW VIEW

5. 1. STATE RESPONSIBILITY FOR GLOBAL CLIMATE CHANGE

5.1.1. International Legal Obligations

One of the fundamental rules of international law is that states shall not inflict damage on or violate the rights of other states. In environmental law, this is referred to as the "no harm rule", which in turn has its foundations in the principle of good neighborliness between states formally equal under the Principle 2 of the 1992 Rio Declaration. Principle 2 echoes Principle 21 of the 1972 Stockholm Declaration, reiterating this rule of customary international law, and outlawing transboundary environmental injury via the following language: "States have, the sovereign right to exploit their resources pursuant to their own environmental and developmental policies, and the responsibility to ensure that activities within their jurisdiction or control do not cause damage to the environment of other States or of areas beyond the limits of national jurisdiction."[799] Although the exact boundaries and elements of this rule are heavily discussed in international law, the basic rule exists, as emphasized by the ICJ in its 1996 Advisory Opinion on the Legality of the Threat or Use of Nuclear Weapons and, for example, in the 3rd Restatement of US Foreign Relations Law. The no harm rule also forms the basis of international environmental law, such as, *inter alia*, the 1992 UNFCCC, and its 1997 Kyoto Protocol. In addition, this rule contains an obliga-

---

799   Boom, *supra* note 46.

tion to minimize risk, i.e. to prevent harm when it is foreseeable.[800] This is of particular importance in the context of adaptation to climate change and the question of who has to bear the costs of such measures. Moreover, in international law, States are responsible for violations of public international law and are obliged to compensate the indirectly or directly affected countries for the damage caused. This rule, extensively explained by Christina Voigt in "State Responsibility for Climate Change Damages" forms the basis of the law of state responsibility, a body of law that has recently been codified by the International Law Commission (ILC, "Draft Articles on State Responsibility for Internationally Wrongful Acts")[801]. The ILC is a United Nations body entrusted with promoting the codification and development of international law. According to Tol and Verheyen, although the rules developed by the ILC do not automatically represent international law, they have to be accepted (e.g., ratified) by states. In addition, they can serve as a useful tool to examine the conditions and consequences of state responsibility for climate change damage.[802]

The following section will break down several necessary steps that are required to establish state responsibility, which in turn, will give the baseline for identifying and testing the appropriate international law. "A claim for damages under international law must involve the following steps: (i) Identifying the damaging activity attributable to a state, (ii) establishing a causal link between the activity and the damage, (iii) determining either a violation of international law or a breach of a duty of care (due diligence), which is (iv) owed to the damaged state, (v) quantifying the harm caused in a court of law and relating it back to the activity."[803]

To hold states responsible for climate change damage, it is either necessary to identify a legally consistent behavior by a country or to attribute the actions of private persons to the state. Regarding state behavior, (i) allowing emissions of GHGs per se or during a particular time, and (ii) not having to put in place the regulatory means to arrest emissions over and above a certain threshold

---

800   Boom, *supra* note 46.

801   Voigt, C (2008). State responsibility for climate change damages. *Nordic Journal of International Law* *(77)*: 1-22. Retrieved from http://papers.ssrn.com/sol3/papers.cfm?abstract_id=1145199

802   Tol, R & Verheyen, R (2004). State Responsibility and Compensation for Climate Change Damages – A Legal and Economic Assessment. *Energy Policy (32)*: 1109-1130. Retrieved from
      https://www.fnu.zmaw.de/fileadmin/fnu-files/publication/tol/enpolliability.pdf

803   Tol, *supra* note 982, at 1111

are both clearly legally relevant state actions or omissions. Moreover, a breach of an international treaty such as the UNFCCC would be attributable to a state regardless of its reasons. However, it could be argued that millions of private persons are responsible for GHG emissions and not the state. The wording of Principle 2 of the Rio Declaration appears to be clear on this issue. It obliges states to ensure that no damage is done from their territory to other countries, and does not differentiate between state and private conduct. Or, as expressed already in 1941 by the arbitrator in the Trail Smelter case: "A State owes at all times the duty to protect other states from wrongful acts by individuals from within its jurisdiction."[804] However, according to Biermann and Boas, many have also argued that states cannot assume "full accountability for the actions of their citizens who, in the exercise of their human rights, are not subject to governmental control." [805]

The customary law rules are somewhat unclear on this issue. Article 4 of the ILC Draft Articles suggests that behavior of private persons, for example, private industry and energy utilities emitting GHGs, cannot be regarded as a conduct of a state. But the majority of emitting activities is subject to a licensing or permits procedure, be it in the energy or transport sector. However, Article 8 of the Draft Articles suggests that, as soon as an activity is allowed or licensed by a state, the resulting behavior is attributable to the state because states must exercise due diligence in control of private persons is an acknowledged principle. This has been argued in particular concerning ultra-hazardous activities. To argue that GHG emissions are not attributable to states would result in significant inconsistencies. For example, it is undisputed that emissions from state-owned electricity plants or other industrial plant are due to the state. In some parts of the world, power plants are now fully privatized, in others the main CO_2 emitting sector is still under direct state control. There is no reason international law would support exoneration of a country simply because of privatization of the polluting activity.[806]

---

804 Trail Smelter Case Arbitration: United States v Canada (1931–1941) 3 UNRIAA, vol. III, p.1965.

805 Biermann, F & Boas, I (2010). Preparing for a Warmer World: Towards a Global Governance System to Protect Climate Refugees. *Global Environmental Politics (10)*: 60-88. Retrieved from

   https://muse.jhu.edu/journals/gep/summary/v010/10.1.biermann.html

806 McAdam, J & Saul, B (2010). An unstable climate for human security? Climate-induced displacement and international law. *Human Security and Non-Citizens*. Retrieved from http://papers.ssrn.com/sol3/papers.cfm?abstract_id=1718865

But more importantly, the discussion becomes academic if one accepts that monitoring and regulation of private person's conduct are still a prime function of states, a function states can fail to fulfill without appropriate care. This must have also been the underlying argument for Canada to assume responsibility in the *Trail Smelter* case, where damage was caused by fumes from the "Consolidated Mining and Smelting Company of Canada, Limited," i.e. a private company. Thus, as a result, at least, the failure to stop, reduce or regulate emitting activities with due care can trigger state responsibility.[807]

It is useful to distinguish between general causation and specific causation, a distinction that is found in most domestic tort laws and which could also be applied to international law. The first type refers to a causal link between an activity and the uncertain outcome. In our case, this concerns the ample proof that anthropogenic GHG emissions change the radioactive forcing in the atmosphere, which results in global warming, and then leads to impacts on ecosystems such as air temperature rise, sea level rise, a shift of climatic zones, etc.[808] This causation chain will be further elaborated on below. Specific causation requires the proof that a particular activity has caused a critical damage in order to put a "figure to a claim" and to link this to a particular actor. This link would be needed to issue specific damage awards.

The following scientific facts can be taken as given and will fulfill all the requirements for general causation. First, there is a universal international scientific consensus that anthropogenic emissions of GHGs cause and have caused changes in the radioactive forcing balance in the atmosphere, which causes climate change. Second, there is a high likelihood that global climate change will lead to impacts on ecosystems and human life. In fact, the IPCC has already found that recent regional changes in temperature have had discernible impacts on many physical and biological systems (Gitay et al., 2001; Smith et al., 2001) and that the observed warming in the past 50 years has contributed significantly to global sea-level rise (Church et al., 2001). Thirdly, some damage will occur, regardless of reduction efforts undertaken by the international community in the framework of the UNFCCC or its Kyoto Protocol.[809]

Moreover, there is relative certainty about the extent to which states, as entities have contributed to emissions of GHGs and there, are scenarios attempting

---

807   Tol, *supra* note 982, at 1112.

808   Idem.

809   Tol, *supra* note 982, at 1112.

to reflect possible contributions for the future. For example, regarding historical emissions of carbon dioxide from fossil fuel combustion (1900–1990), the USA has contributed 30 percent, Europe 28 percent, the former Soviet Union 14 percent, Japan five percent, South and Central America only four percent and Africa was responsible for just three percent. While it is impossible to attribute specific emissions of a particular country to specific impacts (or harm), there is a causal link between each ton of GHG emitted and the change in radioactive forcing. Thus, even though the shares of contributions differ and only lead to the resulting changes in accumulation, they are equally causal in a legal sense. Climate science has also started to estimate damage from the impacts of climate change, thus providing some figures on an aggregate level that can be linked to the level of general causation. One result of these assessments is that damage in developing countries is projected to be significant while impacts in OECD might overall be positive. On the basis of these aggregate figures, it would be possible to assign legal responsibility to countries on the basis of their contributions, and it is also possible to differentiate between countries based on obligations for future harm.[810]

Once the damaging activity and causation have been established, there is usually a requirement in tort or liability law to show some wrongdoing or violation of due diligence. With regard to environmental damage in international law, there are two basic views: (i) a state has to violate a duty of care or a rule of international law to incur responsibility or (ii) where significant environmental injury is a concern, the causal link between injury and activity attributable to the state is enough to trigger state liability and compensation duties.[811] View (i) is reflected in Article 1 of the ILC Draft Articles on State Responsibility. It states that "every internationally wrongful act" entails responsibility while an unlawful act is defined as conduct that constitutes a breach of an international obligation (Article 2). When exactly an obligation is violated depends on the nature and character of the pertinent obligation, but for many international lawyers, there must always be a due diligence test. Therefore, state responsibility can only occur if the respective state has not acted with the appropriate care. In turn, the standard of "adequate care" must be determined according to the

---

810 Kolmannskog, V (2008). Climate change, disaster, displacement and migration: Initial evidence from Africa. *Nordic Journal of Human Rights* 26 (4). Retrieved from http://www.unhcr.org/4b18e3599.pdf

811 Hodgkinson et al. (2009). Copenhagen, Climate Change "Refugees" and the need for a Global Agreement. *Public Policy (4)*:2. Retrieved from http://www.ccdpconvention.com/documents/Copenhagen_And_CCDPs.pdf

actual circumstances and obligation in question. This is the traditional view of state responsibility; it always includes a degree of fault on behalf of the state. However, there has been much discussion about direct or complete state responsibility, i.e. whether states should be liable for any damage caused by certain activities under their control regardless of negligence or fault (view (ii), this is sometimes also called "state liability"). This discussion was triggered when ILC began to develop rules on the harm caused by certain lawful but hazardous activities. These rules became part of the "international liability" project, which has since been modified only to suggest general rules on the prevention of environmental damage. There have also been attempts to apply the polluter pays principle, formerly an economic allocation concept, between states. As a result, responsibility for environmental damage would be generated by the mere causation of harm. Interestingly, during the negotiations of the UNFCCC, it was suggested that the principle could serve as an appropriate legal framework to address issues of liability and compensation. However according to Zetter, thus far the right content of the polluter pays principle remains unclear, and it is doubtful whether it can be regarded as customary international law rule applicable to states.[812]

Finally, regarding the fourth element of the state responsibility test (obligation owed to a particular state), it is crucial to keep in mind that initially, public international law was mostly concerned with delimitating rights and duties of states, for example by defining state boundaries and establishing the law of treatment of aliens. Today, the international law moves more and more towards an act of cooperation. Many multilateral treaties create obligations that do not correspond to preexisting rights of distinct states, but that are much rather owed to the international community as a whole. International environmental law, which in many instances protects global commons such as the oceans and the atmosphere, is the best example of such *erga omnes* obligations (an obligation that is owed to a multitude of states and can thus be invoked by these jointly or individually).[813]

Having shown that it is, in principle, possible to apply the international law of state responsibility to climate change damage, there is an additional need to identify the possible types of damage or costs. To start with, an analysis of

---

812 Zetter, R. (2011). Protecting environmentally displaced people: Developing the capacity of legal and normative frameworks. *Refugee Studies Centre*. Retrieved from http://www.unhcr.org/4da2b6189.pdf

813 Tol, *supra* note 982, at 1113.

national responsibility should distinguish between climate change mitigation, adaptation to climate change, and residual climate change damage. Mitigation is the prevention of anthropogenic climate change at the source by either reducing GHG emissions or enhancing sink capacities (terrestrial or other). Mitigation is the focus of the UNFCCC and the Kyoto Protocol.[814] In the framework of a legal analysis of responsibility for climate change damage, mitigation can be viewed as "indirect" damage prevention, concerned with actually preventing a risk of harm from anthropogenic climate change. As such, the costs or obligations to mitigate climate change do not fall within the scope of this analysis. However, mitigation obligations can form the basis for state responsibility claims. Adaptation, on the other hand, can be legally defined as direct damage prevention, as it can reduce residual damage and thus minimize the risk of such harm. Residual damage occurs when adaptation measures are not possible or are not carried out due to economic or technical constraints. For legal purposes, the obligation to directly prevent damage corresponds with the duty to compensate for any damage done. Since humankind is committed to some climate change regardless of mitigation efforts, both are possible responses to a situation in which the rights or interests of states or/and individuals are affected because of ongoing and past activities (in this case: emissions of GHGs). Therefore, if general legal responsibility for climate change damage is established, such obligation also covers adaptation measures (and costs) as direct damage prevention measures.[815]

Usually, international obligations can be found in either treaty law or customary international law. Customary International Law is developed by state practice and *opinio juris*, i.e. the perception of countries that particular behavior reflects a rule of international law. The already mentioned no-harm principle belongs to this category. Treaty law is the primary source of law in international environmental law, containing much more defined rules as well as differentiated obligations regarding implementation control and enforcement- elements that are widely lacking in rules of customary law (UNFCCC, Kyoto Protocol, the 1982 United Nations Convention on the Law of the Sea (UNCLOS).[816]

---

814 A Survey of Organizations, Providers, and Research Involved in the Effort to Understand and Deal with Climate Change (last viewed June 28, 2013). Retrieved from www.kyotoprotocol.com.

815 Tol, *supra* note 982, at 1113-14.

816 Tol, *supra* note 982, at 1114.

The UNFCCC and Kyoto Protocol provide only a partial answer to the issue of responsibility for damage. The Convention does not address the issue directly. Rather, during the negotiation process of the UNFCCC, industrialized nations emphasized that they would not accept any treaty provisions hinting at state responsibility. This caused several states, upon signature of the UNFCCC and the Kyoto Protocol, to make the following declaration, which refers to state responsibility: "signature of the Convention shall in no way constitute a renunciation of any rights under international law concerning state responsibility for the adverse effects of climate change." This reservation had been proposed by the Alliance of Small Island States for inclusion in the Convention itself during the negotiations but was not included in the final document.[817]

Both UNFCCC and Kyoto Protocol[818] contain some unique provisions relating to adaptation and funding for adaptation. First, Article 4.1 (b) of the UNFCCC obliges all Parties to "formulate and implement national or regional programs containing measures to mitigate climate change and measures to facilitate adequate adaptation to climate change."[819] Thus, adaptation is not a voluntary undertaking but a substantive obligation on all Parties with a view to reducing future climate change damage. However, there is uncertainty as to what constitute "adequate" adaptation measures and when and exactly how the obligation must be met.[820]

Secondly, by ratifying the Convention, OECD countries have accepted a general obligation to assist developing countries in meeting the costs of adaptation under certain circumstances (e.g., Articles 4.3, 4.4, 4.8, 4.9 and 11 UNFCCC).[821] According to Article 4.3 Annex II countries (OECD countries) "shall provide new and additional resources to meet the agreed full incremental costs of implementing measures," which covers "preparing for the adaptation to the impacts of climate change" (Article 4.1 (e) UNFCCC) as well as the duties under Article 4.1(b) mentioned above. Article 4.4 states that Annex II Parties "shall also assist developing country Parties that are particularly vulnerable to the adverse effects

---

817 Tol, *supra* note 982, at 1114.

818 International Committee of the Red Cross. Retrieved from http://www.icrc.org/eng/resources/international-review/index.jsp

819 Harris, P. (2007). Europe and global climate change: Politics, Foreign Policy, and Regional Cooperation. Massachusetts, USA: Edward Elgar Publishing, Inc.

820 Tol, *supra* note 982, at 1114.

821 United Nations Framework Convention on Climate Change. Retrieved from http://unfccc.int/2860.php

of climate change in meeting costs of adaptation to those adverse effects." Thus, while the obligations are neither capped nor time restricted, the treaty does not oblige Annex II countries to bear the full costs of adaptation in all developing countries. Thirdly, the Kyoto Protocol establishes a particular adaptation fund that will receive revenues from the operation of the CDM "share of proceeds" and from voluntary commitments by Parties. New funds for (*inter alia*) adaptation activities were established at the 7th Conference of the Parties to the UNFCCC (COP7).[822]

Conclusively, the wording of the treaty only foresees partial funding of adaptation measures by Annex II countries. The general legal framework of responsibility, as well as saddle sharing issues, is not addressed. Funding pledges made are not directly connected to any accurate assessment of the actual aggregate adaptation needs of developing countries. Even though the financing provisions of the UNFCCC are mandatory, thus far, funding is made available on a constitutional basis without attaching it to legal responsibilities, even though the "polluter pays principle" was suggested by countries as the basis for determining respective countries' shares during the COP 6bis negotiations. Consequently, the UNFCCC and Kyoto Protocol do not resolve issues of state responsibility for adaptation and residual damage, although there are specific law rules and treaty provisions that could serve as the basis for showing that a state has "done wrong" or acted negligent- an essential element of a state responsibility claim.[823]

5.1.2. Establishing Breach

In 2007, at the 13th Meeting of the Conference of the Parties (COP13) of the UNFCCC in Bali, a timeline for a new post-2012 climate change regime was established. Since then, multiple international negotiations have taken place. According to Byrne and Schwartz, the process temporarily peaked in 2009 at COP15 in Copenhagen. However, the negotiations have not resulted in a new legally binding international agreement on climate change.[824]

---

822 Tol, *supra* note 982, at 1114-15.

823 Tol, *supra* note 982, at 1115; UNHCR 2009b. Climate Change and Statelessness: An Overview. Bonn: UNFCCC.

824 Byrne, R & Schwarte, C. (2011). International Climate Change Litigation and the Negotiation Process Retrieved from https://www.ogel.org/article.asp?key=3092

At the Bonn Climate Change Conference in June 2010 both the new and the former executive secretary of UNFCCC were rather pessimistic about the possibility of achieving considerable emission reductions and adopting a new legal framework in the short term. During and in the aftermath of the climate change summit in Copenhagen many officials predicted that it would take around five years to come finally to a binding deal.[825] As a result, billions of extra tons of CO_2 will be released into the atmosphere before the world agrees on how to keep global warming below a certain threshold. Currently, the negotiation process is held up by various factors including new emission reductions targets and the provision of adequate financial resources.[826]

According to Anup Shah, in a domestic, private or business environment there is often a close connection between negotiations and litigation.[827] If individuals or corporate entities cannot settle disputes to their satisfaction through negotiation, relief may be sought from the courts or through other dispute settlement mechanisms. In the international context, under the umbrella of the World Trade Organization (WTO), litigation has been strategically employed by governments to influence negotiations and clarify state obligations.[828]

Contentious litigation is a standard right tool in most jurisdictions. In comparison, the settlement of disputes between states through judicial or adversarial procedures is relatively rare. To address problem issues on the international spectrum, governments instead usually rely on a variety of political means such as bilateral negotiations, discussions in international organizations or mediation by third parties. While domestic law often provides a relatively transparent body of law that governs a particular relationship, public international law is more flexible, being subjected to a constant tension between established rules and the pressure to make changes within a system. The public international law largely

---

825 Bali Climate Change Conference (2007). *United Nations Framework Convention.* Retrieved from
   http://unfccc.int/meetings/bali_dec_2007/meeting/6319.php

826 *Introduction,* CLIMATE-CHANGE-LITIGATION (last viewed July 6, 2013),
   http://climate-change-litigation.wikispaces.com/1.+Introduction

827 Shah, A. (2008). COP13—Bali Climate Conference—Global Issues. *Global Issues.* Retrieved from
   http://www.globalissues.org/article/751/cop13-bali-climate-conference

828 *Introduction,* CLIMATE-CHANGE-LITIGATION (last viewed July 6, 2013), http://climate-change-litigation.wikispaces.com/1.+Introduction; Mike McCarthy and Ben Ferguson, Hopes of global emissions deal at Copenhagen.

overlaps with international politics, and governments often fundamentally disagree about what constitutes the relevant law in a particular case.[829]

Traditionally public international law is described as a system of rules and principles that govern the relationship between states and other subjects of international law (e.g., the United Nations or the European Community). The main primary sources of international law are treaties and customary law. Treaties only bind parties to them and are interpreted through different means. These include the intention of the parties at the time the agreement was concluded and the subsequent practice of the parties in its application.[830] Customary international law is derived from the consistent practice of states accompanied by *opinion juris*—the conviction of states that this practice is required by a legal obligation.[831]

In most cases, the basis for contentious litigation between states would be the alleged breach of an international obligation or a "wrongful act". Such an action results in "state responsibility" (or liability) under international law. To successfully raise an inter-state claim, the wrongful act must be attributable to the accused state and causally linked to any occurring damage. The criteria and terminology employed in this connection differ, and there are significant uncertainties related to the legal and factual underpinning of any potential climate change case. And yet, it may very well provide the basic framework for an inter-state climate change case under the public international law.[832]

The breach of an international obligation can result from the international treaty or customary law, and may be committed by an act or omission. The treaty law relevant in this connection may include the UNFCCC and the Kyoto Protocol, the United Nations Convention on the Law of the Sea (UNCLOS) or other multi- or bilateral agreements. The current literature, however, predominantly suggests that a violation of international law could be based on the so-called "no-harm rule."[833]

---

829 *Law & Literature*, CLIMATE-CHANGE-LITIGATION (last viewed July 6, 2013), http://climate-change-litigation.wikispaces.com/2.+Law+%26+literature.

830 Vienna Convention on the Law of Treaties art. 18, May 23, 1969, 1155 U.N.T.S. 331.

831 *Law & Literature*, CLIMATE-CHANGE-LITIGATION (last viewed July 6, 2013), http://climate-change-litigation.wikispaces.com/2.+Law+%26+literature.

832 *Substantive Law*, CLIMATE-CHANGE-LITIGATION (last viewed July 6, 2013), http://climate-change-litigation.wikispaces.com/3.+Substantive+law.

833 *Substantive Law*, CLIMATE-CHANGE-LITIGATION (last viewed July 6, 2013), http://climate-change-litigation.wikispaces.com/3.+Substantive+law; Patricia Birnie, Alan Boyle and Catherine Redgwell, International Law and the Environment, 3rd ed., Oxford, 2009.

The no-harm rule is a widely recognized principle of customary international law whereby a state is duty-bound to prevent, reduce and control the risk of environmental harm to other states. The legal precedent case usually cited in this connection refers to a Canadian smelter whose sulfur dioxide emissions had caused air pollution damages across the border in the US. The arbitral tribunal, in that case, determined that the government of Canada had to pay the United States compensation for damage that the smelter had caused primarily to land along the Columbia River valley in the US.[834]

The United Nations Office for the Coordination of Humanitarian Affairs has estimated that in 2008 over 20 million people were displaced by sudden-onset climate-related disasters. A recent report of the Global Humanitarian Forum states that per year climate change already causes 300,000 deaths throughout the world, seriously impacts on the lives of 325 million people, and costs USD125 billion globally. In June 2010, the Adaptation Fund established under the UNFCCC approved its first four projects for funding. The projects aim to tackle sea level rise and extreme weather events in the Solomon Islands and the coastal areas of Senegal, flooding from glacier lakes in Pakistan and improve watersheds better to deal with droughts and floods in Nicaragua.[835]

These staggering statistics are proof that, as a result of climate change many countries may already be able to show a certain degree of harm—whether this is the loss of territory, crops or biodiversity. According to the majority opinion amongst writers, the actual occurrence of harm is not a precondition for a violation of the no-harm rule. It is sufficient to show that a state's conduct *will* cause significant damage for its responsibility to be engaged. Thus, the no-harm rule is not only a general obligation to prevent significant transboundary harm, but also to minimize the risk of such harm. The 2007 IPCC report stated that if GHG emissions continued their current trajectory, the earth's temperature would be likely to rise by between 1.8 and 4 degrees Celsius over the coming century, with an outside chance of the increase reaching 6 degrees. The report indicated that

---

834 *Substantive Law*, Climate-Change-Litigation (last viewed July 6, 2013), http://climate-change-litigation.wikispaces.com/3.+Substantive+law; Trail Smelter Arbitration: United States v Canada (1931–1941) 3 UNRIAA, vol. III, p.1965.

835 *Substantive Law*, Climate-Change-Litigation (last viewed July 6, 2013),
http://climate-change-litigation.wikispaces.com/3.+Substantive+law.

some regions will be more affected by climate change than others. These include the Arctic, sub-Saharan Africa, small islands and Asian mega-deltas.[836]

A state can only be held responsible for the breach of an international obligation if this can be attributed to an act or omission of one (or more) of its organs. In most industrialized countries, the majority of GHG emissions have been generated by private entities. In international relations, however, a state remains accountable for activities on its territory and under its effective control. According to Christoph Schwarte, by approving actions that result in GHG emissions, or by failing to put restrictions into place that prevent harm to other countries, its organs are responsible for the resulting transboundary pollution and non-compliance with the no-harm rule. [837] Whether the breach of an international obligation needs to be accompanied by a degree of negligence or fault on the part of the state or its organ(s) to amount to a wrongful act is disputed. Some writers have argued that states are strictly liable for environmental harm. However, in the context of climate change it may seem unfair to make states accountable for activities whose long-term implications have only been gradually understood. Other scholars, therefore, hold that the relevant organs must have violated a particular standard of care. In particular, if the focus of the state's conduct is on an omission (to curb GHG emissions) the need to act must have been apparent to a diligent government.[838]

The precise scope and features of the no-harm rule have been defined by reference to the requirement of due diligence. Due diligence is comprised of at least the following elements: the opportunity to act or prevent; foreseeability or knowledge that an individual activity could lead to transboundary damage; and proportionality in the choice of measures required to prevent harm or minimize risk. If, despite the foreseeability of events, equal measures (which are capable of protecting the environment of other states) were not taken, a state can be

---

836 *Substantive Law*, CLIMATE-CHANGE-LITIGATION (last viewed July 6, 2013),
http://climate-change-litigation.wikispaces.com/3.+Substantive+law.

837 Schwarte, C. (2004). Environmental Concerns in the Adjudication of the International Tribunal for the

Law of the Sea, *Georgetown International Environmental Law Review* (16): 421. Retrieved from https://litigation-essentials.lexisnexis.com/webcd/app?action=DocumentDisplay&crawlid=1&doctype=cite&docid=16+Geo.+Int'l+Envtl.+L.+Rev.+421&srctype=smi&srcid=3B15&key=833ef0a3e511d5e915fe5dfc4d88e9b5

838 *Substantive Law*, CLIMATE-CHANGE-LITIGATION (last viewed July 6, 2013), http://climate-change-litigation.wikispaces.com/3.+Substantive+law; Martin Vermeer and Stefan Rahmstor, *Global sea level linked to global temperature*, Proceedings of the National Academy of Sciences of the United States of America Vol. 106 No. 51, 22 December 2009, pp.21527-21532.

considered careless and held responsible for a wrongful act. Many developed countries have had an opportunity to reduce the risk of transboundary pollution by limiting their emissions of GHGs through, for example, stricter regulations and control measures, the introduction of renewable energies or changes in the lifestyle of their populations. At least, since 1992, when the UNFCCC was put in place to stabilize GHG emissions, parties to that agreement have explicitly acknowledged this link. Given the risks related to global warming previous actions were taken to limit emissions, even at the expense of economic growth and prosperity in already affluent societies, seem only proportionate. Some Annex I governments might, however, vehemently disagree.[839]

To raise a claim of state responsibility, it is further necessary to establish that there is a causal link between the activities complained of and the harm in question. In 2007, the IPCC found that there is a better than nine in ten chance that global warming can be attributed to emissions from industry, transport, deforestation and other human activities. Over the last few years, scientists have also improved their capacity to analyze the role of human-induced climate change on specific extreme weather events. Hence, sophisticated climate modeling may eventually help to determine the extent to which climate change is to blame for the floods in Pakistan and the heat wave in Russia; or desertification in Mongolia.[840]

The legal literature is mainly concerned with the impossibility of attributing emissions of a particular country to specific damages. The problem with damage from climate change is that it is hard to trace back to any one particular state's actions. Due to the compound and synergetic effect of the diverse pollutants and polluters involved, and the non-linearity of climate change, it may be difficult to establish a chain of causation. Contributory factors may intervene, and the complexity of the climate system can almost always be relied upon to assert a possible break in the chain. Hence, the standard of proof applied in respect of causation may be crucial. The international jurisprudence in this regard differs and the test used has ranged from *"clear and convincing"* to *"on the balance*

---

839 *Substantive Law*, CLIMATE-CHANGE-LITIGATION (last viewed July 6, 2013), http://climate-change-litigation.wikispaces.com/3.+Substantive+law; Anil Ananthaswamy, Time to blame climate change for extreme weather, New Scientist, 25 August 2010.

840 *Substantive Law*, CLIMATE-CHANGE-LITIGATION (last viewed July 6, 2013), http://climate-change-litigation.wikispaces.com/3.+Substantive+law.

of probabilities."[841] The precautionary principle has been used as a procedural tool to lower the standard of proof in situations where the complexity of scientific facts leads to a degree of uncertainty. In the existing jurisprudence, partial causation has also been considered sufficient to establish liability. There exist relatively precise estimates of different countries' relative contributions to the absolute tons of GHG emitted globally. It has therefore been suggested that, because of the cumulative causation of climate change, each actor should only be held responsible for its share of the overall wrong. The general rule of international law, however, appears to be that states that are jointly responsible for a wrongful act are jointly and severally liable. Thus, each state is separately responsible. As a matter of principle, this responsibility is not reduced by the fact that other states are responsible for the same wrongful act. A state already suffering from the impacts or increased exposure to global warming could rely on a growing body of scientific research to substantiate the imputation of cause and effect (flooding, drought, extreme weather events, etc.). While a perpetrator of an international legal wrong could be fully accountable, the resulting legal obligations may remain subject to the principle of proportionality. Liability for the entirety of damages (maybe with a burden to then seek contributions from others) would not necessarily result in an obligation to make full reparation.[842]

Under international law, there are some circumstances that preclude the wrongfulness of an act and which may, therefore, be asserted by a state seeking to justify its actions. These are consent of the injured state, proper countermeasures, force majeure, distress, necessity, compliance with peremptory norms and self- defense. As far as self-defense, although a state may indeed act in that way, which does not necessarily mean that all actions taken in self-defense are lawful. The provisions of international humanitarian law and international human rights law will still apply. Notably, addressing whether an action can be considered by a right to self-defense, the International Court of Justice (ICJ)

---

841 Schwabach, A. Transboundary environmental harm, and state responsibility: Customary international law. *International Law and Institutions.* Retrieved from http://www.eolss.net/sample-chapters/c14/e1-36-02-02.pdf

842 *Substantive Law,* CLIMATE-CHANGE-LITIGATION (last viewed July 6, 2013), http://climate-change-litigation.wikispaces.com/3.+Substantive+law; Simon Marr, The Southern Bluefin Tuna Cases: The Precautionary Approach and Conservation and Management of Fish Resources, 11 European J. Int'l Law, 2000, p.815; Alexander Yankov, in Myron H.

Nordquiest & John Norton Moore (eds.), Current Fisheries Disputes and the International Tribunal for the Law of the Sea, Current Marine Environment Issues and the International Tribunal for the Law of the Sea, 2001, p.223.

claimed that "respect for the environment is one of the elements that go to assessing whether an action is in conformity with the principles of necessity and proportionality."[843]

In the context of climate change, the argument that a state can easily use is the necessity.[844] For instance, a rapidly developing state might argue that its emissions are justifiable because of the urgent need for development to lift its population from poverty. There would, however, be obstacles to such an argument. First, a state would need to prove that the act in question is the only way for the state to safeguard the people against a grave and imminent peril, and that does not seriously impair an essential interest of the international community as a whole. Under traditional international public law state, sovereignty and territorial integrity are first principles. It may, therefore, be difficult to argue that the need for development could outweigh the physical existence or the inundation of coastal areas of another state. Another justification, which a state might use, is consent or waiver. Consent arises before or during the act complained of and precluded wrongfulness. Waiver or acquiescence arises after the action is completed and leads to the loss of the right of the complaining state to invoke the responsibility of the perpetrator. The history of states' tolerance of GHG emissions could be relied upon to argue either that they had consented to those emissions, or had waived any claim arising from the damage the emissions had caused.[845]

If a state is found responsible for committing an unlawful act under international law, it is obliged to discontinue the wrongful act, offer guarantees of non-repetition and provide full reparation for the consequences of the breach it has committed. The purpose of restitution is to wipe out, as far as possible, all the implications of the illegal act and re-establish the situation, which would, in all probability, have existed if the act had not been committed. This can take the form of restitution in kind or, if this is not possible, payment of damages, satisfaction or any combination of the three. The claim for reparation may be

---

843 *Substantive Law*, CLIMATE-CHANGE-LITIGATION (last viewed July 6, 2013),
     http://climate-change-litigation.wikispaces.com/3.+Substantive+law.

844 Convention on International Liability for Damage Caused by Space Objects (adopted 29 November 1971 entered into force 1 September 1972) Article IV; UNCLOS Article 139(2).

845 *Substantive Law*, CLIMATE-CHANGE-LITIGATION (last viewed July 6, 2013),
     http://climate-change-litigation.wikispaces.com/3.+Substantive+law; ILC Draft Articles, Article 25(1)(a)-(b).

limited by the requirement of proportionality of measures—their reasonableness and equitability.[846]

To date, the discourse in the academic literature on state responsibility for climate change has very much focused on the question of compensation for damages. However, if the liability of a state for an unlawful act under international law has been established, the primary obligation that arises is to cease the wrongful act and to provide assurance or a guarantee of non-repetition. In the case of a hostile occupation, for example, this would mean the immediate and unconditional withdrawal of troops and abstention from any further military action. Depending on the context it could also entail the immediate release of hostages and prisoners, ending existing discriminations or disturbances to the domestic order of a country, or taking necessary measures to prevent the destruction and theft of property. The demand for cessation is usually accompanied by a request for assurances or guarantees concerned with other potential breaches in the future. Whereas satisfaction and reparation focus on the violation, warranties and guarantees deal with the continuation of the affected relationship. Assurances are commonly given verbally while guarantees require something more. For example, a guarantee may involve preventative measures being taken by the responsible state designed to avoid repetition of the breach.

On March 31, 2008, Ecuador filed a dispute at the ICJ concerning the aerial spraying by Colombia of toxic herbicides at locations near, at, and across its border with Ecuador. Ecuador alleged that the spraying causes severe damage to people, crops, animals and the natural environment on the Ecuadorian side of the frontier, and poses a grave risk of further damage over time. Accordingly Ecuador, amongst other things, requested the Court to declare that Colombia has violated its obligations under international law and shall[847] "...take all steps necessary to prevent, on any part of its territory, the use of any toxic herbicides in such a way that they could be deposited on the territory of Ecuador; and (iii)

---

846 *Legal Consequences*, CLIMATE-CHANGE-LITIGATION (last viewed July 6, 2013), http://climate-change-litigation.wikispaces.com/4.+Legal+consequences; Case Concerning the Land and Maritime Boundary Between Cameroon and Nigeria (Cameroon v. Nigeria: Equatorial Guinea intervening), ICJ Reports 2002, p. 303.

847 International Court of Justice. Retrieved from www.icj-cij.org

prohibit the use, by means of aerial dispersion, of such herbicides in Ecuador, or on or near any part of its border with Ecuador."[848]

On May 31, 2010, Australia initiated proceedings before the ICJ against the government of Japan, alleging that Japan's pursuit of a scientific whaling programme constituted "a breach of the International Convention for the Regulation of Whaling and other international obligations" for the preservation of marine mammals and marine environment. In its application, Australia requested the Court to declare that Japan was in breach of its international obligations, and order that Japan ceases the implementation of its programme, and revoke any authorizations, permits or licenses allowing whaling activities. Furthermore, Japan should provide assurances and guarantees that it will not take any further action under its scientific whaling, or any other similar, programme. These two ICJ cases are still in the early stages and, recent international judgments illustrate the reluctance of international judicial bodies to find for environmental protection claims. However, both applications reflect the general principle that if an international obligation has been breached, the first and foremost legal consequence is the discontinuation of the wrongful act. Cessation of a violation is the first step towards eliminating the consequences of the unlawful act. In the case of transboundary pollution, it has been questioned, however, whether this would entail the immediate and unconditional stop of the unlawful environmental interference. In practice states have often been given a reasonable timeframe to modify or terminate the polluting activities. This may also be considered a question of proportionality between the significance of the international legal wrong and the redress owed. The legal doctrine is divided as to whether cessation is regarded as part of the reparation for a wrongful act or the resumption of compliance with the original obligation. Unlike the concept of restitution, the need for cessation of a breach may not be limited by the principle of proportionality.[849]

Restitution in kind is an ideal form of reparation and comes closest to the general principle that a state must wipe out the consequences of its wrongful act by re-establishing the situation that would have existed if that act had not

---

848 *Legal Consequences*, CLIMATE-CHANGE-LITIGATION (last viewed July 6, 2013), http://climate-change-litigation.wikispaces.com/4.+Legal+consequences; ICJ, Case Concerning Pulp Mills on the River Uruguay (Argentina v Uruguay) ICJ judgment of April 2010.

849 *Legal Consequences*, CLIMATE-CHANGE-LITIGATION (last viewed July 6, 2013),
http://climate-change-litigation.wikispaces.com/4.+Legal+consequences.

been committed. Visible means of achieving restitution would, for example, be to return or repair the property.[850]

If restitution were no longer possible (e.g., property has been permanently destroyed, become valueless or restoration is highly impracticable), compensation would be the next available remedy to consider. In certain cases, full reparation may be disproportionate as far as the responsible state is concerned. Therefore, reparation would be limited to equitable compensation, i.e. to the extent that it is reasonable and fair. In general, the injured state can choose amongst the different forms of reparation and indicate a preference. Compensation is usually calculated by reference to a depreciation of the economic value of the damaged item. Thus, assessing adequate compensation for damage to the environment poses a variety of challenges.[851]

Satisfaction is the remedy for those injuries not financially assessable, such as moral or legal damages. Such injuries are frequently of a symbolic character, arising from the very fact of the breach of the obligation, irrespective of its material consequences. The appropriate form of satisfaction would depend on the circumstances. It can take the form of an acknowledgement of the breach, an expression of regret or a formal apology. A declaration of the wrongfulness of the act by an international court or tribunal is usually considered sufficient.[852]

Once an internationally wrongful act has been committed, a legal relationship between the injured state and the responsible state occurs. An unlawful act does not usually affect the pre-existing relationship and the continuous duty of the wrongdoing state to perform the obligation it has breached. However, in some circumstances the violation of the obligation may put an end to the bond itself, or allow the injured state to terminate the pre-existing relationship (and thereby the continuous responsibility). An injured state may also take countermeasures such as economic sanctions, which would otherwise be contrary to international law. Countermeasures are not intended as punishment but as an instrument of achieving compliance. They are only permissible in response to a

---

850 *Legal Consequences*, CLIMATE-CHANGE-LITIGATION (last viewed July 6, 2013), http://climate-change-litigation.wikispaces.com/4.+Legal+consequences

851 *Legal Consequences*, CLIMATE-CHANGE-LITIGATION (last viewed July 6, 2013), http://climate-change-litigation.wikispaces.com/4.+Legal+consequences

852 *Legal Consequences*, CLIMATE-CHANGE-LITIGATION (last viewed July 6, 2013), http://climate-change-litigation.wikispaces.com/4.+Legal+consequences; Permanent Court of International Justice (PCIJ), Factory at Chorzów, Jurisdiction, 1927, PCIJ Series A No. 9 p.17.

previous international wrongful act of another state and must be directed against that state. If, subsequently, the allegedly wrongful act is found to be lawful, the countermeasures result in state liability.[853] Countermeasures usually take the form of non-performance of an obligation and are temporary in nature. They should be discontinued if the responsible state complies with its obligation of cessation and reparation. States are to choose countermeasures that are proportionate to the wrongful act and, as far as possible, reversible. Certain breaches of international law may be considered so grave that they require multilateral cooperation to bring them to an end. In practice, serious violations are likely to be addressed through the United Nations Security Council and the General Assembly, and sanctions are one form of multilateral cooperation.[854]

Usually, an injured state must actively give notice to the responsible state that it seeks cessation and reparation. This could take the form of an unofficial or confidential reminder of the need to fulfill an obligation. In any event, the injured state must give notice of its claim to the state, which is in breach. If the wounded state is aware of the violation, failure to do so—in part (e.g., omitting to claim interest) or in full—may eventually preclude it from invoking state responsibility because of waiver or acquiescence.[855] States are in general also under an obligation not to recognize or sustain the unlawful situation arising from a serious breach of an absolute duty.[856]

The ICJ is the principal judicial organ of the United Nations and has been described as the guardian of the international legal community as a whole. It may hear contentious disputes concerning an alleged breach of an international obligation if (and to the extent) the States concerned have accepted its jurisdiction. A state may accept the ICJ's jurisdiction in three different ways: by special agreement, through an international treaty that contains a clause providing for acceptance, or by a unilateral declaration. The mechanism of the unilateral

---

853 ICJ, Case Concerning East Timor (Portugal v. Australia), Judgment, ICJ Reports 1995 p. 90; Military and Paramilitary Activities in and against Nicaragua (Nicaragua v the United States of America) Merits, ICJ Reports, 1986 p.14.

854 *Legal Consequences*, CLIMATE-CHANGE-LITIGATION (last viewed July 6, 2013), http://climate-change-litigation.wikispaces.com/4.+Legal+consequences

855 ICJ, Legal Consequences for Sates of the Continued Presence of South Africa in Namibia notwithstanding Security Council Resolution 276, Advisory Opinion of 21 June 1971, ICJ Reports 1971, p.16.

856 *Legal Consequences*, CLIMATE-CHANGE-LITIGATION (last viewed July 6, 2013), http://climate-change-litigation.wikispaces.com/4.+Legal+consequences

declaration (recognizing the jurisdiction of the Court[857] As binding on any other state also accepting it as binding) has led to the creation of a group of countries, which have accepted the ICJ's jurisdiction to settle any dispute that might arise between them in future. In principle, any state in this group is entitled to bring one or more other states in the group before the Court.[858]

Many declarations, however, contain reservations limiting their duration or excluding certain categories of dispute. This means that the ICJ will only have jurisdiction to the extent that the declarations of all parties to a dispute coincide and do not exclude the type of argument raised. Individual countries have, for example, excluded disputes, which concern the delimitation of maritime zones, originate in armed conflict or "*where the parties have agreed on other settlement methods.*" If applicable, the latter reservation is likely to be invoked by a Respondent to argue that the dispute settlement procedures agreed under the UNFCCC limit the jurisdiction of the ICJ.[859] However, where it can be established that prior negotiations have been unsuccessful in the absence of an Annex on UNFCCC arbitration, there is no "other" method to settle the dispute.[860]

Contentious cases brought before the ICJ can take several years from the filing of the case to the reading of the judgment on the merits. Under Article 41 of the ICJ Statute, and Article 73 of its Rules, the ICJ can order provisional measures if it considers that circumstances so require[861]. The objective of provisional measures is to preserve the respective rights of the parties, pending a decision of the Court on the merits. A link must, therefore, be established between the provisional measures requested and the rights that are the subject of the proceedings before the Court as to the merits. Provisional measures will only be granted if the majority of judges believe that there are good grounds for the underlying

---

857 Charter of the United Nations, 1945, Art.92; Separate Opinion of Judge Lachs in Questions of Interpretation and Application of the 1971 Montreal Convention arising from the Aerial Incident at Lockerbie (Libyan Arab Jamahiriya v the United Kingdom), Provisional Measures, Order of 14 April 1992, ICJ Reports 1992 p.26.

858 *Procedural Avenues*, CLIMATE-CHANGE-LITIGATION (last viewed July 6, 2013),
http://climate-change-litigation.wikispaces.com/5 +Procedural+avenues; ICJ Statute, Art.36.

859 The full text of all declarations is available from the website of the ICJ at http://www.icjcij.

860 *Procedural Avenues*, CLIMATE-CHANGE-LITIGATION (last viewed July 6, 2013),
http://climate-change-litigation.wikispaces.com/5.+Procedural+avenues

861 102 ICJ Statute; Rules of Court (adopted 14 April 1978, entered into force 1 July 1978) available at
http://www.icjcij.org/documents/index.php?p1=4&p2=3&p3=0&PHPSESSID=5c407&lang=en&PHPSESSID=5c407.

application and the content and effect of such measures does not prejudice the case's outcome. Thus, the court cannot make definitive findings of fact or imputability. The right of each party to dispute facts and responsibility, and to submit arguments in respect of the merits, must remain unaffected by the decision. Provisional measures are only justified if there is urgency in the sense of an imminent risk that irreparable damages may be caused by the subject matter of the disputed rights. However, it is disputed whether provisional measures ordered by the ICJ under Article 41 of its Statute are binding.

In practice, the record of compliance with interim measures is not encouraging. Following Russia's occupation of South Ossetia in August 2008, Georgia requested the ICJ to order provisional measures to prevent irreparable injury to the right of return of ethnic Georgians (under Article 5 of the Convention on Racial Discrimination) pending the Court's determination of the case on the merits. In its Order of October 2008, the ICJ, *inter alia*, indicated that both parties should refrain from any act of racial discrimination; abstain from sponsoring, defending or supporting racial discrimination; and do all in their power to ensure security of persons, freedom of movement and residence and the protection of property in the region. In the Pulp Mills case (Argentina v. Uruguay), Argentina claimed that by unilaterally authorizing the construction of a pulp mill whose operation would damage the environment of the river Uruguay, Uruguay was in breach of a reciprocal obligation of prior notification and consultation in respect of actions, which may potentially cause transboundary harm. It requested provisional measures including the suspension of all building works.[862] However, the Court dismissed the application (and, in April 2010, to a large extent, the case on the merits), as even if there were a violation of international law, the Mills could eventually be modified or dismantled. In the Court's view, the construction of the mills would not create a "fait accompli" and would not render the current sitting of the mills irreversible.[863]

The IPCC has not indicated a specific temperature threshold for "dangerous" anthropogenic interference with the climate. The international discussion is currently targeting around a 2oC (3.6oF) (corresponding to a concentration

---

862 Tzanakopoulos, A. (2004). Provisional Measures Indicated by International Courts: Emergence of a General Principle of International Law. *Revue Hellenique de Droit International* (57):1-53. Retrieved from

   http://www.peacepalacelibrary.nl/plinklet/index.php?sid=related&ppn=299299996

863 *Procedural Avenues*, CLIMATE-CHANGE-LITIGATION (last viewed July 6, 2013),

   http://climate-change-litigation.wikispaces.com/5.+Procedural+avenues.

of GHGs in the atmosphere of approximately 450 ppm CO2-eq) compared to pre-industrial times to avoid unmanageable climate risks. In this connection, the date of the peak of emissions is vital. The UK Met Office's Hadley Centre for Climate Prediction and Research found that if global emissions peaked in 2016, and then started to decline at an annual rate of 4 percent, there would be a 50:50 chance of keeping the rise in temperature to 20C. For every year that the peak was delayed, the Hadley Centre said the world would be committed to another 0.50C of warming. Economists and climate change experts at Price Waterhouse Coopers[864] Found that one-fifth of the world's carbon budget for 2000-2050 required to limit temperature rise to 20C had been used up by 2008. Hence, the world was already 10 percent off the necessary trajectory to hit the target. If it stays on this course, the entire global carbon budget for 2000-2050 will be used up by 2034. Consequently, some scientists argue that the world is already on course for the worst-case scenario (outlined by the IPCC) regarding climate change with global average temperatures rising by up to 60C by the end of the century. Such a rise would have irreversible consequences for the Earth making parts of the planet uninhabitable and threatening the basis of some societies and multiple species. There is also evidence that the natural carbon sinks that have absorbed CO2 over previous decades on land or sea are beginning to fail as a result of rising global temperatures.[865]

The substantive provisions of UNCLOS may be of potential relevance in connection with possible climate change litigation efforts discussed previously. The Convention also contains an elaborate system for the peaceful settlement of disputes between its parties. When a dispute concerning the interpretation and application of the Convention arises—for example on the mutual obligations to prevent harm to the environment of states under Article 193—they are obliged to exchange views on its settlement expeditiously. Unless they have already agreed to a process in advance, parties must then proceed to settle the dispute using their choice—for example, further negotiations, conciliation or judicial procedures. If parties fail to reach a solution in this way, any dispute must be submitted to UNCLOS settlement procedures leading to a binding decision- possible the ICJ, the International Tribunal for the Law of the Sea (ITLOS) or an arbitral

---

864   ICJ, Pulp Mills on the River Uruguay (Argentina v. Uruguay), Provisional Measures, Order of 13 July 2006, ICJ Reports 2006, p.113; Passage through the Great Belt, Order of 29 July 1991, para.31.

865   *Procedural Avenues*, CLIMATE-CHANGE-LITIGATION (last viewed July 6, 2013), http://climate-change-litigation.wikispaces.com/5. +Procedural+avenues; Low Carbon Economy Index, Price Waterhouse Coopers, December 2009.

tribunal. To which body the dispute goes depends on the choice of the parties on or after signature of the Convention. When the parties involved in the case do not accept the same procedure, it goes to arbitration. [866]At present, 160 states are subject to compulsory dispute settlement under UNCLOS. This includes all the main emitters except the US.[867]

5.1.3. Claims under international law

The climate crisis introduces an existential and moral dilemma of unparalleled proportions. The proliferation of carbon-based emissions in the atmosphere is threatening—and will continue to threaten with greater severity—the ecosystems that support all life and human civilization. The impacts of climate change are experienced unevenly, with the most vulnerable—the "climate vulnerable"—set to suffer first and worst. The current and anticipated impacts demonstrate a grand irony: those who will suffer most acutely are also those who are least responsible for the crisis to date.[868]

Increased concentrations of carbon dioxide in the atmosphere threaten the general stability of ecosystems and civilizations, with a greater effect on the world's poor and those least equipped to adapt. The rising temperatures that result from higher carbon concentrations are linked to changes in rainfall, with attendant impacts on water supply for humans, agriculture, and ecosystems. Rapid melting of tropical glaciers results in severe threats to water supply and hydropower. Additionally, increased fire frequency, ecosystem damage, desertification and irrevocable sea level rise, observed today, will persist for generations and are irreversible[869]. Indeed, observed changes in climate are already occurring with evidence that these changes are due to human activity. Such

---

866 International Tribunal for the Law of the Sea (ITLOS), Southern Bluefin Tuna Cases, Request for Provisional Measures, Order of 27 August 1999.

867 *Procedural Avenues*, CLIMATE-CHANGE-LITIGATION (last viewed July 6, 2013),

   http://climate-change-litigation.wikispaces.com/5.+Procedural+avenues.

868 Maxine Burkett, *Climate Reparations*, 10 Melbourne Journal of Int'l Law 1, 1-2 (2009) [hereinafter Burkett, *Climate Reparations*]; *Ice Bridge Ruptures in Antarctic*, BBC NEWS (April 5, 2009), http://news.bbc.co.uk/2/hi/7984054.stm.

869 Ad Hoc Working Group on Further Commitments for Annex I Parties under the Kyoto Protocol, Consideration of the Scale of Emission Reductions to Be Achieved by Annex I Parties in Aggregate — Addendum: Submissions from Parties, United Nations Doc FCCC/KP/AWG/2009/MISC.1/Add.1 (25 March 2009) 10 (Paper No 2: Submission by Tuvalu).

observed impacts indicate that we have already reached an atmospheric carbon concentration that is in the "danger zone."[870]

The "climate vulnerable" describes those communities or nation-states that have a particular acute vulnerability to present and forecasted climatic changes. Evidence of climate change's disproportionate impacts is well documented and becoming increasingly prevalent. As early as 2001, IPCC stated, "the countries with the fewest resources are likely to bear the greatest burden of climate change regarding the loss of life and relative effect on investment and economy." Growing evidence reveals that climate change will hit two particular groups "disproportionately and unfairly."[871]

Although the UNFCCC "specifically identified past, current and long-term implications of continued, intensive carbon emissions," emphasizing "the need for rapid reduction of CO2 emissions by the major polluters," emissions trends have moved inversely.[872] For example, "despite knowledge of the consequences of increased carbon output and their specific obligations under the UNFCCC, emissions in the developed world increased significantly, with the US among the top increased emitters."[873]

The developed world has agreed in principle that those vulnerable to climate change need substantial financial assistance to adapt to the ravages of climate change, yet the promised funds and monies provided to date have been woefully lacking. Taking into account current and projected international finance, adaptation funding is only in the order of millions of dollars per year. This is compared to the over 50 billion US dollars that Oxfam estimates are required. Attempts have been made to craft a comprehensive approach to achieving compensation based on climate change, both within and beyond the UNFCCC, even if this framework does not address the ethics and justice elements that are key to a useful system of reparation by climate change damages. Verheyen and Roderick in "Beyond Adaptation: The legal duty to pay compensation for climate change" persuasively argue that, at the international level, claims for compensation by the climate vulnerable against specified developed countries would have a firm

---

870 Burkett, *Climate Reparations, supra* note 1056, at 4-5.

871 Burkett, *Climate Reparations, supra* note 1056, at 5.

872 Burkett, *Climate Reparations, supra* note 1056, at 6; "Climate Change and the Poor: Adapt or Die," The Economist (New York, US) 13 September 2008, 57, estimating the population of these two specific groups to be one billion in 100 countries.

873 Burkett, M. (2009). Climate Reparations. *Melbourne Journal of International Law (10)*. Retrieved from http://papers.ssrn.com/sol3/papers.cfm?abstract_id=1539726

basis in international law if brought before the appropriate tribunal. They conclude that many advanced countries have had the opportunity to reduce their emissions, but did not. Such countries most likely have been well aware of the consequences of increased emissions but failed to take appropriate precautions and instead generated "excess emissions." Further, they cite arguments contending that the language of the UNFCCC "amounts to an implicit acceptance by developed country parties of responsibility for causing climate change," yet the "climate regime" lacks rules on compensation that might be used to aid adaptation measures in vulnerable nations. In light of these very plausible claims, Verheyen and Roderick identify the possibility of legal action against the major polluting countries and rightly caution against a "raft of complex, uncoordinated" and "cumbersome" individual cases that might ensue. Instead, they introduce a reliable vehicle for a more comprehensive approach to generally, and its disproportionate impact on the developing world, in particular, is not, however, squarely addressed by this legal mechanism.[874]

Cooperation and negotiation, arguably foundational principles of international law, militate against legal action. However, since there are significant gaps in the international climate regime, to fulfill its promises of avoiding dangerous climate change and providing adaptation support to those vulnerable to climate change, a flurry of legal actions and accompanying theories of liability have emerged. Most claims at the domestic US level have tried to enforce more stringent emissions reductions. The vast majority of applications in the US, however, have not broached the special needs of the climate vulnerable. Claims on behalf of the climate vulnerable and those advancing claims for adaptation are far less frequent, and the plausibility of their success is, even more, remote.[875]

"One such claim, recently dismissed in a US District Court, is *Native Village of Kivalina vs. Exxon Mobil.* In *Kivalina*,"[876] "the plaintiffs sought damages for climate change from oil, coal and electric utility companies, alleging that the defendants' GHG emissions constituted a public nuisance."[877] "Specifically, a

874 *Id.*

875 *Id.*

876 *Native Village of Kivalina v Exxon Mobil Corp,* No C 08-1138 SBA (ND Cal, 30 September 2009) (Order Granting Defendants' Motions to Dismiss for Lack of Subject Matter Jurisdiction) ('*Kivalina*'). See also Complaint about Damages; Demand for Jury Trial, *Native Village of Kivalina v Exxon Mobil Corp* (ND Cal, filed 26 February 2008), http://www.climatelaw.org/cases/country/us/kivalina/Kivalina%20Complaint.pdf.

877 Burkett, *Climate Reparations, supra* note 1056, at 10.

native Inupiat village must now relocate due to melting sea ice that formerly served as a wave barrier for their village."[878] "The loss of that ice has resulted in significant erosion, rendering the village of Kivalina uninhabitable."[879] "Until very recently, courts have deemed climate change and its remedies to be political questions beyond the expertise of the judiciary."[880]

Reparations claimants are entitled to repair because they are primary victims of the injustice or are injured in an identifiable and significant way. As discussed above, the climate vulnerable suffer from anthropogenic climate change to which their contribution is, in most cases, negligible, yet the consequences are life-threatening.[881]

Adding to the tragedy of increased vulnerability to climate change due to climate shifts and circumstance, the climate vulnerable are further injured by: the lack of meaningful participation in international negotiations, at which the major emitters wield ultimate power in setting the agenda; the stringency of the goals; and the very determination of what is considered "dangerous" climate change. Indeed, Angus Friday, who has spoken for small island states at the United Nations, stated that the most vulnerable nations are the least able to participate effectively in the climate talks. The inability to compete effectively results in perilously low emissions reduction goals, an additional injury to which this class is subject. The UNFCCC, at the time of its passage, did not quantify the stabilization level for atmospheric carbon, instead leaving that determination to future discussions at which parties to the UNFCCC would identify what constitutes a "dangerous" interference with the climate system. As described above, vulnerable developing countries and island nations have emphasized that they already experience what they consider dangerous climate change. Nevertheless, the world's wealthiest countries, comprised of the major emitters, have adopted a 2°C increase in global temperature above pre-industrial levels as a goal to limit human-made global warming. This is in contrast to scientists who argue for an increase of no more than 1.7°C, and the island nations' insistence that anything over 1.5°C could prove catastrophic. In spite of this bleak landscape, the developed world has not given severe or appropriate consideration to

---

878 Burkett, *Climate Reparations, supra* note 1056, at 10.

879 Burkett, *Climate Reparations, supra* note 1056, at 10.

880 Burkett, *Climate Reparations, supra* note 1056, at 10.

881 Burkett, M. (2007). Reconciliation and Nonrepetition: A New Paradigm for African-American Reparations. *Oregon Law Review* (1).

suggestions for meaningful contribution to adaptation and sound mechanisms for compensation.

In sum, the harms for which the injured might seek repair are the result of past emission actions described above and contemporary failures in the negotiations arena. A repair effort must focus on correcting the current effects of past wrongs, effectively shifting from *redress to address*. This is especially important in the context of climate change. In fact, the normal time lag between increased carbon concentration's effects is yet another factor that makes the climate crisis such a unique moral and political challenge. For that reason, the impact of current emissions might have to be considered. Continued emissions of carbon may constitute an additional and separate tort though ultimately the groups pursuing the reparations claims would determine their temporal scope, similar to other reparations efforts. However, the assumption is that without immediate and appropriate efforts to repair, the harm may continue and worsen into the future. The parallel hypothesis here is that if immediate measures to mitigate and adapt are not implemented, the ecological destruction will continue and worsen. [882]

Those responsible for repair might be those who have committed the harm, benefitted from the harm and/or are successors to the "harm-doers." In the context of climate change, there is substantial evidence available that demonstrates the disproportionate historical and current emissions of the developed world, which is "plausibly seen ... as a kind of tort imposed by wealthy countries on poor ones." Generally speaking, researchers have found that there is a significant ecological debt owed to low-income nations from wealthy states for various environmental consequences of human activity, including the disproportionate emissions of GHGs. The developed world may contest the period for which they are responsible, arguing that they should not be responsible for emissions that occurred when they did not understand the consequences of those emissions. However, one can make a strong argument that they understood the implications of increased carbon emissions at the time of participating in the UNFCCC, which for most developed countries occurred in the early 1990s. [883]

Under the UNFCCC, Annex I countries have additional obligations, including further requirements for emission reduction and facilitation of climate-friendly technology transfers due to the stark differences in their historical contributions

---

882 Burkett, *Climate Reparations, supra* note 1056, at 19-20.

883 Burkett, *Climate Reparations, supra* note 1056, at 20-21.

to climate change. The subsequent Kyoto Protocol reflects those special and additional commitments, not the least of which was the requirement that Annex I parties reduce their emissions to about five percent below 1990 levels.[884]

Developed countries have failed to take equal measures to reduce excess emissions, remaining intransigent in negotiations for stricter emissions reductions. In fact, developed country emissions have risen at a *greater* rate after becoming aware of the importance of reducing emissions, posing an even sharper risk to all states, but especially those whose livelihoods are immediately and severely threatened. Whether or not the no-harm rule provides adequate legal force, it provides a framework for appropriating responsibility.[885]

Climate reparations would provide an agreed-upon framework for repair while giving voice to the climate vulnerable and moral force to their claims. International law recognizes three forms of reparation. The first — re-establishing the situation that existed before the wrongful act was committed, meaning restitution in kind — is impossible in the climate change context. As discussed above, the impacts of climate change are irreversible and, as such, are forecasted to render communities and entire nation-states nonexistent, if not significantly impaired. Compensation, monetary or otherwise, is also an oft-used remedy and is the second of the three recognized forms of reparation. The third is satisfaction. Satisfaction describes solutions other than restitution or compensation and encompasses the aspects of repair — such as an apology, truth telling and non-repetition — that are of significant value in the climate context. It is a non-standard, although well-established, form of reparation and provides repair for injuries that "amount to an affront to the State."[886]

As mentioned above, an apology, some form of compensation and the guarantee of non-repetition would be the three essential elements of a successful reparations effort — though utilized in various degrees depending on the nature and extent of the harm. Indeed, "full compensation" is accomplished through the flexible use of different reparative mechanisms and, to the extent one form is dispensed with or unavailable — as restitution in kind is in this case — the other methods become correspondingly more important. The apology is the first step in acknowledging the harm resulting from one's actions; forgiveness may, in fact, depend on it. A sincere apology is a voluntary declaration in which

---

884 Burkett, *Climate Reparations, supra* note 1056, at 21.

885 Burkett, *Climate Reparations, supra* note 1056, at 22.

886 Burkett, *Climate Reparations, supra* note 1056, at 23.

the developed world *fully accepts* the responsibility of its excess emissions. The apology reminds the wrongdoer of community norms because the apology admits to violating them." As such, it offers something that trials and monetary reparations cannot — a collaborative acknowledgment of violation and responsibility.[887]

For the climate vulnerable, compensation and non-repetition require discussion of adaptation and mitigation efforts, respectively. Taking adaptation first, numerous formal and informal promises have been proposed to help increase the adaptive capacity of the climate vulnerable. These efforts can be a form of compensation for the acknowledged effects of excess emissions to the extent that they are delivered in lump sum monetary transfers. Adaptation measures, like insurance plans or technology transfers previously floated, are also methods of compensation. In short, the developed world could execute the many adaptation proposals and provide, without delay or distraction, the tens of billions of dollars needed to prepare the developing world. This would also allow developed nations to honor their self-imposed obligations. For example, as signatories to the UNFCCC, the developed world bound themselves to some adaptation provisions that are meant to reflect the acknowledgment of the disproportionate burden of climate change.[888]

Environmental Degradation- a terrorist act?

Furthermore, there is a scenario of the state responsibility analysis under the international law, specifically the legal argumentation between the fight against terrorism and the fight against environmental degradation emanating from outside the country. May the Pacific Islands environmental threat be compared with a terrorist act? May the major countries, sources of the climate change be accused of "climate (environmental) terrorist" acts? The legal parallel could argue the understanding and definitions under international law, particularly regarding the Olympic Games from Germany in 1972 and after September 11, 2001, events. There are no specific conclusions; however the evaluation could become an attractive and appropriate assessment of the facts concerning the similarities and applicability of the two concepts, under the international law umbrella.

---

887 Burkett, *Climate Reparations, supra* note 1056, at 23-24.

888 Burkett, *Climate Reparations, supra* note 1056, at 24.

5.2.1. Actual Status

The Pacific Island nations are well aware of their current situation, and, there-fore, have made it a priority to gain the attention and support of the international community. In the summer of 2001, the 31st Annual Pacific Islands Forum took place in Nauru and a major focus was the increasing threat posed to member nations by rising sea levels. The Pacific Islands Forum is made up of represen-tatives from Australia, Cook Islands, Fiji, Kiribati, Micronesia, Nauru, New Zealand, Niue, Palau, Papua New Guinea, Marshall Islands, Samoa, Solomon Islands, Tonga, Tuvalu, and Vanuatu.[889] In response to the increasing threat, the Pacific Islands Forum has demanded a meeting with U.S. President George W. Bush.[890] President Bush has stated that the United States will back out of the Kyoto Protocol and its call for a reduction in GHG emissions because it places an unfair burden on the United States.[891] The island nations want to urge President Bush to do more to reduce GHG emissions and to back the global emission cuts put forth in the Kyoto protocol.[892] The president of Nauru, Rene Harris, contends that with so many nations threatened by rising sea levels it would be a "modern holocaust" if the world did not address the problem.[893]

The problem of rising sea levels has also been brought up in the global com-munity. In the early 1990s, concern over the impact of increased GHGs on the global climate prompted the adoption of the UNFCCC. By September 2000, 186 nations had ratified the treaty.[894] The UNFCCC does not require parties to reduce

---

[889] Pacific Islands to Sign Trade Pact (2001). BBC NEWS. Retrieved from http://news.bbc.co.uk/hi/english/business/newsid_1490000/1490339.stm.

[890] Mercer, P. (2001). Islanders Press Bush on Global Warming. BBC NEWS. Retrieved from http://news.bbc.co.uk/hi/english/world/asia-pacific/newsid_1496000/149651.stm.

[891] Anderson, K. (2001). Bush Feels Heat on Global Warming. BBC NEWS. Retrieved from http://news.bbc.co.uk/hi/english/world/americas/newsid_1438000/1438089.stm.

[892] *Id.*

[893] *Id.*

[894] UNFCCC: Signatories and Ratification of the Convention, Parties in Chronological Order--Update on Ratification of the Convention, http:// unfccc.de/resource/conv/ratlist.pdf (last visited on Nov. 12, 2001).

GHG emissions, but it does note the particular vulnerability of low-lying atolls and their inhabitants.[895] The first international agreement requiring parties to make a significant reduction in GHG emission was the Kyoto Protocol of 1997.[896] For example, it required some of Annex I states that signed and ratified it to reduce emissions to an average of five percent below 1990 levels during the 2008-2012 period.[897] While the environmental community may have found the Kyoto Protocol to be a very promising beginning, the reality of the Kyoto Protocol has been far less auspicious. Many Annex I nations, including industrialized nations like the United States, who initially agreed to cut GHG emissions, are in fact increasing emissions.[898] In the United States, a change in administrations resulted in a change in support for the Kyoto Protocol. Many commentators cite heavy lobbying and hefty campaign contributions from the oil, gas, coal, and energy industries for this policy shift that favors big business.[899] So, while there is an overall international diplomatic and political support for a reduction in GHG emissions, in reality, the cuts are not occurring at the desired rate.[900]

There are only a few practical options for threatened Pacific Island nations if the other nations of the world continue to ignore the problem and do not cut GHG emissions to a level sufficient to mitigate sea level rise. Retreating to higher ground is not a possibility.[901] These islands simply do not have enough usable landmass that lies out of the reach of the rising sea. The ideal option for small island nations would be to have a global reduction in GHG emissions. But, given the world economic dependence on fossil fuels and industrial processes that produce GHGs, a dramatic reduction is very unlikely. Therefore, to fund relocation and mitigation strategies, these nations must seek financial assistance from the international community. It seems that there are several possible legal

---

895 UNFCCC, supra note 30, at pmbl. ("Recognizing further that low-lying and other small island countries are particularly vulnerable to the adverse effects of climate change.").

896 Kyoto Protocol, *supra* note 369.

897 *Id.*

898 See UNFCCC Greenhouse Gas Inventory Database (2001), at http:// ghg.unfccc.int (last visited May 18, 2007). For example the United States total CO_2 emission (in gigagrams) went from 5,193,841 in 1995 to 5,478,051 in 1998.

899 *Id.*

900 Reed, *supra* note 978.

901 Intergovernmental Panel on Climate Change, Climate Change 2001: Impacts, Adaptation, and Vulnerability, 17.2.2.1, http://www.ipcc.ch/pub/tar/wg2/626.htm#17221

avenues for these countries to find the necessary funding. One option would be to pursue a remedy under the Rio Declaration, which the United States does recognize.[902] Principle 2 of the Rio Declaration states that each state has "the responsibility to ensure that activities within their jurisdiction or control do not cause damage to the environment of other States or of the area beyond the limits of national jurisdiction."[903] Because the Rio Declaration itself is not binding law, an action based on a violation of the Rio Declaration would be an action for a breach of customary international law. Similarly, a tort action could be brought to remedy this harm. Any of the preceding claims would need to be brought in the appropriate court, most likely the International Court of Justice ("ICJ") or a United States district court. The United States, however, does not submit to the jurisdiction of the ICJ.[904] Thus, the best option is to bring an action in United States district court under the Alien Tort Claims Act.[905]

5.2.2. Planning

On December 11, 2011, the seventeenth session of the Conference of the Parties to the UNFCCC yielded the "Durban Package." Durban Package was created to fulfill several objectives of countries that are among the most vulnerable to climate change: the Pacific Island Developing States ("SIDS") and the larger AOSIS. These objectives carried out the hope that the negotiations would produce more ambitious GHG emission reduction pledges by developed countries. They also wanted the institutions mandated by the 2010 Cancun Agreements to become fully operational and to complete the terms of reference for the review of the long-term global goal for emission reductions.

Although the Durban Package aimed to accomplish many of the PSID and AOSIS goals for adaptation, on mitigation, however, it is now clear that the Durban Package did not do what these countries wanted. Action taken on the

---

902 United Nations Conference on Environment and Development: Rio Declaration on Environment and Development, 47th Sess., U.N. Doc. A/CONF. 151/5/REV.1 (1992), reprinted in 31 I.L.M. 874. The Rio Declaration was adopted by consensus by all participants in the conference. Lakshman D. Guru Swamy et al., Supplement of Basic Documents to International Environmental Law and World Order: A Problem-Oriented Coursebook 1268 (1994).

903 See Rio Declaration, supra note 76, print. 2.

904 J. Chris Larson, Note, Racing the Rising Tide: Legal Options for the Marshall Islands, 21 Mich. J. Int'l L. 495, 497 (2000).

905 Reed, *supra* note 978.

Kyoto Protocol's second commitment period is no more than a proposal to formalize pledges made last year in Cancun by Kyoto Protocol developed country parties. Also, it does not include major emitting countries such as the United States, Canada, Russia, and Japan. UNFCCC parties agreed to establish the Ad Hoc Working Group on the Durban Platform for Enhanced Action ("AWG-DPEA") to adopt, by 2015, a new "protocol, legal instrument or agreed outcome with legal force."[906] While the new AWG-DPEA has the mandate to develop proposals on the full range of climate change issues, its focus will clearly be on raising the "level of ambition" on mitigation for all parties.

The views of the parties on emission reductions were as predicted. AOSIS countries wanted to conclude negotiations for a new treaty with substantially greater emissions reductions by the end of 2012. The United States, however, argued that it is unwise to request countries to increase their emissions reduction goals when they just agreed to pledges two years ago in Copenhagen. The United States also insisted on "legal symmetry," that is, comparable commitments from all major economies. However major emitting developing countries like Brazil, South Africa, India, and China refused to commit to any binding obligations.

The United States was not alone in pressing developing countries to increase their ambition through legally binding commitments. Switzerland, the European Union, and others called for parties to rethink the meaning of common but differentiated responsibilities ("CBDR"), the UNFCCC's cornerstone principle. In the climate change regime, CBDR means that developed countries bear a disproportionate responsibility to mitigate climate change given their disproportionate historical emissions. Because China is now the world's largest emitter of GHGs and developing country emissions of carbon dioxide, exceed those of developed countries,[907] These countries argued that CBDR must "evolve" to take into account these current circumstances. As a result, the Durban Package neither increases ambition nor adopts formal amendments to the Kyoto Protocol. Instead, it tentatively establishes a second five-year commitment period running

---

906 Decision -/CP.17, Establishment of an Ad Hoc Working Group on the Durban Platform for Enhanced Action, p 2 (advanced unedited edition). All draft decisions from COP17 and CMP7 are available at the Climate Change Secretariat's website, http://unfccc.int/2860.php.

907 International Energy Agency, CO2 Emissions from Fuel Combustion: Highlights 7 (2011).

from January 1, 2013, to December 31, 2017.[908] Ensuring that the second commitment period will end in 2017 rather than 2020 was a major victory for the SIDS because they did not want to lock in low ambition for an eight-year period, as favored by the European Union.

The second commitment period is tentative because the parties must complete many steps to make it a reality. The Durban Package merely "takes note" of the proposed amendments to Annex B of the Kyoto Protocol, which restate the pledges these countries have already anchored in the Cancun Agreements. In addition, the Durban Package "takes note" of the "intention" of Annex I parties to convert their pledges into quantified emission limitation and reduction objectives. This step is necessary to make pledges comparable to some countries that have chosen different base years from which to measure reductions or that have used different assumptions for calculating emission reductions. The second commitment period will enter into force when three-fourths of the Kyoto Protocol parties ratify the amendments.

The UNFCCC parties made progress on measurement, reporting, and verification of their mitigation commitments. Beginning in 2014, each Annex I party must submit a biennial report that provides information on its mitigation actions and progress towards meeting its targets.[909] Developing countries, known as non-Annex I parties, were expected to complete biennial update reports on GHG emissions and control measures consistent with their capabilities and level of financial support received for reporting, by December 2014, although Least Developed States and Small Island the Developing States may have submitted reports at their discretion.[910] The parties also adopted procedures for verification, called International Assessment and Review ("IAR") for Annex I parties[911] And International Consultation and Analysis ("ICA") for non-Annex I parties.[912] Generally speaking, both IAR and ICA consist of a review of information

---

908 Draft Decision -/CMP.7, Outcome of the Work of the Ad Hoc Working Group on Further Commitments for Annex I Parties under the Kyoto Protocol at its Sixteenth Session (advanced unedited version); *see also* FCCC/KP/AWG/2011/L.3/Add.1, p 1 (Dec. 10, 2011).

909 Decision -/CP.17, Outcome of the Work of the Ad Hoc Working Group on Long-term Cooperative Action under the Convention (advanced unedited edition), 12–22, Annex I. *See also* FCCC/AWGLCA/2011/L.4.

910 *Id.* 39–44, Annex III.

911 *Id.* 23–31, Annex II.

912 *Id.* 56–62, Annex IV.

regarding implementation of a country's pledge. Parties will be invited to pose questions to a party, and that party may respond orally to those questions.

The UNFCCC parties further developed institutions and processes for adaptation, technology transfer, and capacity building. They determined the Adaptation Committee's composition and charged the committee with compiling and sharing information, knowledge, and expertise concerning adaptation.[913] They adopted guidelines for LDCs to prepare national adaptation plans.[914] They also took further steps to launch the Climate Technology Center and Network[915] and established a Durban Forum to share experiences, ideas, and best practices concerning capacity building.[916]

The UNFCCC parties took several steps to channel funding to developing countries for adaptation and mitigation. Perhaps most significantly, they approved the governing instrument for the Green Climate Fund ("GCF"), [917]which will provide a significant portion of the $100 billion per year in long-term adaptation and mitigation finance that developed countries have pledged to mobilize by 2020? Also, the parties also established a new Standing Committee to make recommendations to coordinate the proliferating sources of climate change financing under the UNFCCC and the Kyoto Protocol, including the GCF, the Adaptation Fund, and the Least Developed Countries Fund.[918] The Standing Committee will also provide advice on monitoring, reporting, and verification of support provided to developing countries. The parties will develop a work program as well regarding long-term finance to help scale up the mobilization of climate finance.[919]

The Durban Package reflects a fundamental change in reporting and accounting for LULUCF for Kyoto Protocol parties.[920] Perhaps most importantly,

---

913 *Id.* 92–119, Annex V.

914 Decision -/CP.17, National Adaptation Plans (advanced unedited edition); *see also* FCCC/CP/2011/L.8/Add.1.

915 AWG-LCA Outcome, 133–43, Annexes VII, VIII.

916 *Id.* 144–56.

917 Draft Decision -/CP.17, Green Climate Fund: Report of the Transitional Committee (advance unedited version).

918 AWG-LCA Outcome, 120–25, Annex VI.

919 *Id.* 126–32.

920 Decision -/CMP.7, Land Use, Land-Use Change and Forestry. *See also* FCCC/KP/AWG/2011/L.3/Add.2 (Dec. 10, 2011).

this decision requires developed country Kyoto Protocol parties to account for emissions and removals of GHGs from forest management even though such accounting is voluntary under Kyoto Protocol Article 3.4. However, the parties adopted rules to account for emissions and removals from forest management that Tuvalu and others consider a "loophole." Under this regulation, emissions are calculated about a reference level based on a country's projection of its anticipated emissions and removals. If actual emissions are below this figure, then the party will have net withdrawals. Only if emissions exceed this reference level will a party incur emissions. Based on this methodology, a party could have substantial emissions from forest management—that is, it cut more forest than it replanted—but the party may show no emissions or even removals because it factored this into its reference level. Although the rules now require Annex I parties to calculate emissions from wood products, they may use estimates for changes in the carbon stored in these products based on the *2006 IPCC Guidelines for National Greenhouse Gas Inventories* or use country-specific data, provided that verifiable and transparent data are available. However, wood products resulting from deforestation must be accounted for as rapid oxidation. In addition, imported wood products are excluded from this accounting.[921]

As the negotiations shift from Durban to Doha, the site of COP18, Pacific Island States will likely turn their attention to obtaining steep emissions reductions through the new AWG-DPEA. However, they will likely face significant obstacles. First, parties will not even be halfway through implementation of their Cancun pledges before they are asked to adopt new commitments. Second, the Review Mechanism, which will review the adequacy of the long-term global goal for emissions reductions, and the latest report of the IPCC, may not be completed in time to inform governments. Third, the AWG-DPEA will inherit the seemingly intractable issue of whether any future climate deal should take the form of a "protocol, legal instrument or agreed outcome with legal force." As such, it will take a substantial breakthrough to avoid business-as-usual political and emissions trends.

5.2.3. The right to self-determination as customary international law

Self-determination is a principle with a long history that has been used and throughout the 20th century. It has evolved into a norm in customary

---

921 *Id.* Annex I, 4, 16, 26–32.

international law, and its components represent viable alternatives for minority groups seeking to self-determine their fate.[922] On the one hand, self-determination rights for a minority group may involve political and representative rights within a central state, but on the other it may amount to remedial secession and eventual independence.

There are a few case studies that illustrate the link between concepts such as self-determination, state sovereignty, and intervention. These studies include East Timor, Chechnya, Kosovo, and Georgia. In each of these countries "people" struggled for self-determination and ultimately independence. Only the Timorese and the Kosovars were successful in their plight for self-determination, primarily because the Great Powers determined that their cause was legitimate. The Chechens and the South Ossetians and Abkhazians were not as lucky: their struggles for self-determination remained unsupported by the Great Powers and these regions remain governed by the same ruling regimes.[923] The example of East Timor will be discussed in more detail below and Kosovo and will illustrate the idea of a minority movement aided by the world community in its quest for independence.

East Timor forcibly became a part of Indonesia in 1976, when Indonesia claimed East Timor as its 27th Province. Before 1976, East Timor had been colonized and administered by Portugal.[924] The international community was swift in its condemnation of Indonesia following the 1976 takeover and the United Nations continued to recognize Portugal as East Timor's official administrator.[925] The Indonesian rule over East Timor "imposed a military force that viciously led to human rights and humanity violations,"[926] And was often marked by extreme violence and brutality. Estimates of the number of East Timorese who died during the occupation vary from 60,000 to 200,000.[927]

---

922 Castellino, J. (2008). Territorial Integrity and the "Right" to Self-Determination: An Examination of the Conceptual Tools. *BROOK. J. INT'L L.* (503): 557.

923 Milena Sterio, *On the Right to External Self-Determination: "Selfistans," Secession, and the Great Powers' Rule,* 19 MINNESOTA JOURNAL OF INT'L LAW 137, 140 (2010), *available at* http://minnjil.org/pdf/Sterio.Web%20PDF.pdf.

924 Purnawanty, J. (2000). Various Perspectives on Understanding the East Timor Crisis. *14 TEMP. INT'L & COMP. L.J.* (61).

925 Charney, J. (2001). Self-Determination: Chechnya, Kosovo and East Timor. *VAND. J. TRANSNAT'L L.* (34): 455, 465.

926 Idem note 166.

927 Sterio, *supra* note 1120, at 158.

In 1999, the East Timorese people voted in a United Nations-organized referendum to separate from Indonesia.[928] Indonesia protested the referendum results and was accused of backing violent militias to attack and intimidate the East Timorese populations. The United Nations Security Council, in Resolution 1264, established the International Force for East Timor, a peacekeeping force to safeguard the country.[929] East Timor was then administered by the United Nations, with substantial support from other countries. East Timor became the first new sovereign state of the 21st century by obtaining independence on May 20, 2002, when United Nations Secretary- General Kofi Annan handed over the authority of the country to the new government.[930] A few months later, East Timor joined the United Nations as a new, independent state.[931] Although sporadic outbreaks of violence have plagued East Timor since its independence, the constant military involvement on behalf of the international community has helped to contain the spread of violence.[932]

The East Timorese struggle for independence perfectly illustrates the paradigm of how the Great Powers' support, or lack thereof, influences the result of such a self-determination struggle. The East Timorese people fought for independence during several decades. During the Cold War era, however, their struggle was unsupported by some of the Great Powers, and the East Timorese were not able to assert independence from Indonesia on their own, as they lacked the political, economic, and military capability to do so. After the end of the Cold War, the Great Powers began supporting the East Timorese, which was reflected in the Security Council decision-making process, when virtually all Security Council members agreed that the East Timorese should no longer

---

928 Idem note 166, p. 67.

929 Purnawanty, *supra* note, p. 276.

930 East Timor: Birth of a Nation (2002). *BBC News World Edition*. Retrieved from http://news.bbc.co.uk/2/hi/asia-pacific/1996673.stm.

   See also Timor-Leste: UN Admits Newest Member State, UN NEWS CENTRE Sept. 27, 2002, http://www.un.org/apps/news/infocusRel.asp?infocusID=27 (declaring East Timor the first new country of the millennium).

931 United Nations NEWS CENTRE, *supra* note.

932 Sterio, *supra* note 1120, at 159.

remain governed by Indonesia.[933] Thus, the United Nations Security Council authorized the deployment of peacekeepers to East Timor and helped organize the popular referendum and elections, which ultimately paved the way to Timorese independence. If there was no support in the post-cold war period from the Great Powers, it is doubtful that East Timor would have gained independence from Indonesia as quickly.[934]

5.3. INTERNATIONAL ACTION IN THE PACIFIC

5.3.1. New Zealand

Immigration to New Zealand began around the 10th century with Polynesian settlement in New Zealand. The role of Moriori settlement is currently disputed, with some saying that the Moriori arrived in New Zealand before the Maori, while others believe that the two groups were related, with the Moriori being a sub-group of Maori. European migration provided a significant influx following the signing of the Treaty of Waitangi in 1840. Subsequent migrants have been arriving from the British Isles, Europe, the Pacific, the Americas, & Asia.[935] Currently, "New Zealanders welcomes some citizens of Kiribati, Tuvalu and Tonga to settle in New Zealand each year under the Pacific Access Category."[936] "Work opportunities, education and family are some of the reasons people

---

933 Chaulia, S. *A World of Selfistans?* (2008). Global Policy Forum. Retrieved from

http://www.globalpolicy.org/component/content/article/171-emerging/29875.html ("As long as General Suharto [the Indonesian leader] was necessary for the West's Cold War agenda, the United States, Britain, and Australia helped Indonesia to annex and control East Timor. Once Indonesia lost the support of the great powers, these same states ganged up to recognize East Timor's right to self-determination and acted as midwives for its birth as an independent state.").

934 Sterio, *supra* note 1120, at 159-60.

935 Helping empowers people from refugee backgrounds to achieve their goals and contribute to their new home in New Zealand. *New Zealand Red Cross – Refugee Programs.* Retrieved from http://www.refugeeservices.org.nz/

936 *Pacific Access Category,* Immigration New Zealand (June 17, 2013), http://www.immigration.govt.nz/migrant/stream/live/pacificaccess/.

choose to leave the Pacific Islands and start a new life in New Zealand, and many have found New Zealand a great place to live, work and raise families."[937]

People of Pacific ethnicities have a long history of settlement in New Zealand, and ongoing migration from the Pacific, which started several centuries earlier with the first flows from Polynesia.[938] Several waves of migration occurred from various parts of the Pacific throughout the last century and a half, with significant periods of immigration during the 1960s and 1970s. Pacific people in New Zealand are now a diverse group with ancestral links to many parts of the Pacific. The communities have settled throughout New Zealand but prefer to live in particular areas, such as South Auckland. The majority are New Zealand-born.[939]

More than 47 percent of people of Pacific ethnicities have moved within New Zealand between 2001 and 2006.[940] "In 2006, there were 266,000 people who identified with one or more ethnicities in the Pacific ethnic grouping."[941] "Of these, 255,000 people told us where they had lived five years earlier at the time of the 2001 Census."[942] "Among the people aged five years and over who have disclosed this information, 47 percent had moved at least once in NZ within the previous five years, 44 percent had not moved, and 9 percent had arrived or returned from overseas."[943]

"The Pacific grouping of ethnicities includes people of several distinct ethnicities. They have different migration histories and different characteristics, such as settlement patterns, age structures and rates of intermarriage."[944] "These

---

937 *Pacific Access Category*, Immigration New Zealand (June 17, 2013),
http://www.immigration.govt.nz/migrant/stream/live/pacificaccess/.

938 *Id.*

939 *Overview of Pacific Migration*, STATISTICS NEW ZEALAND (last viewed July 9, 2013),
http://www.stats.govt.nz/browse_for_stats/population/Migration/internal-migration/pacific-mobility.aspx.

940 *Overview of Pacific Migration, supra* note 1137.

941 *Overview of Pacific Migration, supra* note 1137.

942 *Overview of Pacific Migration, supra* note 1137.

943 *Overview of Pacific Migration, supra* note 1137.

944 *Diversity in the Pacific Population*, STATISTICS NEW ZEALAND (last viewed July 9, 2013). Retrieved from
http://www.stats.govt.nz/browse_for_stats/population/Migration/internal-migration/pacific-mobility/diversity-in-the-pacific-population.aspx.

affect mobility either directly or indirectly."[945] "The three largest Pacific populations in New Zealand are people of Samoan, Tongan and Cook Island Maori ethnicities."[946] "In each case, the majority were born in New Zealand: 60 percent for Samoan, 56 percent for Tongan and 73 percent for Cook Island Maori."[947]

The Niuean population in New Zealand is over 14 times the size of the population of Niue and 74 percent of the group was born in New Zealand. It is a highly integrated community with high levels of inter-ethnic partnering. Only 22 percent of couples in New Zealand with at least one person of Niuean ethnicity have both partners who are Niuean. Moreover, 60 percent of Niueans also identifies with other ethnicities. Consequently, their mobility pattern is very similar to the social model and different from most other Pacific groups. While almost half of those in New Zealand five years ago had moved to New Zealand, just over half had not moved. Conversely, Fijians are a more recent migrant community. Less than half were born in New Zealand, and almost a quarter of the group was overseas five years ago. Fijians continue to be highly mobile with more than half of those in New Zealand five years ago having moved.[948]

"Between 2001 and 2006, 48 percent of the Pacific population who had been living in New Zealand in 2001 had not moved, and a further 43 percent moved within the same region council area. Inter-regional movers accounted for 9 percent of the Pacific population."[949] Auckland region dominated because of the portion of the Pacific population living in that region (67 percent). Between 2001 and 2006, 52 percent of the Pacific population in Auckland who had been in New Zealand in 2001 had not moved, and a further 44 percent moved within the region. Although the exchange of Pacific people between Auckland and other areas was largest for Auckland, Auckland lost only 3 percent of this population to other regions. Movers into Auckland region contributed five percent of the region's Pacific population aged five years and older who had not been overseas in 2001.[950]

---

945 *Diversity in the Pacific Population, supra* note 1143.

946 *Diversity in the Pacific Population, supra* note 1143.

947 *Diversity in the Pacific Population, supra* note 1143; http://www.refugeehealth.govt.nz/aboutus/refugeenz.asp

948 *Diversity in the Pacific Population, supra* note 1143.

949 *Where are Pacific People Moving to?,* STATISTICS NEW ZEALAND (last viewed July 9, 2013), http://www.refugeeservices.org.nz/refugees_and_new_zealand

950 *Where are Pacific People Moving to? supra* note 1150.

Mobility within Auckland region has contributed strongly to the level and nature of internal migration among people of Pacific ethnicities. Manukau and Auckland Cities had the highest proportion of non-movers among their Pacific populations. Manukau City is home to the majority of the Auckland Pacific population and is the preferred location for many, as shown by the low proportion of people who chose to move out of the territorial authority (TA) and the large proportion of movers who decided to remain in the TA. Manakau City also drew substantial numbers of internal migrants from other TAs in the region than it gained.[951]

The vast majority (87 percent) of Pacific internal migrants who moved between 2001 and 2006 moved within or between main urban areas. The remaining 13 percent, approximately a third of whom are of both Maori and Pacific ethnicities, involved the exchange of people between the various urban and rural area types. The main urban areas gained more internal migrants than they lost to other area types. The majority of the net gain to main cities was from population moving between main urban and minor urban areas. This contrasts with small net losses to other area types. However, in general, the size of the outflows is very similar to the size of the inflows.[952]

Main urban areas exchanged people of Pacific ethnicities with all other area types, resulting in an overall net gain in the main cities. The significance of the exchange of people between area types becomes evident when we consider the source of internal migrants for each area type. Pacific movers into central urban areas came from minor urban and rural areas, which is also the case for Maori movers. However, unlike Maori, secondary urban areas contributed a similar number of Pacific people to main cities. Outflows from main urban areas also differed from Maori in that Pacific movers added almost equal numbers to secondary urban, minor urban and rural areas. International migration has a significant relationship with internal migration. People who migrate or return to New Zealand tend to settle initially in the major centers—primarily in Auckland but also in significant numbers in Christchurch and Hamilton. Many subsequently move, contributing to internal migration patterns. Similarly, other people may choose to move to another country rather than to another part of New Zealand.[953]

---

951 *Where are Pacific People Moving to?, supra* note 1150.

952 *Where are Pacific People Moving to?, supra* note 1150.

953 *Where are Pacific People Moving to?, supra* note 1150.

Pacific people are highly urbanized and new migrants and individuals returning from overseas tend to settle in main urban areas. This explains the higher proportion of the Pacific population in main urban areas, which had been overseas five years ago in 2006, compared with other area types.[954]

Auckland is the key point of entry for the majority of people arriving in or returning to New Zealand. Auckland region, in 2006, accounted for 68 percent of people of Pacific ethnicities who had been living overseas five years ago. Wellington region was the next most popular region with 12 percent of this group living in that region.[955]

The age distribution of those who were overseas five years ago who were living in the Auckland territorial authorities shows quite distinct location preferences. Manukau City attracted more people of Pacific ethnicities in all age groups than other areas. The relationship between the 5–14 years ago group and the 30–49 years age group suggests that family migration was critical in Manukau and Waitakere Cities, with a bias towards student and young working adults in Auckland City.[956]

5.3.2. Australia

Canada's decision to formally withdraw from the Kyoto Protocol because the protocol did not cover the world's largest emitters—namely China and the US, represents a great example Australia wants to follow. Australia argued at Durban it would not be part of a second commitment period under Kyoto until a broader agreement was reached covering all major emitters including both developed and developing countries. The European Union, Switzerland and Norway were among the very few parties to agree in South Africa to new commitments under Kyoto.

The new treaty is scheduled to be concluded no later than 2015. It will then come into effect by 2020. Australia considers that this is "not that far off at all" and has not avoided legislating a carbon tax from mid-2012.

---

954 *Where are Pacific People Moving to?, supra* note 1150.

955 *Where are Pacific People Moving to?, supra* note 1150.

956 *Where are Pacific People Moving to?, supra* note 1150.

Australia openness to Pacific Islands- a proposed solution

The 2006 Temporary and Circular Labor Migration Programme (TLCM) for Columbians during the time when the Galeras volcano erupted, targeted different vulnerable communities and was used to provide a migration opportunity for affected people. This programme allowed them to temporary migrated to Spain, where they could have earned an income in the seasonal harvest.[957] "Afterwards, the programme was also expanded to rural populations, whose crops and land are particularly vulnerable to floods, droughts and other environmental disruptions."[958] "During their working period in Spain, the temporary migrants acquired knowledge and skills to diversify their income upon return to Colombia."[959] "In this way, they could reduce their vulnerability to environmental disruptions, without being forced to permanently relocate."[960] "Furthermore, their absence allowed the recovery of their fragile land (Engelman 2009; Irin Humanitarian News and Analysis 2010)."[961]

In 2007, the IOM joined the TCLM project, with the aim of strengthening it, and making it replicable. The IOM also wanted to promote certain targeted communities to benefit from the programme. Thanks to funding of the European Commission's AENEAS programme, the IOM expanded the initial project, increasing the number of beneficiaries and the number of Spanish employers taking part. The organization also provided technical assistance to national institutions developing a migration policy and legislation (IOM 2010). While the UP had initiated the project as an opportunity for economic welfare and development, the IOM added the perspective of "migration management," as required by the AENEAS programme (Magri 2009).[962]

In the last years of functionality, the TCLM programme offered Colombian workers the possibility to work in Catalonia by doing seasonal labor for one of the employers associated with the UP. The goal of this programme was twofold:

957 Moor, N. (2010). Temporary Labour Migration for Victims of Natural Disasters: The Case of Colombia. UNIVERSITEIT GENT. Retrieved from http://www.ehs.unu.edu/file/get/5403; http://www.iom.int/jahia/Jahia/colombia.

958 Moor, *supra* note 1159, at 7.

959 Moor, *supra* note 1159, at 7.

960 Moor, *supra* note 1159, at 7.

961 Moor, *supra* note 1159, at 7.

962 Moor, *supra* note 1159, at 7;

Firstly, it aimed at effectively managing seasonal labor migration. The programme was an answer to Catalonia's demand for low-skilled labor and was meant to regulate legally labor migration flows. Secondly, the programme also aimed at supporting "the generation of wealth in both countries" (Magri 2009: 28). In other words, it intended to enhance the impact of migration on the development of local communities in Colombia (IOM 2010). Since the experience of seasonal migration could provide skills and resources, migrants could be made "innovators and entrepreneurs in their country of origin" (Magri 2009: 13). This way, the seasonal worker could not only improve his personal income and social status but the economic welfare of his home community as well. The idea was to provide the migrants with temporary residence and work permits, to allow them to earn a living and acquire knowledge and skills, making them more resilient when returning to Colombia. As for the beneficiaries coming from environmentally-affected regions, the programme offered a limited income alternative, while the affected regions can recuperate. According to Koko Warner, the TCLM programme was "an important source of post-disaster rehabilitation" (Irin Humanitarian News and Analysis 2010).[963]

To achieve these ambitious goals, strategic alliances with third countries were needed (Magri 2009). Furthermore, the participating workers needed to be well prepared and guided during the whole migration process. Through various training activities, the TCLM programme prepared migrants to generate economic and social development in their region of origin. Participating workers were supported in the planning, coordination, formulation and management of community projects, and in the structuring and follow-up of business plans. They were also encouraged to achieve self-sustainability through marketing, services or import/export activities. Moreover, remittances were channeled towards productive initiatives or the purchase of goods improving the socioeconomic status of the community of origin. IOM's local partners were responsible for some of the preparation work in the country of origin, as the selection of the migrant workers, and the identification of job-generating initiatives.

Could the TCLM programme model be implemented between Pacific countries and other hosting countries like the European member states or Australia? As the programme was considered to be a "best practice," it is interesting to

---

963 Program on Forced Migration and Health. Retrieved from http://www.forcedmigration.columbia. edu/faculty/wessells.html

investigate the possibility to copy this model, taking into consideration national specificities and improved safeguards.

Various prerequisites for the replication of the TCLM programme can be identified: Firstly, the political, economic and institutional context of the host region is decisive for the implementation of any labour migration programme. The political will to support temporary labour migration with a focus on co-development is imperative for the replication of the TCLM project. A gap between labour supply and demand in the destination country is another fundamental factor for a labour migration programme. Seasonal labour migration is furthermore stimulated by an economic sector with a calendar linked to the circularity of the temporary migrant. The TCLM project was implemented in the Spanish agricultural sector, where there is a large demand for seasonal migrant workers for the harvesting and processing of fruit. In 2006, foreign workers counted for 74.1 percent of the labour forces in this sector[964]. Also, a big employer's organisation, with a coordinating and mobilizing management role, facilitates such a project[965]. Furthermore, the way in which countries deal with irregular migration and with sanctioning employers hiring irregular migrants plays a vital role[966].

Legally speaking, the TCLM programme was implemented under a specific legal framework, allowing third country nationals to undergo temporary labour migration, and encouraging circularity of foreign workers. The conditions and procedures for (seasonal) labour migration may vary between the EU Member States. And/or Australia,[967] however, the replication of the TCLM programme is only possible for those states that allow seasonal labour migration for low-skilled workers. Furthermore, the issuance of residence and work permits for third country nationals is in some countries limited to nationals of certain third countries. In Italy for example, the seasonal quota is mainly reserved for citizens of listed countries or countries that have signed a cooperation agreement with Italy, aimed at fighting irregular migration and repatriating irregular migrants.[968] Countries like Spain and Italy, with a large demand for seasonal labour, tend to

---

964 Zapata- Barrero, Ricard; Faundez Garcia, Rocio and Sanchez Montijano, Elena 2010.

965 Ibid.

966 MAGRI, 2009.

967 Laws for Legal Immigration in the 27 EU Member States, International Migration Law N° 16, International Organization for Migration (IOM), 2009.

968 MAGRI 2009.

facilitate seasonal migration through bilateral agreements on migration management with third countries.[969] Moreover, according to some national legislation, labour migration can only take place within certain quota established by the government. This means that some countries only allow migrant workers to be employed in certain sectors or certain jobs while others apply a more broad approach regarding the employment of third country nationals. For those countries where labour migration is limited to nationals of certain third countries, the introduction of a TCLM programme will likely be preceded by a cooperation agreement with countries of origin.

Another important aspect is the support of the circularity of the migrant in national policy and legislation. As discussed above, the Spanish legislation has introduced various incentives for the migrant to return to his country of origin after his working period in Spain. The Italian migration law also aims at guaranteeing the return of temporary workers, giving obeying workers priority for re-entrance during the following season[970]. Of course, a lot depends on the contents of bilateral agreements between home and host countries.

A programme like the TCLM model furthermore requires some flexibility in national migration law. Employers in the agricultural sector, where Colombian beneficiaries were employed, are exposed to sudden changes in production and need to be able to respond to changes in the demand for workers. Spanish legislation allows for a temporary permit extension, according to changes in the seasonal work planning. This means that employers can choose to employ a person longer than the period that was initially authorised. In some countries (e.g., Italy), such an extension is not possible. Another aspect of legal flexibility is the possibility for a seasonal migrant to work for more than one employer within the allowed period. In some countries, such an authorisation can even be given after the worker has entered the country[971]. A legal framework allowing for such flexibility is better suited to introduce a seasonal labour migration programme, by the TCLM model. The efficiency of the migration procedure is significantly important. Inefficient procedures even act as a stimulus for employing irregular migrants already residing in the country[972]. Both the swiftness and reliability of

---

969 Laws for Legal Immigration in the 27 EU Member States, International Migration Law N° 16, International Organization for Migration (IOM), 2009.

970 Magri 2009.

971 Ibid.

972 Ibid.

the institutions, in the country of origin as well as in the country of destination, contribute to the effectiveness of the recruitment process.[973]

It is clear that a flexible legislation, combined with a migration policy linked to co-development, is a *condition sine qua non* for this model of programmes. The programme acted as an opportunity to address some of the underlying motives of forced environmental displacement, such as the lack of resilience to disasters and underdevelopment of environmentally-fragile communities like the Pacific, for example. For certain affected populations, planned environmental migration (whether preventive or post-disaster) might be a more durable solution than mere emergency relief. It also connects migration policy with environmental and development policy. Governments could integrate environmental migration into their development policy, by enhancing migrants' contribution to the sustainable socio-economic development of their countries of origin, through recognizable local and community projects. Migration could moreover be mainstreamed into national and international adaptation plans, as it can relieve pressure on destructed or degraded regions, and provide alternatives to the affected population. Finally, environmental motives could be included into a coherent migration policy. By creating programmes of short-term legal migration, and prioritising people affected by environmental degradation, we can both manage migration when migration pressure rises, and offer relief to the affected persons.[974]

5.3.3. United States

When the Kyoto Protocol was written in 1997, it was mainly the US and its lobbyists that were against the protocol because of economic concerns. Developing countries did not want to agree to any commitments unless they first saw progress from industrialized nations.[975] And yet, *they were* making reductions and transitions showing developed countries that it can be done, and applying

---

973 Verge Oms 2010

974 Temporary and Circular Labor Migration: Experiences, Challenges and Opportunities. *IOM International Organization for Migration.* Retrieved from
http://www.upf.edu/gritim/_pdf/Temporary_and_Circular_Labour_Migration_Experiencesx_Challenges_and_Opportunities.pdf

975 U.S. Cities and their Cities working together to address climate change. *KyotoUSA.* Retrieved from
http://www.kyotousa.org/

the concept of "common but differentiated responsibilities," which the US still ignores.[976]

Relations between the USA and Tuvalu are very good, but there have been notable disagreements regarding the issues of climate change and the Kyoto Protocol. The main point of friction between Tuvalu and the United States has been the latter's non-ratification of the Kyoto Protocol. Tuvalu is suffering severe environmental damage due to climate change and has repeatedly urged the United States to do more to reduce its pollution levels. In 2002, Tuvaluan Prime Minister Koloa Talake threatened to take the United States to the International Court of Justice for its refusal to ratify the Kyoto Protocol. He was prevented from doing so by his subsequent defeat in that year's general election. More recently, in 2007, Tuvalu's Deputy Prime Minister Tavau Teli called upon all countries to "make an effort to reduce their emissions before it is too late for countries like Tuvalu."[977] On other matters, Tuvalu supports American positions very often, such as human rights and security measures and development.

In some parts, the US agencies and national security have recognized the seriousness of the threat posed by global climate change. The US Department of Defense, for example, included the climate threat as a key pillar of its most recent Quadrennial Defense Review. Even the CIA has established a Center for the Study of Climate Change. And yet, the US' response to climate change has been viewed as feeble when compared to the country's greater and faster responses to arguably less likely or smaller scale risks.[978] For example, in 2010, the US spent about 1.7 billion on international climate change financing, a figure that might seem large at first sight but which in reality pales in comparison to other financial responses.

The agreements the US has entered, including the Copenhagen Accord, rely on an unenforceable international honor system to combat emissions. The US government has invested trillions of dollars in preventing and mitigating the risks of weapons of mass destruction, global terrorism and systemic economic

976 Shah, A. (2012). Reactions to Climate Change Negotiations and Action. GLOBAL ISSUES. Retrieved from http://www.globalissues.org/print/article/179#src-48.

977 Millard-Ball, A. (2011). The Tuvalu Syndrome. Can Geoengineering Solve Climate's Collective Action Problem? *Climatic Change (110)*: 1047-1066. Retrieved from http://papers.ssrn.com/sol3/papers.cfm?abstract_id=2028166

978 Climate Change: The 'Feeble' US Response to the "Enormous Security Threat " (2011). Retrieved CLIMATE PROGRESS (Jul. 21, 2011), http://thinkprogress.org/climate/2011/07/21/274010/climate-change-security-threat/

crises because the consequences of inaction would be considered unaccept-able. These investments were made despite significant uncertainty about the frequency with which these catastrophic events might occur. When it comes to climate change, however, the required certainty is there, and the conse-quences of failing to manage risks appropriately should also be unacceptable. Meanwhile, the scientific community is as close to certain as humanly possible about the prospects for the global crisis. Without action, the scientific consensus is that climate change threatens billions of lives, and a catastrophe will almost surely occur. Such a security threat calls for an urgent and financially signifi-cant response from US policymakers. [979] The policymakers need to understand finally that climate change is a global issue that requires an urgent international response. Cooperation on this worldwide issue is critical: governments, indus-tries, communities and organizations across the globe must work together to develop and implement measures to reduce GHG emissions and avoid danger-ous consequences of climate change.[980]

---

[979] What EPA is Doing about Climate Change. *The EPA United States Environmental Protection Agency.* Retrieved from http://www.epa.gov/climatechange/policy/index.html

[980] *Id.*

CHAPTER SIX

CONCLUSION AND DE LEGE FERENDA PROPOSALS

Environmentally speaking, the book concludes that greenhouse gasses will continue to threaten our world for the years to come, and, therefore, the developed countries (and leading polluters) need to take clear actions. Success, however, is only possible if all countries undertake action. One solution should focus around lowering the percentage of gas emulsions through the Kyoto Protocol. Another would be to cut off the tropical hardwood use by a minimum of 20 percent. Alternative solutions concerning renewable energy sources (a change from fossil oil to increased renewable energy) are not yet agreed upon by the oil supporting countries and hence cannot be implemented. The high polluting countries, not parties to the Kyoto Protocol, should follow the Road Plan discussed in Cancun, Durban, Doha and lately in Paris, offering to the achievements made at last COPs a chance to success. There is no reason to adhere to the Kyoto Protocol anymore because its validity expired at the end of 2012. However, these countries should nonetheless start acting in the right direction, which represents cutting carbon emissions. The Sinking Islands would have to obtain an international acknowledgment from the countries involved in the fight against global warming and international programs. Alternative resettling projects that may transform into sustainable and durable solutions with limited impact on the islanders' rights should be considered, as well.

Climate change is a global challenge. Advances in science are making it easier to identify and project the current and future impacts of climate change on the global environment and economy. However, many have noted that scientific evidence has often failed to translate into stringent and efficient policies. This can be seen in both adaptation literature and in examining the numerous international agreements on climate change that have not yet produced any significant results. To help us move forward, changes need to be made in both mitigation and adaptation efforts as described below:

Strengthening Mitigation Measures

If we implement various mitigation measures over the next decade, we can potentially close the existing emissions gap (mentioned under the Kyoto section) by[981]

1. Strengthening pledges: This can be done via stringent emission accounting rules for Annex I countries, raise ambition among all governments to move forward on emission cuts and have a process in place to avoid "double-counting" of emission credits.

2. Improving technical mitigation: One option is to reduce fossil-fuel consumption subsidies[982] Worldwide,[983] Increase the share of renewable energy production globally, and have a climate policy in place for renewable energy.

3. Improve energy efficiency: This will require a policy focus on household building standards, commercial building standards, industrial operations, transport and investing in a smart energy future.[984] It can result in a more cost-efficient measure, which

981 Niklas Hoehne et al., *After Durban: Risk of Delay in Raising Ambition Lowers Chances for 2°C, while Heading for 3.5°C*, CLIMATE ANALYTICS (Dec. 11, 2011),

http://climateactiontracker.org/assets/publications/briefing_papers/CAT_Durban_update_2_20111211.pdf

982 It must be noted that any measures to reduce fossil fuel subsidies can have serious political repercussions, especially in fragile states. *See Eleven Nations with the massive fossil fuel subsidies*, NATIONAL GEOGRAPHIC (last viewed July 10, 2013), http://news.nationalgeographic.com/news/energy/2012/06/pictures/120618-large-fossil-fuel-subsidies/

983 IEA World Energy Outlook provides a global overview of the fossil-fuel consumption subsidy rates for 2010. This helps to show the difference between countries and to see which country needs stronger policies/ more support to move towards a carbon-neutral economy. *See* IEA World Energy Outlook (2012), http://www.iea.org/subsidy/index.html.

984 *See Australia's Environment Groups: Climate Change Policy Agenda* (last viewed July 10, 2013), http://www.sustainablelivingtasmania.org.au/content/documents/NGOjointpolicyagenda.pdf (recommending that Australia makes solar hot water systems compulsory for all homes built after 2008 and that least efficient appliances should be banned).

in turn can help incentivize governments to transform to a more sustainable energy system.

4. Eliminate deforestation: Mature forests store enormous quantities of carbon, but when forests are logged or burnt, that carbon is released into the atmosphere, increasing the amount of carbon dioxide and other GHGs and accelerating the rate of climate change. [985] Thus, land-use changes need to be regulated and monitored more carefully.

While reducing or "mitigating" GHG pollution remains/should remain a top priority for the international community and governments worldwide, it is inevitable that climate change is real, and its impacts are already beginning to pose problems, especially for the most marginalized communities. Thus, it is equally important to talk about preparing for or adapting to the harmful effects of climate change.

Measures needed to prepare adequately for climate change

The array of potential adaptation response available to human societies is vast ranging from technological, through behavioral, to managerial and policy:

- Technological: Infrastructure such as roads, bridges, and housing-can play a critical role in building communities coping capacity to deal with both long-term and short-term impacts of climate change. To move this forward, future initiatives need to include local governments and participation from citizens and community organizations (who often have the necessary knowledge about the local conditions).[986]

- Behavioral: Our consumption behavior can act a long way to both mitigate and adapt to future climate change. For instance,

---

985 *Deforestation and Climate Change*, GREENPEACE (last viewed July 10, 2013), http://www.greenpeace. org.uk/forests/climate-change.

986 *6.5 Land Use Planning and Building Regulation*, GLOBAL ASSESSMENT REPORT (2011), http://www.preventionweb.net/english/hyogo/gar/2011/en/how/index4.html.

reducing our consumption of meat can decrease our GHG emissions significantly. As the head of the U.N.'s Nobel Prize–winning Intergovernmental Panel on Climate Change, Pachauri urged people to cut back the consumption of on meat to combat climate change, stating: "Give up meat for one day [per week] at least initially, and decrease it from there. Regarding immediacy of action and the feasibility of bringing about reductions in a short period, it clearly is the most attractive opportunity."[987]

- Managerial: For centuries, farmers have learned to adapt their livelihoods to a wide variety of disturbances caused by environmental variability and change, through local coping strategies, and there is a broad range of case studies documenting this occurrence.[988] In perceived changes in climate, farmers can alter their farm practices by planting crop varieties that, for example, are more resistant to floods.

- Policy: As we saw in the case of the Pacific, many countries worldwide are proposing national plans to help them adapt to the impacts of climate change. These should begin to focus on how other levels of government, such as local and regional, can participate in both the decision-making and the implementation of such plans.

Despite the numerous measures that are currently taking place or will shortly, little has been written about how effective various options are at reducing risk. Moreover, environmental, economic, informational, social and behavioral barriers still exist to the implementation of adaptation.[989] Thus, we have to take larger steps and offer long-term criteria when measuring success in our society. In addition, we have to realize that investments in transforming our economies are not costs, but rather investments in our future.

---

[987] Bryan Walsh, *Meat: Making Global Warming Worse*, TIME (Sept. 10, 2008), http://www.time.com/time/health/article/0,8599,1839995,00.html#ixzz26MYuYbzC.

[988] Mirjam Macchi, et al., *Indigenous and Traditional Peoples and Climate Change*, IUCN, at 10 (March 2008),

http://cmsdata.iucn.org/downloads/indigenous_peoples_climate_change.pdf.

[989] *Climate Change Adaptation and Mitigation*, FOOD AND AGRICULTURE ORGANIZATION, at 15 (Sept. 2012), http://www.fao.org/docrep/016/i2855e/i2855e.pdf.

Under the refugee perspective, the conclusions extracted from this book emphasize the key renewing and modernization of the refugee definition, as it is expressed at this time through the 1951 Refugee Convention. As demonstrated in multiple arguments, the definition of the „refugee" is long-standing and outdated regarding the refugee law evolution and the progressive interpretation of law, *per se.* New/old terminology like "Climate Refugee," "Environmental Refugee" or "Economic Refugee," is entitled to "official" worldwide recognition, regulation and promotion coming from the leading international authority, the United Nations High Commissioner for Refugees. Furthermore, regional comprehensive plans of action in Pacific for climate scenarios, with a direct involvement of the United Nations High Commissioner for Refugees should be elaborated. A high-level engagement and the use of science to support decision-making are necessary to avoid a predicted confrontation with a massive, unprecedented and unregulated by law migration.

The human rights conclusions would promote the recognition of the right to (a clean) environment, as the first step at international level. Although regulated by some regional human rights conventions (Americas and Africa) the right to the environment requires a wider and spread appreciation, as customary law, for a better implementation and enforcement of the domestic legislations, regardless of involvement in international agreements, treaties or conventions. Accordingly, the states would be forced to act in this regard, the implied (implicit) rights resulting from the right to environment, obtaining a higher applicability at national, regional and international levels. Regionally, an actualized human rights approach by the international bodies would be recommended, in particular the United Nations Office of the High Commissioner for Human Rights, as the majority of the Pacific Islands, including the Sinking Islands, are parties only to conventions under the United Nations authority, the inexistence of regional human rights agreements representing a critical factor of the human rights violations occurring in these countries.

Lato sensu, to control the situation in Pacific, under international law (in general terms) there is an evident necessity for political and financial commitment. Immediate action is required, from all international actors, state actors and non-state actors to avoid the eventual environmental catastrophes, refugee and human rights related difficulties in the case of the Sinking Islands. The state of the Sinking Islands is aggravating, and the people involved in the process are becoming more and more affected by the climate change in general and the international unresponsiveness in particular. With political and financial support their situation could be improved, and the international law should be adjusted to prepare for future climate change effects.

In addition to what was stated above, this book goes further and tries to recommend general law or particular relevance law, in relation to Pacific and future evolution of the Sinking Islands problem. Respecting the principles of international law, the legal proposals intend to stimulate more the action towards the Sinking Islands, attributing more international responsibilities and constraints for rapid responses. Unquestionably, the Sinking Islands status quo is not satisfactory as regard to the legal options the Pacific Islands have in general and as regard to the reluctant position of the international law-making actors, in particular.

The virtual inexistence of a high regional legal authority in the Pacific move all the potential law- making process towards the United Nations and its mechanisms, as the only body with direct influence over the legal aspect of the Pacific Islands. For example, there is already known that Asia as a continent represents the only region (including Pacific via Oceania) without a regional human rights mechanism. More political implication coming from the United Nations Office of the High Commissioner for Human Rights would transform the 1993 Bangkok NGO Declaration on Human Rights into a veritable regional human rights convention, for more than four billion people, representing more than 60 percent of the actual world population. More, it will have a direct implication for the Pacific community, transferring the United Nations authority to a regional more comprehensive and better-working mechanism.

It is clear that the United Nations High Commissioner for Refugees, as a humanitarian actor cannot solve the Sinking Islands problem by itself. Therefore, a hybrid mechanism must be formed between the environmental body of the United Nations, the human rights body, and the United Nations High Commissioner for Refugees, under the direct supervision of the Secretary-General. A new instrument of this kind would facilitate the unification of these three actions as one next act, a single interpretation, and adaptation of the Sinking Islands case. Nevertheless, the General Assembly decisions would support its activities with decisions aimed to address the problem of Sinking Islands strictly or in general the problem of the communities affected by climate change.

It is less probable that the 1951 Refugee Convention would have added a new annex or a protocol, which would redefine the refugee definition under the new changing circumstances. However, this book argues for creating a new document, which will focus exclusively on the environment, a topic that 1951 Convention avoids addressing.

Finally, this book expresses eventual suggestions for the existing international law, *mutatis mutandis* urging the local, regional and international actors to act for confronting a new generation of challenges the humanity faces today, mainly environmentally related. These actions should concern the Sinking Islands and the Climate Refugees implied in the process, as well as the international law-making society, in general.

CPSIA information can be obtained
at www.ICGtesting.com
Printed in the USA
BVOW06s0841250517
484582BV00015B/26/P